BORDERS OF BELONGING

BORDERS OF BELONGING

STRUGGLE AND SOLIDARITY

IN MIXED-STATUS

IMMIGRANT FAMILIES

HEIDE CASTAÑEDA

STANFORD UNIVERSITY PRESS • STANFORD, CALIFORNIA

Stanford University Press

Stanford, California

Printed in the United States of America on acid-free, archival-quality paper

Library of Congress Cataloging-in-Publication Data

Names: Castañeda, Heide, author.

Title: Borders of belonging : struggle and solidarity in mixed-status immigrant families / Heide Castañeda.

Description: Stanford, California : Stanford University Press, 2019. | Includes bibliographical references and index.

Identifiers: LCCN 2018018752 | ISBN 9781503607217 (cloth : alk. paper) | ISBN 9781503607910 (pbk. : alk. paper) | ISBN 9781503607927 (epub)

Subjects: LCSH: Immigrant families—Texas—Lower Rio Grande Valley. | Immigrants—Family relationships—Texas—Lower Rio Grande Valley. | Illegal aliens—Family relationships—Texas—Lower Rio Grande Valley. | Immigrants—Texas—Lower Rio Grande Valley—Social conditions.

Classification: LCC JV7100 .C37 2019 | DDC 306.85086/912097644—dc23

LC record available at https://lccn.loc.gov/2018018752

Typeset by Westchester Publishing Services in 10/14 Minion Pro

Cover design by Rob Ehle

Cover photo: AP Images

CONTENTS

PREFACE

On an unusually chilly Sunday evening in South Texas, I sat outdoors with family and friends, talking and laughing into the night as the smoky mesquite aroma of backyard barbeques lingered around us. Now and again the unmistakable sound of a Border Patrol helicopter passed in the distance. We were less than a mile from the international border, separated only by the Las Palomas Wildlife Management Area, which began just a few yards from where we were sitting. As the evening wore on and the laughter slowed, some bid farewell to return to their homes on the other side of the river, across the U.S.–Mexico border. As the sound of helicopters faded in and out, my mind wandered as I contemplated families who are at once united and separated. Divided by a political boundary, in the morning they would wake to different realities as sure as the sun peeked through the blinds. People the same, but stratified by borders, passports, visas, legal status.

While I remember a specific chilly evening when the idea for this book was first born, it has always been a work in progress, tapping into my family's history and my own transnational upbringing. Borders, citizenship, and belonging—and the various physical and social im/mobilities associated with them—shaped my early understanding of the world and, later, the trajectory of my career. Throughout her life, my mother carried with her the joy and pain of leaving her home country, returning, and leaving again. Since birth, I too have been on the move—my first 5,000-mile transatlantic migration was at just four weeks old—and while I grew up primarily in Germany, I was also regularly in South Texas following my parents' separation. It was in these locations and landscapes that I witnessed the impact of migration and the militarization of borders on family life.

Growing up during the Cold War of the 1980s, we lived not far from the border with East Germany, with many families and communities split apart on either side. Unable to see each other for decades, they were separated by a wall, or, in the region where I lived, a heavily fortified but largely invisible line surrounded by a no-man's-land of tranquil birch forests. On either side of this dividing line were barbed wire, guard towers, tanks, and nuclear missiles tucked stealthily underground, as signs warned, "*Achtung! Zonengrenze*" (Warning! Border Zone). The trauma that accompanied the separation of families and entire communities was always present, but was rarely talked about openly.

During the summers, I visited with my father's side of the family in South Texas, spending time in both San Antonio and the Rio Grande Valley. Some of my earliest memories are of scorching late afternoons wandering dry arroyos with him, looking for fossils in the limestone banks. I fell in love with this region—and neighboring Mexico *lindo y querido*—as a young girl, and was always drawn to the border that divided it. This was a highly visible boundary, physically marked by a river, but while the separation was incredibly palpable, it also seemed nonsensical. Here, the Spanish language dominated, and food, commerce, and politics, it seemed, were always binational affairs. Some of my childhood friends were undocumented, or had parents who were, although I didn't really understand what that meant at the time.

As an adult, I have continued to travel between these sites, listening to migrants with precarious status. Throughout my own life, and especially during the research described in this book, I have learned to appreciate deeply what migrant parents give up for their children's futures. They make difficult decisions, and this shapes subsequent generations and their ideas of belonging—about forms of citizenship, but also about their positionality within larger structures of family. At the same time, I remain acutely aware of my own privilege, including the flexible forms of national belonging that are the chance outcome of a specific historical moment and geopolitical circumstance. This book, *Borders of Belonging*, is an attempt to tell a story that has been a spectral presence in my head and my heart for many years. It seeks to represent the stories of the people I met, to whom I am deeply grateful.

ACKNOWLEDGMENTS

This book is dedicated to the families in the Rio Grande Valley who shared their stories with me. I feel privileged and humbled to know each of you and wish I could thank you by name, which is not possible for reasons of confidentiality. I hope that I have reflected your experiences in all their complexity, and that this book can contribute in some small way to a better future.

Milena A. Melo was the research assistant for the series of studies upon which this work is based, in addition to being a dear friend. Without her knowledge, perseverance, and thoughtful input, the collection of this data would not have been possible. Thank you for the conversations, insight, and support over the past several years. My fantastic writing partner, Wendy Vogt, was a constant source of camaraderie, keeping me on task and providing critical feedback throughout the process. Thank you, Wendy, for your friendship and support, and the many insightful conversations about migration theory and ethnographic writing along the way. Many others were generous in lending their time and expertise to comment on portions of the manuscript. I thank Elizabeth Aranda, Jill Fleuriet, Helen Marrow, Sarah Smith, and Angela Stuesse for reviewing early drafts of chapters. I am especially grateful to Ryan Logan for his assistance with many elements of this project over the years, especially analysis and manuscript preparation. Several other graduate students at the University of South Florida provided crucial support with project development, transcription, and analysis: James Arango, Nora Brickhouse Arriola, Carla Castillo, Paola Gonzalez, Seiichi Villalona, and Aria Walsh-Felz. In addition, thank you to undergraduate researchers Yessica Chavez Grimaldo and Juliana Leon.

For thoughtful scholarly exchanges about many aspects of this project over the years, I want to thank Sabrina Balgamwalla, Deborah Boehm, Jennifer Burrell, Lauren Carruth, Leo Chavez, Nicholas de Genova, Tara Deubel, Hansjörg Dilger, Whitney Duncan, Karin Friederic, Christina Getrich, Ruth Gomberg-Muñoz, Roberto Gonzales, Margaret Graham, Lauren Heidbrink, Josiah Heyman, Seth Holmes, Elizabeth Hordge-Freeman, Sarah Horton, Christine M. Jacobsen, Sharam Khosravi, Nolan Kline, William Lopez, Sarah Luna, Lenore Manderson, Girsea Martinez, James McDonald, Emily Mendenhall, Juan Manuel Mendoza, Nelda Mier, Anne Millard, Jessica Lavariega Monforti, Shanti Morell-Hart, Jessica Mulligan, Faidra Papavasiliou, Brianda Peraza, Anne Pfister, James Quesada, Robin Reineke, Thurka Sangaramoorthy, Adam Schwartz, Jeremy Slack, Carolina Valdivia, Elizabeth Vaquera, Linda Whiteford, Sarah Willen, Kristin Yarris, Rebecca Zarger, and so many others. In addition, the Steering Committee of the Anthropologists Action Network for Immigrants and Refugees (AAINR) has been a positive source of supportive peers and engaged scholars developing concrete actions to lift up the communities with whom we work.

This research was funded by the National Science Foundation (#1535664, jointly through the Law & Social Sciences Program, Cultural Anthropology Program, and Sociology Program), as well as by a grant from the Wenner-Gren Foundation for Anthropological Research. Pilot data collection was made possible by a grant from the University of South Florida Humanities Institute. In addition to this generous assistance, I am fortunate to work with a wonderfully supportive group of colleagues in the Department of Anthropology at the University of South Florida.

In the Rio Grande Valley, I am grateful for the time and support of several organizations over the years, including La Union del Pueblo Entero (LUPE), Nuestra Clinica del Valle, Fuerza del Valle, Access Esperanza, El Milagro Clinic, ARISE, Sacred Heart Refugee Center, MHP Salud, Hope Family Health Center, RGV Focus, Proyecto Azteca, Valley Interfaith, and Children's Defense Fund. For taking the time for conversations I also appreciate individuals associated with the Hidalgo County Health Department, La Joya Independent School District, Pharr–San Juan–Alamo Independent School District, Teach for America, South Texas College, Texas A&M Colonias Program, and the University of Texas–Rio Grande Valley.

Michelle Lipinski of Stanford University Press shepherded this project to completion with unwavering support and encouragement. Thank you, Michelle, for reading over my manuscript and for all the thoughtful feedback along the way. Thank you also to Nora Spiegel, John Donohue, and the fantastic production staff at the Press. In addition to the scholars named above, I am indebted to the anonymous outside reviewers of this manuscript; I appreciate your thoughtful comments and recommendations, which have greatly strengthened the book. Portions of Chapter 6 have appeared in Castañeda, Heide, and Milena A. Melo. 2014. Health Care Access for Latino Mixed-Status Families: Barriers, Strategies, and Implications for Reform. *American Behavioral Scientist* 58(14): 1891–1909.

My deepest gratitude is reserved for my family, because of their unwavering love and support. Thank you especially to my mother, Kriemhilde, for inspiring and encouraging me, for always being my champion, and for being genuinely interested in my wild ideas and travels. I am grateful for my exceptional partner and best friend, Valentín, whose companionship makes life beautiful. And to Drake, thank you for understanding my work; I hope you always remain a person with integrity and compassion for others, and speak up and demand justice for those who cannot.

Any royalties that I receive from the sale of this book will be donated to organizations that provide legal support for immigrant families.

INTRODUCTION

ILLEGALITY AND THE IMMIGRANT FAMILY

AFTER MICHELLE MARTINEZ gave birth to a baby girl in a South Texas hospital, she went to the county clerk's office to pick up the birth certificate, the same way as she had with her first child. But officials told Michelle, an undocumented Mexican immigrant, that the rules had changed. Without specific documents, she would not be able to get the vital record showing that her daughter was a natural-born citizen. When I met Michelle, her daughter was three years old and still had no birth certificate. She said,

> I need to get it before they take everything away from her. I don't have a Social Security number, and I can't get an ID from here. I have the *matrícula consular* [identification card issued by the Mexican consulate], but they don't want to take it like before. With everything that's going on right now, they can take Mexican parents away, deport them. I'm scared. They want a specific ID I can't get here. You actually need to go over to Mexico for that. But if I do, I can't come back.

Like many other mothers, Michelle was asked to present a Mexican driver's license or national identity card. Since she came to the United States when she was four years old, she had neither. Because she is now undocumented, she can't travel to Mexico and return; if she did, she would be stopped at the border and refused entry since she no longer has a valid visa. And at the time, consulates in the United States only issued the *matrícula consular*, which numerous states, municipalities, and businesses across the country accept as an official identification card. The federal government allows it to be used to obtain an Individual Taxpayer Identification Number (ITIN) in order to pay income taxes, many states consider it valid proof of identity for obtaining a driver's license, and financial institutions accept it for critical activities such as banking. It is a lifeline for the more than 5.6 million undocumented Mexican nationals in the United States. For undocumented parents like Michelle, the *matrícula consular* is often the only form of identification they can obtain.

Michelle continued, "So I asked them, 'Is there any other way?' But they didn't want to help me. I'm like, what do I do? Next year she starts school. She was supposed to start Head Start this year, but she couldn't because I don't have the birth certificate."[1] The baby's father, a U.S. citizen, was not listed on the birth certificate even though he was present at the birth. The hospital staff wouldn't let him sign the paperwork, since he did not have an ID with him at the time. "So, his mom went home and got the ID," Michelle told me. "And then he signed everything. He went into the office of the lady that did the paperwork. Gave her the ID and everything. We thought that was done." However, when they tried obtaining the birth certificate, they were told he had still not been listed as the father. She said, "It looked like someone had whited out his name. We were shocked!" To correct the clerical mistake, the county then asked Michelle to complete an application for child support. She was incredulous: "Why am I going to file for child support? We live together. Just because they didn't list him on the birth certificate? So now we had to go get all these papers signed and notarized again, and wait while they send it up to Houston. Then we have to pay again."

To speed up the process, the clerk suggested that Michelle drive to Houston and visit the main office of the Texas Department of State Health Services in person, where she could obtain the birth certificate the same day. However, to get there, Michelle would have to pass through one of the U.S. Customs and Border Protection checkpoints set up between 25 and 100 miles from the international border along all major highways leading to the interior of the United States. Because of these checkpoints, since 2001, Michelle has been unable to leave the region where she resides. She is one of 1.7 million undocumented immigrants living in Texas, many of whom are concentrated within a 100-mile-wide buffer strip along the border that forms a secondary boundary to the interior of the United States.[2] These checkpoints affect not just recent border crossers but also those who have lived here for decades. Michelle was trapped between two boundaries: she could not return to Mexico to obtain another form of identification for herself, nor could she drive to Houston to expedite the process for her daughter.

In 2015, two dozen parents sued the State of Texas, saying they could not obtain the documents that officials were demanding.[3] The lawsuit argued that the state had violated the Fourteenth Amendment of the Constitution, impacting U.S.-citizen children's rights by ordering county registrars to no longer recognize as proof of identification their parents' *matrícula consular* or foreign passport without a valid visa. The State of Texas, on the other hand, argued that the issuing party (the Mexican consulate) did not routinely verify the documents used to obtain the *matrícula*. But as the lawsuit stated, "By denying the Plaintiff children their birth certificates, Defendants have created a category of second-class citizens, disadvantaged from childhood on with respect to, inter alia, health and educational opportunities." It cited opaque and irregular processes at vital statistics offices—particularly inconsistent in the Rio Grande Valley of South Texas—that prevented undocumented parents from being able to present adequate proof of their own identities in order to secure documents for their children.[4]

This example highlights what has been termed "bureaucratic disentitlement," which targets marginalized groups, such as the U.S.-born children of undocumented immigrants. Bureaucratic disentitlement is "the insidious process by which administrative agencies deprive individuals of their statutory entitlements and infringe on their constitutional rights."[5] In everyday practice, it takes the form of withholding information, providing misinformation, isolating applicants, and requiring extraordinary amounts of documentation for simple administrative procedures. In doing so, it inhibits the transformation of statutory rights into tangible benefits. This example goes one step further, hinting not only at disentitlement but also at the attempted bureaucratic erasure of an entire generation. These practices highlight the power of rhetoric around "anchor babies" in the United States today, which frames the U.S.-born children of immigrants as undeserving and suspect citizens, and underscore the ways in which the state can disregard their rights.[6] Despite widespread misconceptions, U.S.-born children do not "anchor" families by providing automatic pathways to citizenship to their parents, nor do they provide protection from deportation; instead, mixed-status families remain entrapped in a "labyrinth of liminality" and precarity.[7]

A year later, I caught up with Michelle again. My first question was: What happened with the birth certificate? "I barely got it last week," she told me

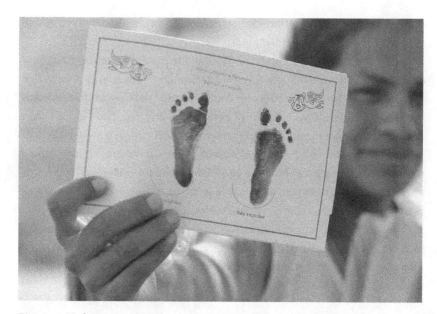

Figure 1. Undocumented mother in the Rio Grande Valley who was denied a birth certificate for her U.S.-citizen child. Source: AP Photo/Eric Gay.

(see figure 1). On social media, she had found a community of mothers similarly affected by the change in policy. One person had suggested an alternative process, by which a "person acting under contract for the registrant" could obtain the birth certificate after submitting a particular form. In this way, her boyfriend—acting "under contract for the registrant" rather than in his rightful capacity as the child's father—was able to request the birth certificate. Michelle explained,

> I went and tried again. "She's starting school, I need her birth certificate!" They said no again, that I couldn't get it. But they also didn't tell me, "Oh, we have this certain form you can fill out." So that's when I said, "Ok, I need that form giving permission for someone else to get it." They were surprised I knew about it. Her dad filled it out, we had it notarized, and that's how we got the birth certificate. A huge weight was lifted off my shoulders. She's four years old, and still didn't have her birth certificate. I wasn't allowed to enroll her in Head Start. We were going to baptize her, but we couldn't. And now it's the last week of registration for elementary school, so just this morning I went to sign her up.

In July 2016, the Texas Department of State Health Services agreed to a settlement that expanded the types of credentials that parents could present, including Mexican voter identification cards—now obtainable at Mexican consulates in the United States—along with a list of additional, newly specified supporting documents more readily available to undocumented persons such as utility bills or paycheck stubs. While Michelle had already found a less-than-ideal alternative solution on her own, other mothers would no longer have to struggle with these inconsistent, arbitrary, and unjust bureaucratic requirements.

Parents like Michelle live in constant fear of having their families torn apart, and without a birth certificate they cannot prove their relationship to their U.S.-born children if stopped by authorities. Undocumented parents struggle with accessing basic education, health, and other services for their families, as all the while the specter of deportability hovers over them. While it comes as little surprise that undocumented persons face such limitations, Michelle's story shows how U.S.-born citizens are also affected—disenfranchised, even—by a family member's legal status. At the far end of the spectrum of possibilities, without a birth certificate a child can also become "undocumented" in the most literal sense of the word, even though they are a U.S. citizen. The refusal to issue birth certificates, as well as inconsistent rules and de facto disentitlement practices of state officials, highlights the precarity of rights even for citizens. A parent's undocumented status can affect their children from the very start, even if they actively pursue every avenue to protect them, as Michelle did.

This book argues that the construction of "illegality" for some members in a family influences opportunities and resources for all, including legal residents and U.S. citizens. Like other contemporary studies of the lived effects of law, I use the term "illegality" to refer to a sociopolitical condition, juridical status, and relationship to the state.[8] This book follows the experiences of 100 mixed-status families to understand how this illegality impacts the entire family, what it looks like on a day-to-day basis, and how people respond. In order to explore these broad and cumulative ripple effects of undocumented status, the book reframes how we think about contemporary migration by focusing on a social unit—specifically, the family—rather than individuals. Illegality impacts opportunities for everyone, since individuals are always embedded within these complex social units. Mixed-status families have become "collateral damage" in enforcement efforts and are relegated to a life of indefinite uncertainty.[9] A better understanding of these effects is needed to help redirect contemporary debates that assume anti-immigrant policies only affect the undocumented.[10] This book illustrates why political efforts toward reform must take into account the experiences of mixed-status families, now a primary and enduring feature of the contemporary immigrant experience in the United States.

While illegality impacts everyone in the family, people are not simply passive recipients of this fate. They mobilize intimate ties to challenge the effects of illegality and deportability.[11] Thus this is also a book about the resilience and creative responses of people in mixed-status families, such as Michelle turning to social media for advice and then demanding an alternative form at the county clerk's office. While life in the United States is made difficult for them, a return to their country of origin is generally out of the question: they have established deep roots in the United States, including strong familial ties, and many would face challenging conditions upon return to a country they no longer know well. This book highlights not only the enduring effects of the condition of illegality but also how people actively strategize and resist juridical categories as part of legal consciousness, in which the law's meanings are frequently amended and contested as part of everyday experience.[12]

Finally, this book argues that all these experiences are significantly framed by place. This research was conducted in the Rio Grande Valley of South Texas (see Map 1), in a county where more than one in ten people are undocumented.[13] There are a significantly high proportion of mixed-status families like Michelle's, whose members not only interact with one another but also come into daily contact with bureaucrats, doctors, teachers, law enforcement agents, and others in their community. While their experiences are largely generalizable to mixed-status families in other parts of the United States, they are also framed by the characteristics of a specific place. The borderlands between the United States and Mexico encapsulate a number of contradictions in regards to mobility, ethnonational identity, political participation, economic practices, education, and health care. Communities on both sides of the river have been variously conjoined and split apart through a violent history of multiple conquests and intentional marginalization. Today, the Rio Grande Valley retains a number of geographic and social features that set it apart from adjacent regions, including its ethnic makeup, the dominance of the Spanish language, and a strong binational frame of reference. However, while large numbers cross the border daily for work and recreation, this mobility is only afforded to some segments of the population.

The region is particularly unique in terms of immigration enforcement, as undocumented persons are trapped both in and out of the region, to the south and to the north. Those who are undocumented may be relegated to life within

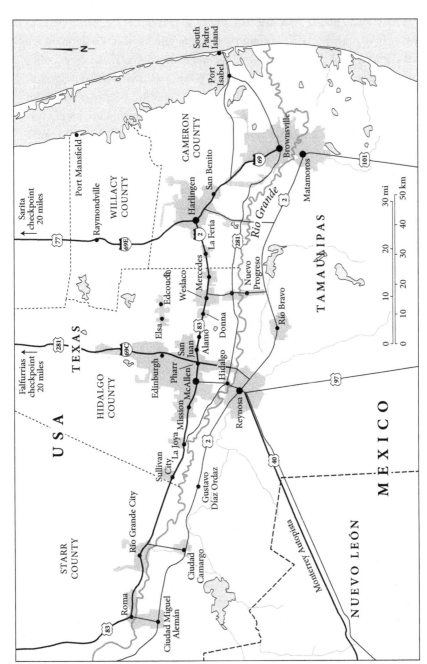

Map 1. Map of the Lower Rio Grande Valley of South Texas.

this small strip along the border. Unable to reenter the United States if they cross back into Mexico, they are also unable to travel north to other parts of the state or to other parts of the country, as this requires inspection at one of the fixed Border Patrol checkpoints along the major highways. These checkpoints trap people within a distinct space, while temporary roadblock checkpoints further fuel fear and uncertainty within it. This intensive border enforcement creates what has been referred to as a "second river," or a secondary border further impeding mobility into the interior of the United States.[14] This has a range of negative effects, not only on undocumented individuals themselves but also on their citizen family members and communities.

The border region of South Texas is an important site in which to study the lives of mixed-status families as it is one the poorest and most heavily enforced areas in the country, where a high proportion of people are undocumented. It is here that the effects of national policies are experienced more discordantly than in the interior, and thus it is an ideal place to understand the lived effects of law, to challenge conceptualizations about their impact, and to explore terrains often not considered in the design of policy. It is a harbinger site that can offer lessons to the rest of the United States on two issues: (1) the incorporation experiences of a growing demographic—namely, people living in mixed-status families; and (2) the impacts of increased interior immigrant enforcement on communities.

Mixed-Status Families in the United States

"Everybody is undocumented in my family, so that's all I really grew up knowing. Even though I'm a U.S. citizen, I got used to those norms, so in a way it was like I was undocumented myself." This is how Lisa, a twenty-two-year-old college student, explained growing up in a mixed-status family and how it impacted her everyday experiences and outlook on life. We are currently witnessing a demographic shift in the United States. Never before have so many citizen children been affected by the illegality of a family member as in our current historical moment. While immigration has shaped the United States from the nation's inception, it remains a perennially divisive issue. Both popular and scholarly attention has generally neglected to account for this growing population and the contradictory and perhaps unexpected experiences of families like Michelle's or Lisa's.

Attention to mixed-status families is urgently needed, as they now constitute a primary feature of the contemporary immigrant experience. Over the
past two decades, the number of families in the United States with complex
legal status configurations has sharply increased. Nationwide, at least 16.7 million people are part of mixed-status families, living with at least one undocumented family member in the same household.[15] There are now an estimated
4.6 million mixed-status family households in the United States, which con-
tain varied constellations of citizens, permanent legal residents, undocumented
immigrants, and individuals in legal limbo through temporary protected
status or deferred action programs.[16] The majority of those in mixed-status
families—6.6 million—are U.S. citizens.[17] Most children in these families are
U.S. citizens, comprising three-quarters of all children of unauthorized immigrants.[18] These numbers highlight the profound impact of policy on children and
youth, regardless of their own citizenship or migration status.[19] These "forgotten
citizens" may not enjoy fully the benefits of citizenship or feel that they belong.[20]
In addition to intergenerational differences, there are 450,000 foreign-born siblings of citizens, whose experiences have remained largely underinvestigated
and unaddressed.[21]

The sharp and measurable increase in mixed-status families over the past
two decades is the result of two interrelated exclusionary developments. First,
increased border militarization has made it more difficult for people to circulate between the United States and Mexico as they did in the past. For most of
the twentieth century, people who migrated to the United States for work
returned home for parts of the year or to remain permanently after several years.
But, beginning in the 1990s, increased Border Patrol presence and its accompanying technologies—sensors, drones, aerostat radar systems, and coordination
with local law enforcement departments—have made this circular movement
more difficult. Routes for entering the United States were shut off, redirecting
people into deadly desert passages.[22] Because of these amplified barriers, many
people stopped returning to Mexico and instead opted to either bring relatives
over or establish their families in the United States. In addition, a visa backlog
has made entering the country legally a daunting, almost impossible, process.
Because of the large number of family ties to the United States, there are many
more Mexicans waiting for green cards than those from other countries. Obtaining a family-sponsored green card can take up decades for those living in
Mexico, a country that is considered "oversubscribed" because it has exceeded

its allocation of visas.[23] At the time of this writing, the U.S. Citizenship and Immigration Service was still processing applications that were submitted twenty-one years ago. With this in mind, it is perhaps no wonder that even those who are eligible for a visa may forfeit the wait and attempt entry in another manner to reunite with family.

A second trend has been the decline in opportunities to regularize one's legal status. In prior decades, the overall experience of illegality was shorter and affected fewer people. Through the late 1980s, there were a number of mechanisms and easier processes for undocumented people to become legal, including marriage to a citizen, petitioning through a family member, and amnesty programs. By the mid-1990s, however, policy changes greatly restricted the ability to legalize status. These shifts in both immigration and enforcement policy disproportionately impacted Mexican nationals; as a consequence, more than half of Mexican immigrants in the United States are undocumented today.[24] As a result of these ever-shifting terrains, mixed-status families represent a complex web of migration histories, legal statuses, and national identities. This complexity means that we must move beyond binaries of "documented" and "undocumented"—or "authorized" and "unauthorized"—to a spectrum that captures various dimensions of people's legal ambiguity.[25]

By examining how the construction of illegality for some members in a family influences opportunities and resources for all, including legal residents and citizens, this book contributes to scholarship on deportability, precarity, and how they relate to constructions of citizenship.[26] It illustrates how lives are repeatedly mediated by the condition of illegality, the impact of which can be examined in everyday, embodied experiences, even for those who are lawfully present.[27] A myopic focus on individuals in U.S. law and policy to date has grossly neglected historical and geographical factors resulting in mixed-status families. As a result, cumulative effects on families are overlooked. Members are sharply separated on the basis of rights and opportunities, even though they share lives and occupy the same spaces on an everyday basis. Juridical categories of legal status stratify resources and shape members' socialization in relation to institutions such as education and health care, as well as within the domestic sphere of the household. By examining the experiences of mixed-status families, we can examine the functioning of the contemporary state and its penetration into institutions of kinship,[28] as well as how policies, institutions, and agents interpret, implement, and/or extend immigration laws.[29]

Immigration law in the United States has failed to keep pace with the fluid and complex configurations of migrant families; rather than preserving families, law has become a mechanism for dividing them. The ways individuals are categorized by law—which has the power to demarcate boundaries and define inclusion—establishes the very contours of the family. For instance, while current U.S. immigration laws privilege family membership in the re-unification process, it simultaneously undermines those structures through specific state-defined constructions of kinship (that is, who is included as "family") in addition to the designation of some members as unauthorized. Illegality and its counterpart, deportability, are thus constituted and reconfig-ured through intimate relationships. Although experienced as personal and private, intimacies are material sites that are always connected to larger rela-tions of power and governance.[30] States have historically utilized intimate ties to create and reinforce deeply unequal relationships at various scales.

While I utilize the term "family" throughout this book, it is important to not take this social construct for granted and to recognize that it has particular meanings and implications in the law. Which intimate relationships are ac-knowledged as constituting "family"—and which are not—is a deeply political and constantly shifting question. As Luibhéid, Andrade, and Stevens argue, "When states designate certain intimate forms as constituting 'families,' this may carry access to rights, opportunities, and protections for those involved. Yet, these recognized ties also become the basis for state authorities to govern, subjectify, and often dispossess people in multiple ways that demand cri-tique."[31] The state derives power to define and divide families precisely by sin-gling out and interacting with the individual.[32] Mixed-status families, thus, are the result of isolating the individual as the site for regulatory enforcement, and obscuring the central role of the state and its agents in defining legitimacy.

A major theoretical concern of this book is the character of relationships with state regimes, requiring a focus on the concept of citizenship. Citizenship, here, refers to a complex set of practices that constitute political belonging; this concept has evolved to expand beyond the nation-state context to incorporate claims making in various sites and scales. Social scientists view citizenship as more than the rights and membership determined by the nation-state. Rather, they are spaces of belonging that can surpass or supersede legal membership. There are many forms of political and cultural membership beyond possession of a passport; people also assert membership by residing and participating in

a community. They can sustain a sense of belonging even if they are excluded in other ways. Despite the central role of legal status in this book, the stories presented here are framed through a broader consideration of relational citizenship, emphasizing that it is a dynamic institution of both domination and empowerment, governing who is citizen, subject, and abject within the body politic.

Transnational migration poses a basic challenge to citizenship because it interrupts the relationship between territorially bounded states and political subjectivity. Since its inception as a field of study, examinations of citizenship practice have focused on the individual. Meanwhile, studies of immigrant families have hitherto focused on their transnational nature or on the incorporation experiences of the second generation.[33] This book offers theoretical insights on illegality and the practices of citizenship, bridging the experiences at the micro-household and policy levels to better understand how the state shapes differences at the family level. Illegality is typically viewed as a process, in which the end point is becoming legal. However, it is frequently an open-ended condition, and it also touches the lives of those who are "legal."

Scholarship on citizenship and migration has long focused on the immigrant family as a way to understand incorporation processes—especially of the second generation—over time. For this reason, the family has generally been defined by the presence of dependent children. However, this definition, while entrenched in U.S. law, does not capture all dimensions of family variation.[34] "Mixed-status families" have been distinguished in a number of ways. Three decades ago, Leo Chavez[35] introduced the concept of the "binational family" to describe such kinship structures—that is, families that include both undocumented members and also U.S. citizens, remarking on the implications of status differentiation for political belonging. The Pew Hispanic Center defines them as families with at least one undocumented parent and at least one U.S.-citizen child.[36] Other scholars have broadened the utility of the term, such as Ruth Gomberg-Muñoz, who uses it to mean any self-defined family with different immigration and/or citizenship statuses.[37]

In this book, I use "mixed-status" to refer to families comprised of at least one undocumented member and at least one other person with any authorized legal status (i.e., U.S. citizen, legal permanent residency) or precarious status (e.g., deferred action or temporary protected status). Because the focus is on the effects of illegality on others, at least one undocumented person must be

present for an analysis of how this impacts the social unit of the family. However, the inclusion of *precarious status* as part of the definition (rather than only citizens) is unique and results from the increased impact of deferred action in the United States over the past several years. Precarity refers to the politically induced condition of indeterminacy, or as Anna Tsing describes it, of "life without the promise of stability."[38] In 2012, President Barack Obama initiated the Deferred Action for Childhood Arrivals (DACA) program, which provided temporary reprieve to undocumented young adults. Some 800,000 individuals benefited from this program before it was rescinded. The temporary status shift out of illegality for these young adults was so impactful, I argue, that it created incorporation experiences and family dynamics that must be analyzed in ways similar to mixed-status families with citizens. However, at the same time, it was temporally limited and experienced as a precarious status in which people were lawfully present but still deportable.

This book also recognizes a *wider range of relationships*, including extended family members and the presence of multiple generations in the household, relying on participants' own designation of who constitutes family. This is particularly important since the book examines how people negotiate legal categories, which often have a more narrow definition of what constitutes a family and may not recognize the same range of relationships as individuals do. Here, the concept of mixed-status incorporates same-sex households. It considers equally the experiences of couples who have obtained new opportunities for legalization through the Supreme Court ruling *United States v. Windsor* in 2013 that declared the Defense of Marriage Act (DOMA) unconstitutional and allowed same-sex spouses to receive the same immigration benefits under federal law that "traditional" marriages had long received. The experiences of these households have been neglected in scholarship on immigrant families to date, although they can shed light on the legal double bind that existed between their own and the state's definitions of family (or intimate ties).

The analytical focus in the coming chapters is not limited to intergenerational relationships (i.e., parent/child); rather, this book includes a rare look at the implications of *status differences between siblings*. While most scholarship on immigrant families is concerned with intergenerational dynamics,[39] the focus here is on a broader set of relationships in order to understand their impact on the immigrant experience. Sibling relations—and how they influence dynamics of exclusion, material support, and emotional connection—remain an

understudied area.[40] Attention to gendered experiences further highlights the ways in which they are a critical determinant of the distribution of resources and responsibilities within families.

Finally, the composition of mixed-status families is not static, as members may move between statuses and in and out of households over time. Notably, there is significant overlap between the family—a concept that references kinship structures—and the household as a strategic social grouping of co-residing individuals who may be, but are not necessarily, related. Households are a critical locus of negotiation, where collective decision making is in tension with often conflicting interests of individual members.[41] This results in complex power dynamics, as households are units not only of collaboration but also of contention and inequality. Those in mixed-status families have a clear understanding of the resources afforded to various members and are engaged in constant negotiation with state power, feeling the profound impact of the law in both their private and public lives.[42]

The Study

This book examines the experiences of 100 mixed-status families, based on five years of ethnographic study in a U.S.–Mexico border county where an estimated 11.7 percent of the general population is undocumented,[43] and which has a high percentage of mixed-status families. The study relied on a unique approach: rather than interviewing one person from each family, which would have resulted in a limited and subjective snapshot of experiences and dynamics, it sought greater depth by focusing on multiple members of the same family in order to produce novel empirical and theoretical insights. Between two and five members were interviewed per family.[44] Participants were recruited using purposive referral (snowball) sampling after initial individuals were identified with the assistance of local community-based organizations. In other words, each participant was asked at the end of the interview if they could recommend others that fit the study criteria.

Research assistant Milena A. Melo was a critical part of the data collection process. A doctoral student in anthropology at the time, she was also conducting fieldwork for her dissertation, which compared the experiences of Mexican-born dialysis patients at the fringes of the U.S. health-care system.[45] During our trips, we frequently visited participants in either study, and, in a few cases, people were involved with both projects. My understanding of these

dire life-and-death health situations was deeply enriched through this complementary fieldwork. A DACA recipient from a mixed-status family herself—as well as a native of the Rio Grande Valley—the rapport Milena brought in recruiting participants was invaluable. It also offered the opportunity for thoughtful discussions as we traversed the region for hundreds of miles together, as she reflected on her own experiences compared to the stories of participants. While we split interviewing tasks, we were generally both present for every encounter.

Interviews took place at a location of the participant's choice, typically in their homes (in the kitchen, in the living room, or, to take advantage of the breeze on hot days, in the front yard). Many participants lived in *colonias*, unincorporated neighborhoods that are distributed all across the county though not always distinguishable from other housing developments except for a lack of street signs and paved roads. Most commonly, people were interviewed individually rather than as a group, which allowed the triangulation of multiple, independent perspectives and reduced bias that may be introduced by power differentials among family members. However, because of the sustained interactions with families across years, some of the later interviews evolved to include multiple family members at the same time, which provided a more natural conversational setting and allowed participants to complement or question one another's accounts of events. Between 2013 and 2017, interviews were conducted with a total of 167 individuals—in Spanish, English, or both languages—and audio-recorded with the participants' consent.[46]

A second central component of this study's methodological approach was longitudinal interviewing across several years. The experiences of multiple family members were followed over time, which permitted a more in-depth understanding of dynamics by generating data to compare perspectives. Following up with people a year or two (or three) later, we met new babies, learned about recent marriages, heard about changes in employment, watched as houses were built or renovated, congratulated people on high school and college graduations, commiserated with families' experiences of death and deportation, and traced shifts in legal status and the complex processes associated with obtaining them. Beyond the formal interviews, many participant families stayed in touch in other ways, including phone calls, messages, and updates on social media, providing an ongoing glimpse into important events in their lives. This kind of deep and long engagement is an effective way to understand, as Roberto Gonzales notes, "how vulnerable populations make sense of, contend with, and respond to the material conditions of their lives."[47] Of the 167 persons interviewed, 75 completed a follow-up interview one to two years after the first, while 10 completed two additional interviews and were followed for more than four years. This resulted in a total of 252 interviews, which provided the longitudinal picture of their lives that forms the foundation of this book.[48]

Even with this large set of data resulting from following families over several years, a triangulation of multiple sources was utilized to ensure robust findings. These included informal interviews with sixty-two health-care providers, teachers, caseworkers, social workers, nonprofit and nongovernmental organizational staff, public-health officials, researchers, and other key stakeholders. These interviews provided background information about resources and major challenges and successes in the region. These formal methods were supplemented by extensive on-the-ground participant observation in communities, including activities ranging from those in more intimate spaces (such as sharing meals with families) to very public forms of engagement and support (such as participating in events advocating for immigrant rights).

Outline of the Book

This book illustrates the effects of illegality on families by underscoring that law and policy do not only affect the undocumented. It uses ethnographic evidence to examine many aspects of daily life to reveal the production of differential outcomes within the same family. Each chapter addresses the three interrelated main arguments of the book: (1) that the construction of illegality for some members in a family influences opportunities and resources for all, including legal residents and U.S. citizens; (2) that families and individuals actively contest their exclusion and develop a set of strategies in response to limitations that arise; and (3) that unique features of the border region shape these experiences and responses. Each chapter investigates a different but interrelated aspect of their experience. Throughout each chapter, I juxtapose the accounts of multiple members of the same family to contextualize the snapshots of social dynamics and to provide novel insights on their experiences.

The book unfolds over eight substantive chapters and a conclusion. Chapter 1 describes the geographic, cultural, and political landscape of the Rio Grande Valley of South Texas, arguing for the importance of place in understanding the ways in which illegality is experienced and negotiated. It includes stories of why and how people decided to cross the border, and the ways in which this mobility directly resulted from and/or produced mixed-status families. Arriving in this region, families are welcomed into a familiar binational cultural space; however, this familiarity is tempered by a long history of violence against and disenfranchisement of Mexicans and Mexican Americans, contemporary anti-immigrant discourse, and relentless surveillance associated with the militarized border. Individuals living in mixed-status families develop layered, intertwined, and contested identities, framed within the history of ethnic politics in South Texas. Chapter 2 examines the dynamics of mixed-status families, including their shared norms, interpersonal tensions, and systems of mutual support. As legal status stratifies the household, creating divisions and even resentment, the central pattern is nonetheless family unity. Chapter 3 turns outward to explore relationships between mixed-status families and others in their communities. Disclosure—that is, to whom, when, and why people talk about their own or their family's status—is a major focus here, with both undocumented persons and U.S. citizens describing "little lies," acts of concealment, and feeling as if they must live a double life. Even close friendships and intimate romantic relationships are affected. Chapter 4 explores the limited physical mobility along the U.S.–Mexico border, within the 100-mile buffer zone, and how this affects mixed-status families in unique ways compared to the rest of the United States. Many people are relegated to life within this small strip along the border, and describe feeling "trapped in a cage" and unable to leave the region, often for decades. Differences in legal status within the family thus become embodied as stratified forms of mobility. Chapter 5 examines the social mobility of children—including U.S. citizens—who grow up in mixed-status families, and the additional borders they encounter as they attend college, obtain jobs, and become independent, as well as the ways in which they overcome these obstacles. Health is the focus of Chapter 6, especially the stark differences in access to medical care between citizens and their undocumented parents and siblings. Health policies have multiple direct and indirect impacts on mixed-status families, and may result in a hesitancy to enroll citizen children in public programs due to fear of deportation or to avoid jeopardizing future regularization opportunities. As formal systems fail to meet the needs of a large segment of the population, alternative and informal channels of care proliferate. Simply being part of a mixed-status family can result in poorer physical health and unequal access to care. Chapter 7 turns to the threat of family separation through deportation. The families in this book know well the fear and costs associated with detention and deportation, since it has affected the majority of them at some point. This chapter follows several families whose members have faced deportation, the elaborate "emergency planning" measures to be enacted in the case of family separation, and the return of family members using smugglers. Finally, Chapter 8 focuses on processes of legalization and status transitions. It illustrates that mixed-status families have an intimate relationship with the law, and follows those who have engaged with the legalization process—both successfully and unsuccessfully—including by petitioning through a spouse, child, or sibling. By pure coincidence, the data collected for this book covered the full term of the DACA program, and this chapter also provides rich stories of their trajectories from undocumented to precariously "DACAmented." Finally, it illustrates another social peril: jealousy, stratification, survivor's guilt, and hierarchies created within families and communities as some obtain legal status while others are left behind.

The book concludes with a reflection on the lessons learned from the 100 families, arguing that political efforts toward reform or social integration must take into account mixed-status family configurations, since they are a primary and enduring feature of the immigrant experience in the United States today. From the outset, this research was committed to informing policymaking through robust, theoretically grounded findings. Through deeper understanding, we can work toward policies that lift communities up rather than exacerbate inequalities.

CHAPTER 1

BELONGING IN THE BORDERLANDS

"HONESTLY, I'VE NEVER met a family where everyone is from the United States," twenty-five-year-old Manuel began. "There are a lot of people here with Mexican parents, but who already have legal status. Here, every family is mixed-status." We were in the kitchen of his parent's house, children from the neighborhood chasing past us, in and out of the back door. The kids laughed and shouted to one another in English, but when addressing their parents switched effortlessly into Spanish. A soccer game played on the television in the background, as Toluca tackled the reigning Liga MX champions, Club America. For me, soccer on TV has always been the definitive and comforting sound of a Saturday afternoon, so I was feeling quite at home. The smell of a wood smoke permeated from the backyard, as someone prepared coals for a barbeque later in the evening.

Manuel had come to the United States from Michoacán, Mexico, with his parents when he was three years old. He and his mother are undocumented, but his father is a lawful permanent resident (that is, a green card holder). His younger brother and sister were born in South Texas, and both are U.S. citizens. Manuel ended up marrying his high school sweetheart, a U.S. citizen, and the couple have a baby girl, who is also a U.S. citizen. I already knew Manuel's father's sister's family, and had briefly met his mother's brother and sister, and knew that all their relatives—the spouses, children, cousins, and in-laws—had a mix of legal statuses.

Manuel's younger brother Eric walked up to the table we were sitting at and asserted, "We're all Mexicans here," he laughed. I raised my eyebrows and asked, "So, you were born in the U.S., but you identify as Mexican, more than American?" "Yeah, because I grew up with my people. Even though some of them are citizens, they're all, like in a cultural way, Mexicans. We go to *quinceañeras, carne asadas, pachangas*." His broad smile faded, and he continued, "But sometimes I don't even feel American. I mean, look at how they treat my parents, my family. The discrimination. But here in the Valley it's different compared to up north, the way they see immigrants. Here, we don't see them as these illegals taking jobs or harming people. We see them as like, hey, they are our neighbors. They are family members. They're the people we know."

I knew Manuel's claim that "here, every family is mixed-status" was exaggerated, but it certainly often seems that way in South Texas. In the county where Manuel lives, at least one in ten persons is undocumented, and their lives are deeply enmeshed in families and communities with people from varying migrant backgrounds and legal statuses in addition to large numbers of U.S. citizens. This binational frame of reference makes sense: this used to be Mexico, before the borders were reorganized through the 1848 Treaty of Guadalupe Hidalgo and residents of the area were granted U.S. citizenship. For the next century and a half, the dominant population has remained Latinos of Mexican origin.[1] But there are also recent arrivals, drawn to the area by a combination of kin ties and factors pushing them to leave their home country, especially violence and economic instability. Of the estimated 100,000 undocumented people in this county, 98 percent are from Mexico.[2] Even for these individuals, their connections to the United States are deep; besides existing family ties, more than a quarter have lived in the United States for twenty years or longer.[3] As a result of these enmeshed lives, in this county, more than half (51.3 percent) of all U.S. citizen children live with at least one noncitizen parent.[4] The fact that 97 percent of people living here speak Spanish at home further underscores how binational ties extend into subsequent generations.[5] In many parts of the United States, but especially in the U.S.–Mexico border region, the relationships between kinship, legal status, citizenship, race, ethnicity, and belonging are complex—simultaneously contemporaneous and deeply historically embedded.

Place matters. This chapter examines how local context uniquely shapes pathways of incorporation and impacts the everyday experiences of mixed-status families. Local configurations of laws, practices, and attitudes reflect how specific geographic settings offer unique mobilities, resources, opportunities, and disadvantages.[6] While other studies have sought to counter the overwhelmingly urban focus in the literature by examining the socio-geographical and structural conditions of rural America to understand the role of regional context,[7] this book turns its focus to the U.S.–Mexico borderlands. Across the United States, processes of illegality do not unfold evenly; they are in constant interplay with local barriers and facilitators of belonging. As this chapter illustrates, there are pockets of inclusion. At the same time, the historical marginalization and illegalization of Mexican migration through U.S. immigration laws, along with contemporary militarization of the region, provides an important backdrop for understanding the experience of illegality for families.

A number of geographic and social features set the Rio Grande Valley apart from adjacent regions, including its ethnic makeup, the dominance of the Spanish language, and a strong binational frame of reference. These features are tempered by the relentless and constant surveillance associated with the militarized border. In particular, the geographical layout of border enforcement checkpoints supplements and intensifies the extensive interior enforcement that is becoming commonplace in other parts of the United States, including through roadblock checkpoints and raids on jobsites. The case of the U.S.–Mexico border region foreshadows the effects of the merger between immigration enforcement with the criminal justice system that has been developing in the rest of the country, and for understanding what life looks like in an area militarized early and vigorously.

Borderlands

Rafael and I met to catch up over breakfast one Friday morning at a popular downtown diner. Opened in 1947, it had changed little since. The original green-and-white neon sign still hung outside the two-story brick building. Vinyl stools were bolted in front of the old soda fountain, where servers hustled to refill coffee. A glass case next to the cashier stand brimmed with pan dulce: pink, white, and chocolate *conchas*; empanadas filled with pineapple, strawberry, or sweet potato; piglet-shaped *marranitos*; pink-and-white twisted *cuernos*; pecan *polverónes*; buttermilk biscuits; and sugared donuts. The smell of griddled potatoes and bacon scented the air. A mural on the south wall depicted life in the 1940s, highlighting the importance of the railroads to the city and honoring Narciso Delgado, a pioneer of Tejano music who hailed from the region.

The restaurant was full. Octogenarians, all regulars, lingered over coffee, catching up on gossip, reading papers, and entertaining handshakes and conversations with local politicians and funeral directors. Since no tables had opened up for us after a few minutes of waiting just inside the door to escape the 95-degree morning heat, an elderly gentleman waved us over, insisting that we sit at the table he shared with his wife. He wore a bright printed shirt bearing the American flag and eagle, and a baseball hat indicating he was a U.S. Army veteran. His weathered skin was the color of the *café con leche* he was drinking. His wife stacked their finished dishes of *chilaquiles* and eggs to a corner of the table to make room for us. The conversation was friendly and casual, alternating seamlessly between English and Spanish, often in the same sentence. After Rafael asked if the couple were local, the stranger explained that they had lived here since the 1950s. He spoke of first coming to the United States: "Back when we came over," he told us, "no one cared if you had that card. They just cared that you were a good worker. There was always work. We worked in the fields, and then I joined the service." Indeed, until the 1990s, the border was quite porous. For generations, cross-border mobility was not only unrestricted; it was a vital part of daily life.

Despite increased surveillance and regulation in spaces of the nation's interior in recent years, the U.S.–Mexico border remains an analytically powerful construct for examining historical patterns of inclusion and exclusion and is an important reminder of the enduring territorial authority of the state.[8] The Texas border is unique because of the geophysical separation created by the Rio Grande and the twenty-six bridges connecting the two countries. More than 11.5 million people live in interdependent communities along the 2,000-mile border, where transnational living strategies have always been integral components of daily life.[9] These interactions are rooted in early settlement patterns, adaptive cross-border linkages, and ties with recent immigrants, all defying efforts to categorize populations along simplistic lines.[10]

Communities on both banks have been variously conjoined and split through a violent history of multiple conquests and changing ethnic and political identities. Transnational practices and kinship ties have created a regionalism that has often subverted state attempts to control and divide the population.[11] This regional history has shaped local perspectives on immigration to the present day. Here, residents frequently identify more with the border region itself than with each nations' respective social and political core.[12] However, political subjectivity and cultural identity in the borderlands manifests in ways that carry the legacy of specific ethnoracial histories.

The physical U.S.–Mexico frontier remains a space of continuous economic, social, political, and cultural negotiations.[13] While border studies theories have contributed an understanding of underlying and often counterhegemonic relations that take place in such interstitial spaces, this focus can also shroud the specificities that shape the dynamic particularities of the region.[14] While one dominant perspective in migration scholarship argues that bordering processes can now be found everywhere, borders must also be conceptualized not just as parametrical limit points but also as actual spaces of residence and sites of resistance. In other words, the border is and remains exceptionally locationally robust, and in South Texas it is particularly deep and intense.[15]

Map 2 depicts the 100-mile-wide buffer zone along the border that forms a secondary boundary to the interior of the United States. Over the past decade, U.S. Customs and Border Protection has doubled the number of agents along the immediate border as well as in areas up to 100 miles away from it, as part of a layered approach known as the "defense in depth" strategy. Immigration checkpoints, staffed 24/7 and located between 25 and 100 miles from the border along all major highways that lead into the interior of the United States, are one vital element of this strategy.[16] These checkpoints affect not just recent border crossers but also those who have lived here for decades.

Borders represent the ultimate regulation of mobility, creating uneven landscapes of movement. They illustrate not just how particular modes of such are enabled, but also how some forms of mobility are regulated, policed, prevented, and forbidden.[17] In recent years, scholars have challenged the taken-for-granted idea that human populations are inherently sedentary and that movement is only a temporary or extraordinary condition. Instead, migration has always been a part of human behavior. No nation has been untouched or unchanged by human mobility. Meanwhile, dislocation, disjuncture, and zones of social exclusion have come to the fore in the study of mobility.[18] The convergence of critical migration studies and mobility studies allows a focus on embodied politics of difference and an exploration of the ways in which some mobilities are facilitated while others restricted.[19]

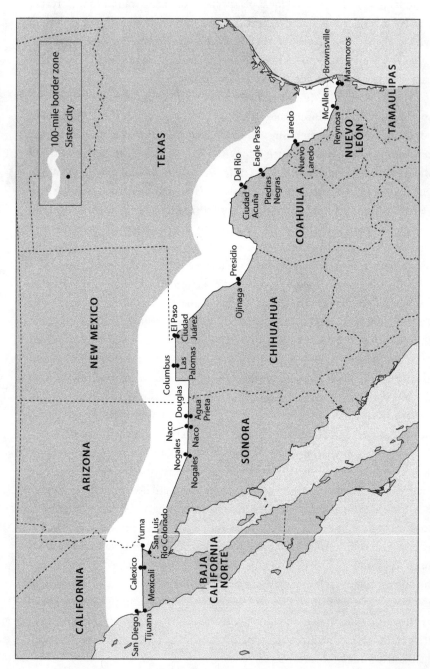

Map 2. The 100-mile-wide border zone, including sister cities on both sides of the international boundary.

A History of Exclusion

Categories of race and the exclusions they create are historically produced and evolve over time. In the uneven and complex landscape of immigration law and enforcement in the United States, Mexicans have been targeted in specific ways.[20] What follows is by no means a comprehensive history of these policies and practices; rather, it is a broad stroke to provide context for the ethnographic moments in this book.

During the nineteenth century, gendered and class-based barriers dictated the outcomes of U.S. citizenship policies. Racial dimensions of immigration and citizenship laws became more prominent after the Nineteenth Amendment to the Constitution granted women the right to vote in 1920. Shortly thereafter, the Immigration Act of 1924 (also known as the Johnson-Reed Act) introduced widespread restrictions on immigration and a national-origins quota system for admission to the United States. The quota system provided visas to 2 percent of the total number of people of each nationality that was living in the United States at the time, based on the 1890 national census. In doing so, this legislation attempted to reproduce the desired composition of the United States and preserve homogeneity, largely discriminating against those who were not northern Europeans. It also included a provision excluding the immigration of those who were considered ineligible for citizenship by virtue of race or nationality, most notably those of Asian heritage.

Mexicans were initially not formally excluded in this same way. The Treaty of Guadalupe Hidalgo, signed in 1848 following the end of the Mexican–American War, gave the northern half of Mexico to the United States and provided U.S. citizenship to those living in the conquered territories (land that makes up all or parts of present-day Arizona, California, Colorado, Nevada, New Mexico, Texas, Utah, and Wyoming). However, the previously loose conflation of race and nationality was also realigned in new and uneven ways through the Immigration Act of 1924, specifically in constructing a white American race for those of European descent. Although Mexicans were initially included in the "white" category, this legal status was highly unstable.

By the late 1920s, a confluence of tensions related to commercial agriculture, immigration, and segregation practices led to the development of a perceived Mexican "race problem" in the U.S. Southwest. The result was greater population management directed at immigrants from Mexico. By 1930, the U.S. Census Bureau established "Mexican" as a distinct racial category, thereby

guaranteeing their exclusion in the national-origins quota system. This rein-
forced the conflation of race, ethnicity, and national origin as tools of oppression and labor extraction. The Immigration Act of 1924 had also established
the foundation for processes that unfolded in the following decades by casting
Mexicans, specifically, as "illegal aliens" and Asians as permanent foreigners.[21]
In times of high demand for labor, Mexicans were repeatedly recruited to the
United States under a series of programs and then repatriated. The most no-
table effort was the Bracero Program, initiated in 1942. This bilateral set of
agreements brought millions of Mexican guest workers to the United States,
particularly as agricultural labor. Operation Wetback, implemented in 1954
by the Immigration and Naturalization Service, was a tag-team effort with the
Mexican government to round up undocumented workers and funnel them
into this program. In 1964, the Bracero Program was terminated.

The Immigration and Nationality Act of 1965 (also known as the Hart-Celler
Act) replaced the quota system with per-country caps, removing the prior racial and national barriers to immigration. In doing so, however, the United
States for the first time put caps on Mexican and other Latin American immigration, and the number of available visas did not meet the demand. This
Act did not actually lead to a decrease in migration levels, but it did foster
undocumented migration in the decades that followed, as people continued
to arrive but with no legal mechanism. While explicit mention of race was removed from immigration law, it was replaced with a central concern with "illegal immigration," and thus effectively increased the likelihood of illegality
for newly excluded Mexicans.[22] This set the stage for the substantial growth in
the number of undocumented Mexicans in the decades to follow.

In the 1980s, several forms of relief were made available to undocumented
persons and their family members, to which heavy-handed anti-immigrant
policies responded in the 1990s. In 1986, the Immigration Reform and Control
Act (IRCA) provided temporary legal status, and eventually green cards, to an
estimated 2.7 million undocumented people. This amnesty was coupled with
the "Family Fairness" executive action under Presidents Ronald Reagan and
George Bush, Sr. (1987–1990), which protected an important group left out of
the IRCA: the spouses and children of individuals who were in the process of
legalizing their status. However, the Illegal Immigration Reform and Immigrant Responsibility Act of 1996 (IIRAIRA), an effort to strengthen and
streamline U.S. immigration laws, was introduced as the most draconian immigration measure to date. It imposed criminal penalties for smuggling and

the use or creation of fraudulent immigration-related documents, and required employment eligibility verifications with sanctions for employers who failed to comply. It also set strict guidelines for the disbursement of government aid to immigrants. Overall, the law made more people deportable—in fact, it created the preconditions for using deportation as a plausible and constant threat, and made it easier to deploy—with the possibility for even lawful permanent residents to be deported for minor offenses.

A more recent trend has been the convergence of immigration policies with border enforcement practices. Heavy militarization of the U.S.–Mexico border began in the 1990s, with the erection of portions of a wall, fencing, drones, blimps, underground sensors, and increased presence of Border Patrol agents. This deterrence strategy was employed especially in areas that are easier to cross, forcing migrants to take more dangerous routes and leading to an increased number of deaths along the border.[23] Jason de León, in *The Land of Open Graves*, argues that this "Prevention through Deterrence" program was part of a strategic federal plan that essentially weaponized inhospitable landscapes—particularly the Sonoran desert—to prevent illegal migration. The deaths that resulted, rather than being unintended consequences of policy, were clearly recognized by the government as both a possibility before its implementation and as evidence that the program was working to presumably deter new migrants.

While this made it more difficult to enter the United States, policies and practices such as these also made it harder to leave and return, disrupting circular migration between the two countries. As a result, many people ultimately settled and started families in the United States rather than return home. This is one of the factors that led to an increase in mixed-status families. A second factor has been the absence of any large-scale legalization program since the mid-1980s. In the meantime, an entire generation of children has grown up without legal status.

The concentration of enforcement efforts at the Southern border has sharpened the association between "illegal immigration" and Mexicans, in particular. The historical and contemporary operation of the border not only restricts the physical movement of Mexican workers but also denies them rights and renders them vulnerable to exploitation by designating them as illegal if they manage to enter U.S. territory. The growing trend of immigration detention has converged with and further racialized these border enforcement practices, relying on and benefiting private prison corporations.[24] The Criminal

Alien Program, which began as an initiative to purge noncitizens from dangerously overcrowded jails, has today become one of the chief mechanisms driving federal prosecution and the imprisonment of people for immigration-related offenses.[25] After the attacks of September 11, 2001, interior enforcement was increased through federal programs like Secure Communities and 287(g), which encourage coordination between local law enforcement agencies and U.S. Immigration and Customs Enforcement. These programs were joined by a number of state and municipal laws, some favorable and some restrictive to immigrants. As Gomberg-Muñoz summarizes, these developments have produced three effects: (1) they pushed deportation to record levels; (2) they shifted enforcement activities to the interior of the United States; and (3) they created a patchwork of varied and inconsistent local and state policies.[26]

Border enforcement plays a critical role in maintaining global inequalities by producing separate social, political, and economic spaces, and by restricting the ability of impoverished residents to move from one region to another.[27] Today, this region experiences heavy policing that extends beyond the border itself, to include what Guillermina Gina Núñez and Josiah McC. Heyman refer to as a "dense web" of enforcement practices that range from inspection at ports of border entry to fixed interior checkpoints and mobile patrols in both urban and rural areas.[28] Along the U.S.–Mexico border, this creates zones of "entrapment,"[29] in which people restrict their movement or face arrest and deportation, thus limiting everyday activities as well as access to services and goods. Margaret Dorsey and Miguel Díaz-Barriga have argued that this, combined with mass incarceration and internal checkpoints, results in a "state of carcelment" for the entire region.[30] This concept highlights the intersection of racial and spatial dynamics emerging from current policing practices, as well as the actual effects on people's mobility and everyday lives. Through the intensifying carceral state, an entire region of the United States is interred.

Today, contemporary Mexican migration to the United States remains a predominantly undocumented story. Mexicans have long been the largest origin group among unauthorized immigrants, peaking at 6.9 million in 2007, or 57 percent of the total unauthorized population.[31] More than half of current immigrants from Mexico are undocumented, a direct and deliberate result of the laws, policies, and practices described here.[32] However, as a result of improved economic conditions in Mexico, there has been a sharp decline in undocumented migration from that country since 2005.[33] Coupled with the recession in the United States, by 2016 the percentage of unauthorized immigrants from Mexico fell to 50 percent of the total.[34] With more Mexicans leaving than coming to the United States, the overall flow between the two countries has been at its lowest point since the 1990s. Nonetheless, Mexicans remain the majority of the nation's undocumented immigrant population, estimated at 5.8 million.[35]

The Decision to Cross

This book is not about the migration process; rather, it is about what happens afterward. Nonetheless, crossing borders is necessarily both the starting point and a constant presence in the lives of mixed-status families. Given the unwelcoming legal landscape for Mexican immigrants in the United States, why do people decide to come? Perhaps unsurprisingly, many people migrate to the United States to find work, especially given the deteriorating economic situation in Mexico in prior years. This is coupled with a desire to improve the situation for their family and to ensure the best possible education for their children. Seventeen-year-old Michael reflected on his mother's gamble to cross through the Rio Grande and subsequently live in the United States as an undocumented person, in contrast to his aunts, who waited to obtain a visa but who can now only visit temporarily. As he sees it, his mother's gamble paid off for the family:

> My mom's sisters thought ahead so they can come here legally. They got their visas, so now they can come visit. But my mom wanted to give us a head start, so we could have a better future. She risked it all by coming over faster. As a result, my cousins didn't go to school over here. So we got a better opportunity than them, because they're still studying in Mexico, which is not as good as here. But on the other hand, they can come legally. Our mom sacrificed her ability to go back and forth so we could be here. She crossed in the middle of the night, risking her life in the coldness of water. The river can take you under. You can drown. She did it all for us, so we all can be together and be united and be strong.

For many others, especially those who arrived in the 2000s, the decision to come to the United States was linked to the increasing violence in Mexico. One important feature of the Rio Grande Valley is its proximity to Tamaulipas, known as one of the most violent states in Mexico because of its intense drug cartel activity (especially the deadly turf wars between the Gulf Cartel and Los Zetas).[36] Local law enforcement has been almost entirely replaced by the

Mexican military and Federal Police, who patrol with assault vehicles and armored trucks. Rates of homicide, armed robbery, carjacking, kidnapping, extortion, and sexual assault are among the highest in Mexico. As a result, many people have left for reasons of personal safety, which is often inextricably tied to economic security. Felipe and his wife, Herminia, decided to leave Tamaulipas in 2002. As he shared:

> I had my own business over there in Reynosa. Then things began to get difficult with the *narcotraficantes*. So I sent my wife and kids to the U.S. We struggled with the decision, because we were doing financially well at the time. The bank had just given us a loan to buy a house. So, they came over here, and I stayed to work in Reynosa, but then the violence increased. They assaulted me at gunpoint in my store. They stole our money. They sold drugs in front of my store. In the end, all of us fled the violence. That is the reason we came here—it is a safe place, and we have to fight to give our children a good life. Over there in Mexico, it's a very, very, very, very, very sad situation. My wife likes to say we are like lions defending our cubs. We had to make drastic choices, but we looked at our options and we can't return to Mexico.

His wife chimed in: "It's still very difficult for our family over there, and we are always wondering how much danger they are in. I have family in Reynosa and they tell me all the time about the shootouts [*balaceras*] that happen in their neighborhoods. Their children are traumatized. They have been outside playing when a gunfight starts, and they see people fall down dead. It's terrible, so terrible." Stories like these have shaped what anthropologist Sarah Luna refers to as the "affective atmospheres of terror" on the Mexico-U.S. border. This is especially the case as Reynosa has become further militarized in attempts to combat narco-trafficking and the torture, killings, and threats that accompany it.[37]

U.S. citizen Jennifer's parents decided to stay in Texas for the same reason, after crossing over to the United States for a temporary visit on a visa. She told me, "In 2005, that's when the cartels started. We went over to visit family in Texas one summer, and two weeks later, my uncle was killed. People told my mom that since he had been seen a lot with my brother, that my brother was at risk too. So we decided to stay here." Her mother nodded in agreement and added, "My plan was *not* to stay and live here, but I made that decision after everything in Mexico changed, with the violence. But we never thought we would enter without documents and stay here. No. We thought there would be a way to fix it somehow, but they never gave us the opportunity." While many have fled violence, Mexican nationals continue to find it difficult to obtain humanitarian visas and to seek asylum status under U.S. law.

Family stories about crossing are complex, often stretching across many years and multiple entries, with different family members arriving and returning at different times. Most of all, these stories are interwoven with difficult memories and emotions. Maricela Gomez and her husband left their Central Mexican home because they could not find well-paying work. They decided to leave their three children behind with her mother.

> My mom had a *comadre*[38] in Texas, who arranged a job for us. "Great," I said, "but what about the kids?" My mother said, "Well, if you want, leave them here with me for now. Go get the job, and then later I will bring them or you can come get them." And so my husband and I left. I told him, "We're just going to go for a year and work, and then come back home." We planned to return and buy some land and build a house. At the time, we had been living with his parents, so we just wanted to buy our own property and be independent. A year passed, and we hadn't saved enough. But I missed my children so very much. So I went back and brought them here to be with us. By the time I returned, he had bought a trailer [mobile home] for us, and we enrolled the children in school.

In a separate conversation, twenty-four-year-old Deisy, Maricela's daughter, relayed what it was like for her mother to leave her and her siblings behind in Mexico with their grandmother:

> One day, my mom said, "I'm going to go buy some groceries en *el mercado*," but she was crying, my dad too. In my mind, I'm like, "They're going to leave us, why are they taking luggage?" And then they didn't come back. I was four at the time. They came over here and worked for a whole year. I don't know how they did it. She would always send us stuff. We would get new toys, but we weren't happy, because we didn't have the love of our mom. She would call us every day, but she would cry. She wouldn't eat. She was depressed.

At this point, Deisy stopped and took a deep breath. The emotions took over. She said, "It's hurtful talking about that. Missing your mom for a whole year, when you're little. It's hard." She sniffled and wiped away tears. "We couldn't understand why." She got up and walked over to the kitchen to pour a glass of water. The subject changed for a while, and she joked about two little dogs poking their heads into the windows from outside, begging to be let in. After gathering herself, she continued.

> So one day my mom came home. It was my sister's birthday, and over there in Mexico, they throw you a big party at age three. That same night we came over here. We didn't know we were going to leave. So we did the party, *todo*, and then at the end of the night we left. Leaving my grandma was the hardest thing, because I never thought that I was going to see her again. We were angry because we left our grandma over there, and she had become like our mom. So once we crossed the river to the U.S., us kids were all mad. My brother was so mad, "Look at *este cochino país* [this filthy country], I want to go back to my grandma. I want to go back with my mom."

In her account, Deisy talks about how her grandmother had become like a mother to them, following her own mother's absence. A common pattern in transnational migration, children are frequently left behind with family members. Caregiving by grandmothers especially makes them, as Kristin Yarris argues in the case of Nicaragua, central actors in global migration today.[39] Recognizing grandmothers' critical role in the mixed-status family dynamic helps to further extend our understandings of transnational families from an intergenerational perspective.

Family reunification is another constant theme in stories of crossing over. Maria, a twenty-two-year old Deferred Action for Childhood Arrivals (DACA) recipient, recalled seeing her mother for the first time in six years. After a harrowing journey with smugglers, she was reunited with her mother. "When I came here and saw my mom, I thought all the stress was worth it! When I saw her, it was like, 'Is this real? Am I really standing in front of my mom?' We just cried together. Then I took a shower and noticed all of the cuts and cactus thorns on my back." These bittersweet stories of reunification often served as the flip side of accounts of extended anxiety and loss, as borders separated families indefinitely.

Crossing Over the "Easy Way" Versus the "Hard Way"

While there are several ways to enter the United States, people joked that these could be divided into crossing the "easy way" and the "hard way." The difference is essential because it impacts the legalization process, if an opportunity becomes available in the future. Administratively, the distinction is between "entering with inspection" versus "without inspection," and centers on whether or not state officials documented the person's entry into the country. Those entering without inspection face stiff penalties that can impact their ability to regularize, as well as lengthen their processing time, as we will see in Chapter 8. The bureaucratic designation of entry with or without inspection overlapped with people's ideas about crossing the "easy way" or the "hard way."

The "easy way" consisted of either overstaying a visa, using someone else's papers, or (especially for young children) appearing to be asleep when passing through inspection points. All of these were more common in the past than they are today, in the age of tighter security and biometric documents. The average time since migration for the people in this study was eighteen years, so many had entered during a time when the "easy way" was still fairly feasible. As Eva recalled, "It was me and my younger brother. We were a little nervous. They told us, 'Okay, just pretend you're asleep.' While crossing the border, I remember the lady that was bringing us over gave them some papers. She had two children about the same age as us. That's how we crossed." In this case, their parents had arranged for Eva and her brother to use the documents of a stranger's children. Despite all the emphasis on militarized border strategies—especially building a wall to purportedly stem migration—the "easy way" of entering the United States actually remains the most common. An estimated two-thirds of those who arrived in recent years did not cross a border illegally, but were admitted on non-immigrant (temporary) visas—often arriving at airports—and then overstayed the period of time they were provided by the terms of their visas.[40] This trend toward increasing percentages of visa overstays is expected to continue in the future.

The "easy" crossing method also reflects some important regional characteristics. A common form of mobility is via a Border Crossing Card (BCC, also called a "laser visa" or *mica*, B1/B2 visitor's visa issued for ten years at a time). This visa allows Mexican nationals to cross back and forth for short-term visits. It recognizes the interdependence of border communities, permitting people to cross frequently to spend time with relatives, shop, or pursue recreational activities (but not work). To qualify, applicants must demonstrate sufficient business, employment, family, or property ties in Mexico, which presumably encourages their return. While it does not permit residency in the United States, the visa does allow frequent, short-term trips. Holders are allowed to travel inside the current BCC border zone—within 25 miles of the border in California and Texas, within 55 miles in New Mexico, and within 75 miles in Arizona—for up to 30 days.

In the study that forms the basis of this book, almost all visa overstays occurred with the BCC, and thus represented a common way through which people found themselves becoming undocumented. Michelle, the young mother introduced at the start of the book who was unable to obtain a birth certificate for her daughter, recalled, "When I first came in here, I had the visa, but then it expired. Then that's when we just stayed here." Jennifer, who was born in the United States, but whose family returned to live in Mexico for a few years, remembers crossing in 1996: "Back then they wouldn't check as much; sometimes they would just wave you through. We all came together in the same car across the bridge. My parents crossed over using their *micas*, the visas. I had my [U.S.] birth certificate and Social Security number. My sister and my aunt were around the same age, so she had my aunt's documentation." As this example demonstrates, different family members held different opportunities for entry, with Jennifer's sister "borrowing" a relative's paperwork.

Entering the United States the "hard way," by contrast to the "easy way," refers to entry without inspection, typically by crossing the Rio Grande. (In a few isolated cases, people had made the journey through the Sonoran Desert, but this was rare in this region.) The decision to cross without inspection was the direct result of more rigid policies and fewer opportunities for legal entry to the United States.[41] Angelica is now a senior in college. She crossed with her mother when she was eight years old:

> I remember waking up, and my mom said, "Oh, you're not going to school today." And I was like, "Okay, that's weird." That was just days after 9–11 [September 11, 2001], and I think that was why my mom decided to make the move so suddenly, even though she was saving up money to cross. Obviously, they were going to increase security, so my mom was like, "You know what, let's go. Because if we don't go now we're probably not going to make it." So, we came over that day.

In a coffee shop near the local university, Carla and her brother José recounted crossing the border as children, a crossing that had also happened because of their parents' abrupt decision. Carla was now a graduate student and had just finished a shift at her professor's lab—which is why we met close to campus—and José was preparing to graduate with a degree in engineering.

They were born just across the border in Reynosa, Mexico, but have lived in the United States for more than fifteen years. After we sat down with our cups of coffee, Carla talked about how they came to the United States. She began, "I was seven when we came over here. I think he was five." José nodded and continued, "I still remember the day. I remember walking to school, and then I saw my dad at the corner, right?" Carla agreed, "Yeah, he was taking us to school. Our dad told us to get ready for school that morning. But actually, he was going to bring us here." "Did you come through the river?" I asked. Carla said, "Yes. We swam across, but I wasn't old enough to comprehend what was going on. I've always been attached to my dad. As a kid you're kind of like, 'He has it under control.' It wasn't until years later that I understand what actually happened." After a thoughtful pause, José recalled,

> I remember coming over here and then we stopped at a store, waiting for someone to pick us up. I remember drinking Dr. Pepper. I still have the taste of Dr. Pepper in my mind. That's why I've always liked Dr. Pepper. It reminds me of the bittersweet type of thing that it was, that day. We didn't know we were coming to the U.S. We didn't know what the hell we were doing.

Carla and José, like many of the so-called 1.5 generation—those who arrived in the United States as children but grew up undocumented—often had only small fragments of memory about their crossings. Those memories vacillated between the banal everyday (going to school, listening to their parents, the taste of a soda) and moments of violence. Many remembered unrelenting mud, cactus thorns, dangerous river waters, and being chased by dogs. Angela, for instance, recalled,

> It was scary, because you're little and you see this big river. And then you are taking off your shoes. All the gooey mud. The *pollero* [smuggler] had us walking like four hours; he was lost, and we were just walking and we're tired. The sugarcane fields cut us, because they are sharp. It was raining. There were a lot of fire ants. It was not a good experience. . . . As we were crossing the river, you had to leave all your clothes there on the other [Mexican] side. You don't have nothing, and then for you to leave your clothes there. It's part of you. I think I left something there since the beginning.

Like Carla, José, and Angela, many young adults described very specific but loosely connected sensations, feelings, and details, often in the present tense, as they searched for fragments of memory. They described confusion and loss, bittersweet upon reflection. Those who were apprehended also had vivid memories of violence and detention. For example, Olivia recalls being apprehended along with her mother and sister during their multiple crossing attempts:

> They took us to a very cold room. I'm not saying that we should get special treatment, but it was super cold. They gave us small cookies, the kind you get from vending machines. My sister and I are crying. We're small. "Where's mom? We want our mom!" We actually see her, because they're fingerprinting her and all that. So they begin to ask us, "Who guided you across? *Quien los está llevando por el otro lado*?" And we're like "Our uncle." "What is his name?" "We don't know." "How old is he? Is he from your mom or your dad's side?" We were like, "We don't know anything, only that he is our uncle." We just stuck to the story.
>
> So that was the first time. They threw us back across. And then the second time, we got caught again. "Get up! Get up!" And here we go again, crying, crying, crying. "Where's my mom?" And my mom is yelling from the other side, "Don't be scared, it's okay, don't be scared!" and I'm like, what is going to happen to us? So, they take us again to the detention center, and then again they throw us back across. And then the last time, when we thought it wasn't going to ever happen, there goes the American Dream, we made it across successfully.

The results of crossing attempts are often tragic and brutal. Maricela, the mother in the Gomez family introduced earlier in this chapter, decided to leave her children with their grandmother in Mexico for several years before she returned to bring them to the United States. Their family history took a heartbreaking turn. Several years later, Maricela resolved to bring over her mother, the children's grandmother, whom they missed dearly and who was now aging alone in Mexico. The journey, however, ended in tragedy. Maricela and her daughter Deisey only hinted at the full story, but Richard, her twenty-two-year-old son, recounted the following:

> Since we were always with my grandma, my mom's mom, she was like our second mom. So we would always encourage my grandma to come over [to the United States] because she didn't have anyone; she was alone. She was always afraid, but eventually decided, "I'm going to go over. I'm going to cross the river." So, she started talking to people to cross her over to this side. It had been years since we had seen her, so we were happy that she was going to come over. Like I said, she was like our second mom. She took care of us when my mom left to work. She was always there for us. My mom was so excited. "I have a surprise for you. Your grandma's going to come!"

But my grandma had an accident trying to cross the river. She panicked in the water, and she drowned, and so did the *pollero* [smuggler]. They both drowned. My uncle's mother-in-law was with them and saw everything, so that's how we know what happened. She couldn't help, because she was old, too, and she was just screaming for help and nobody came. Eventually, she walked until she got to Border Patrol. But they couldn't find my grandma's body. It was a whole week, and we were desperate to find her. Finally, they found her and we identified the body. It was pretty sad. I was eight at the time. I remember it was very hard because we were so excited to see my grandma—I'm starting to get emotional.

Richard sighed, stood up, and started moving toward the kitchen, much like his sister Deisy had when the tears welled up in her eyes. I shifted in my seat and asked quietly if he wanted to take a break. He shook his head and, after a minute, he turned to me and finished the story: "They took us to see my grandma at the funeral home. Well, it was actually just a cold morgue, because they were sending her body back to Mexico. We only had an hour to say good-bye. Until today, we haven't had the chance to go visit her grave. I would like just to go to visit her grave."

While the remainder of this book focuses on the lives of mixed-status families in the United States, it is important to understand the antecedent motivations and experiences associated with the migration process. These stories of border crossings serve as the backdrop upon which people's lives are built in the United States, and they frame the reasons why and the mechanisms behind how they ended up as mixed-status families. It is impossible to separate their lives in the United States from life in Mexico.

The Rio Grande Valley of South Texas

The Rio Grande Valley is an ideal place to understand the lived effects of law and policy. This region experiences the effects of national policies more harshly than the interior and encapsulates a number of extreme contradictions. It has been argued that residents here have historically been "the first affected and the last consulted" by decisions at the national level.[42] As such, it is a prime site for firsthand observation of social change to illuminate wider processes and to trace the contradictions of law.

Often simply referred to as "the Valley"—although it is actually a river delta—the four counties in the southernmost tip of Texas have an estimated population of 1.3 million people (and rapidly growing). It is physically isolated from other parts of the United States; the nearest metropolis, San Antonio, is a four-hour drive through flat brushland and isolated cattle ranches. More than 90 percent of the population is Latino, of whom 26 percent are foreign born, primarily in Mexico.[43] The population is predominately bilingual, with Spanish serving as the primary language.

It is a site of several contradictions. While large numbers of people cross the border in both directions on a daily basis for work and recreation, this mobility is only afforded to some segments of the population. Others, having entered on an unauthorized basis or having overstayed a visa, are restricted to life within a small strip along the border. Many define their lives by the distance they can travel before reaching a permanent checkpoint or other spatial boundary. For undocumented people, this means roughly two hours to the west, through sparsely populated brushland; thirty minutes to the south, until stopped by the U.S.–Mexico border; an hour and a half to the east, until stopped by the Gulf of Mexico; and only forty-five minutes to the north, where they end up facing permanent highway checkpoints. Unable to reenter if they cross back into Mexico, they are also unable to travel north to other parts of the state, as this requires inspection at U.S. Customs and Border Protection checkpoints along major roads. Many families describe being "trapped" in the region for decades, and their Mexican town of origin—as close as a ten-minute drive for those who can cross—may seem hundreds of miles away.[44] For many young people, the true frontier is the one they cross when leaving for colleges further north, without the certainty of being able to return.[45] These permanent checkpoints are supplemented by hundreds of temporary but strategic roadblocks placed in communities where immigrants live and work, operating as an additional level of inspection and creating an environment of entrapment.[46]

This particular stretch of the border has a long history of conquest, poverty, racial segregation, and ongoing militarization. While the local history follows larger patterns of Mexican exclusion, there are some regional particularities. Most notably, despite their U.S. citizenship, ethnic Mexicans remained socially inferior thanks to "Juan Crow" segregation laws and a dual wage system, de facto well until the 1970s.[47] Unlike the strict racial divides of the Jim Crow South, in Texas the structure of Mexican segregation could be partially overcome with lighter skin color, language skills, fluency with Anglo culture, and higher socioeconomic status. When the railroad arrived in 1904, it transformed the economy from a focus on ranching to one reliant on commercial farming. As a result, the Mexican ranching elite began to lose their status as social, economic, and political leaders in the region. As new class and ethnic relations solidified, intermarriage between Mexicans and Anglos, previously common, declined as the shift to commercial farming propelled new practices of segregation. As Jennifer Nájera has argued, "Though the law granted people of Mexican origin certain rights that other nonwhite races did not have, physical and symbolic violence against Mexican people relegated them to the margins of the nation-state."[48]

The historical pattern for this region has been extractive, as benefits of development flow toward the center of each nation, while border residents on both sides absorb the costs.[49] The Rio Grande Valley is also a site of social reproduction of labor. Many people work as seasonal agricultural workers in other parts of the United States while maintaining a primary household in the Valley. As such, it has long functioned as both a territorial and institutional space in which some proportion of the costs of reproducing labor are transferred; that is, it is a space to which politically disenfranchised migrant labor returns for refuge and renewal.[50] Meanwhile, significant costs are absorbed by underfunded local governments, who must pick up the cost of health, education, and welfare programs, while the net benefit from taxes (including those paid by undocumented workers[51]) flow up and profit the federal level.

Despite being a node of major international commercial activity, with billions of dollars flowing through it each day, the Rio Grande Valley is one of the most disadvantaged areas of the United States. In Hidalgo County, the study site, 33.5 percent of residents live in poverty.[52] Many families reside in one of 2,300 *colonias*—unincorporated neighborhoods often lacking roads, water, electricity, and sewerage systems. More than an expression of rural poverty, *colonias* are a phenomenon intimately linked to the border and have their own unique cultural, economic, and geographic features.[53] They are advantageous in the maintenance of multigenerational households, delivering low-cost housing and providing inhabitants with the ability to combine multiple sources of income.[54] A vast informal economy fostered by the international border presents opportunities for persons without legal status, formal education, or English skills, which eases incorporation of newcomers.[55] High poverty and inequality together produce and reproduce a setting with high levels of informality in labor markets and economic exchanges.[56]

The Rio Grande Valley is frequently marginalized in public discourse as a "third world" within the "first world." Representations in the popular media

often portray the region as a lifeless and desolate site in need of federal surveillance,[57] and propagate notions of an area filled with people characterized
as dangerously noncompliant with American ideals of citizenship, prosperity,
and security.[58] Due to its proximity to Mexico, the region is framed as both an
unruly internal colony as well as a racialized periphery, a characterization that
neglects the agency and lives of border residents. For these residents, the Rio
Grande Valley is vastly more than this narrow depiction. While there are high
rates of poverty, there is also low unemployment in the rapidly growing service, manufacturing, and aerospace sectors. There are high rates of medically
uninsured, but there are also established, successful networks of local advocates revitalizing downtowns, fighting for infrastructure and housing improve-
ments, and building community health centers nationally recognized for
excellence.

One of the many contradictions in the region is the high rate of homeownership. While instable housing is often referenced as a major constraint for
immigrant families across the United States,[59] an estimated 57 percent of undocumented persons in Hidalgo County are homeowners.[60] Land is plentiful
here, and in the 1970s and 1980s developers carved up ranchland and sold the
parcels at bargain prices. However, in many places, the land was unprepared
for human habitation, and lacked paved roads, electricity, and water and sewerage systems—in some neighborhoods, they still do. In some of these *colonias*, the rightful owners may be unclear because many paid cash for their land
and did not have it formally mapped out and deeded. Nonetheless, homeownership opportunities are everywhere and highly valued by many immigrant
families. Herminia described the importance she attributed to owning her
own home:

> I told my husband: "We are getting a house, even if we have nothing to eat. We
> have to tighten our belts. Even if it's just a little house with the basics, so our
> children won't have to suffer." I had always heard that people that don't have doc-
> uments have problems renting an apartment. My children need to have peace
> and quiet so that they can concentrate on their studies. That was our motive for
> coming here. So we've sacrificed a lot, but we bought a little house.

Finally, the Rio Grande Valley is a region with a strong history of community organizing, with high rates of formal and informal participation in local
politics by immigrants and citizens alike. One primary example has been the
successful advocacy by community-based organizations to improve conditions

in the *colonias*—organizing for streetlights, improved drainage, and garbage services. More recently, efforts have focused on protesting the proposed border wall extension and its negative impacts in the region, including harm to a major wildlife refuge and private land seizures by the federal government using eminent domain laws. Other organizing efforts have focused on assisting refugee families from Central America—since 2014, a humanitarian respite center overseen by Catholic Charities of the Rio Grande Valley has assisted up to 300 people a day after they are released from Border Patrol custody—as well as protesting the separation of children from their parents when they arrive at the border, seeking asylum after having crossed illegally.

Many mixed-status families in the study were highly involved with such activism. Elizabeth, a U.S. citizen, described her motivation for becoming involved: "I am from Mexican parents who aren't citizens, so I feel like I need to do something. I have a little bit more power and can do more because I am a U.S. citizen. I do feel like I have a bigger responsibility because I am part of this country. We have to be united. I encourage people to vote." Juana is an undocumented mother of three whose entire family participates when there are immigration-related protests or marches. She said, "My seven-year-old son would be affected a lot if they took me. His older sister takes him to rallies and events and he holds up a sign that says, 'Don't separate my parents from me!' He's only seven years old, but he knows that if they want to deport us, the whole family is on a tightrope."

"The Culture Is Always Both"

The Rio Grande Valley has a number of sociocultural features that set it apart from adjacent regions. Many participants commented on the intimate connection to Mexico, and specifically the dominance of the Spanish language. As thirty-seven-year-old Alex, who arrived in the United States at age four from the neighboring state of Tamaulipas, explained, "We are our own people. Majority Hispanic. Between two borders. Separated from the rest of the country. Most speak Spanish. The culture is always both." This was echoed by Marco, a twenty-one-year-old DACA recipient and junior in college. He elaborated on the role of the Border Patrol checkpoints along major highways: "The Valley is kind of like a bubble, because there are checkpoints around it, like literally separating it from the rest of United States and Mexico." Many described growing up "between two borders"—namely, the international border and the highway checkpoints that prevent people from traveling and integrating into other parts of the United States.

Ivan, a twenty-two-year-old engineering student, described the strong binational frame of reference in everyday life as akin to a separation from the rest of the United States: "The Valley, basically it is like our own little country. It is like 'Little Mexico' down here. Everyone speaks Spanish, everyone is comfortable, everyone knows each other." On the other hand, some participants preferred to emphasize the Americanness of the region. Nineteen-year-old Alan commented: "We carry a normal American life; we're very Americanized. The way we eat, the way we talk. We've adapted. Our culture, we've transformed it to where we're mixing both of them, and we're comfortable like that." This mixed binational and bicultural frame of reference is reflected in the name of one of the local high schools, Benito Juarez-Abraham Lincoln High School, named after iconic presidents of both Mexico and of the United States.

Alan, who came to the United States at a very young age, went on to say that, "There's a common sense of helping each other out, because you know that if my family's suffering, like, what are the other families going through? We know families where the kids have died on the way, or their grandparents have died trying to come over here to have a better life. The Valley, it's not very individualistic; we help each other out." Many participants described the Valley as a "comfortable" place to live because of strong social support systems.

Relentless Yet Normalized Surveillance

Despite being a site of cultural blending and robust social networks, the Rio Grande Valley is also a highly militarized community under constant surveillance. Many people commented on the risk of deportation that accompanies random traffic stops, a fear that was heightened when the Texas Department of Public Safety set up networks of roadblocks. Another frequent sight are Skywatch surveillance towers, set up by local police departments to monitor activity along the sole highway in the region. These hover over parking lots in major shopping areas. Permanent shiny blimps are also frequently visible low in the sky: these are tethered aerostat radar systems, unmanned moored balloons that provide airborne surveillance data to U.S. Customs and Border Protection. In many places, the location of the international boundary can easily be traced by looking toward the Western horizon. As Angelica noted, "A lot of people don't understand what it is to live here on the border growing up and seeing the increase of militarization. Seeing Border Patrol everywhere. You can't be like, 'Let's go to the movies.' No, you have to be watching out. It's uncomfortable."

Others commented on the general sense of insecurity in the region, punctuated by spillover violence from cartel activity in Mexico. Alex, who arrived at age four, described growing up close to the border: "We were about two miles from the river; you could hear the gunshots, shootouts. You could hear and see choppers [helicopters] on both sides. You could see people crossing. Sometimes you see truckloads, carloads of people with drugs coming across being chased by state troopers or Border Patrol and local police." Miguel, a twenty-three-year-old U.S. citizen, stated that, "The neighborhood we grew up in, pretty much everybody was undocumented." His family lives in a rural *colonia* with run-down trailer homes and graffiti-tagged street signs. Windswept palm trees dominate the skyline, towering over dirt yards, packs of stray dogs, and citrus groves. "One way you could tell was that there would be violence, and nobody would call the cops, because they were afraid that they would get deported. So the neighborhood was insecure because of that."

Jennifer described interacting with guests from outside the region, who were unfamiliar with the heavy Border Patrol presence. As a member of an immigrant rights organization, she recalled the reaction of other advocates on a visit to the Valley.

> We live, we eat, we drive right next to Border Patrol every single day. And it's become so normal for us. Last summer we hosted DREAMer advocates from other parts of the U.S., and they were so surprised. We went to a restaurant, and Border Patrol was sitting right next to us, having lunch. And our friends were like, "Oh my God, Border Patrol is in here!" and panicking. When you see Border Patrol in other states, it's because something is going to go down, some sort of raid. But when you see Border Patrol here in the Valley, they're just having lunch, just like you. So I think that's what makes us so unique.

Ni de aquí, ni de allá: Overlapping, Contradictory, and Contested Identities

Identity for those living in the Rio Grande Valley is complex, often contradictory, and contested. Undocumented youth who grew up in the United States may have a commitment to American cultural values while at the same time feeling excluded by legal structures and ethnoracial criteria that position them as outsiders.[61] One way in which they contest their liminal status is by becoming actively involved in their communities and participating in civil society.[62] Others emphasized their patriotism. Selena, who received DACA, said, "I've used the terms 'Mexican American,' 'Latina,' 'Hispanic' to describe my identity. I've used 'Chicana' too. 'American,' because I have a lot of patriotism, like when I wear my JROTC uniform. I'm very patriotic."[63] Scholars have elsewhere commented on the deep U.S. patriotism of Mexican Americans in South Texas.[64] Yet this extends beyond U.S. citizens to also include immigrants. Take, for instance, Maria, another DACA recipient:

> I remember it was in eighth grade and it was Fourth of July. They were doing fireworks, and I was like, "Oh my gosh, I love this country." I felt so patriotic, you know? I was singing the national anthem, "Yeah, this is my country, I love it here." I have my life here, my friends here, my family here, my dreams here. My dreams are here, not in Mexico, not anywhere but here.

I asked twenty-three-year-old Daniela, mother of two U.S. citizens, how she self-identified. She responded:

> Well, I don't know what to consider myself really, because what's a real American—how do you define an American? Do you define it as somebody being born in the United States, or you have some traits? If you say, "Oh, they speak English," well, I speak English. "They live in the U.S.?" I live in the U.S. So, I am in the middle. I kind of consider myself Mexican American, 'cause I was born in Mexico but I've been raised in the U.S. I have an identity crisis [laughs]. I feel American, because this is all that I've known. But I live in South Texas, close to the border. And then people ask me, like, "Are you a Tejana?"[65] I'm just like, "Don't ask me!" I'm trapped in between three different things.

In the opening to this chapter, U.S. citizen Eric commented on the fact that he often did not feel "American" and rather prefers a regional ethnic identity as a "Mexican."[66] In fact, many U.S. citizens from mixed-status families did not identify as "American." In part this is because of how their families are treated in this country (which makes them feel marginalized, too) and in part it is a racialized distinction that is informed by the social and ethnic history of Texas described earlier. But it also reflects strong ties to the unique region they grew up in, contrasted with the rest of the United States, and the regional identity that develops because of it.

But there was little consistency around this self-identification of nationality. When I first interviewed Michael, a U.S. citizen living in a mixed-status family, he was getting ready to graduate high school and had set his sights on joining the Border Patrol. The fact that he has undocumented parents already made this an interesting career choice (and is discussed in Chapter 5), but he also held complex ideas of ethnicity, nationality, and belonging. As he told me, "Normally when someone asks me, I say I'm Mexican. Like, here in the Valley, we're all from Mexico. You just got to say that. But if I were to travel up north and they were to ask me, I might say I'm Mexican American, or American Mexican. I'm from here, but my roots are from Mexico." His ideas of belonging, as this quote illustrates, are relational and shaped by where he is and to whom he is speaking.

The children of immigrants have long held a tenuous place in U.S. society, and are often racialized in a way that they are characterized as perpetual foreigners, as these quotes illustrate.[67] U.S.-citizen children of immigrants have been derided as "anchor babies"—especially in recent years—and treated as undeserving. As "suspect citizens"[68] they may be constructed as a racial threat to the nation; because their parents broke the law to arrive, their very birth is potentially unacceptable. Nilda Flores-González describes Latino millennials' experiences of belonging as "citizens, but not Americans."[69] This is reflected well in Eric's comments at the start of this chapter. Their everyday experiences (including spatial segregation, microaggressions, and anti-Latino rhetoric) belie their status as American citizens, underscoring the persistent role of race in notions of belonging to this imagined community. "They hesitate to call themselves Americans," she writes, "because that is neither how others define them nor an identity they can claim without raising eyebrows."[70] This disconnect from national identity stems from their inability to meet its ethnoracial criteria. Mae Ngai describes this experience as that of "alien citizens"—that is, citizens by birth but whose immigrant ancestry renders their status as citizens dubious—as they are cast as perpetual foreigners.[71] Even having U.S. citizenship does not protect them from having their Americanness questioned.

While race is a powerful social category attached to notions of belonging, these issues play out in slightly differently ways in border regions that are predominantly Latino. Somewhat different from other parts of the country—where the reference population may be African American, as Flores-González describes for Latino youth in Chicago—people position themselves not only along a color line of a racial order but also within hierarchies created by their own or their family's legal status.

Mixed-Status Families and Belonging in the Borderlands

This chapter has highlighted how the illegality of some can influence all family members, including legal residents and citizens. However, illegality is a construct that first had to be produced; over time, it has become central to U.S. immigration policy, and with it, to ideologies and practices related to race, citizenship, and state authority. At different historical moments, different groups of undocumented persons became "impossible subjects,"[72] persons whose presence is a social reality but also a legal impossibility. Because of increased border enforcement and its accompanying technologies, people are no longer able to circulate between the United States and Mexico as they did in the past, influencing decisions to clandestinely enter, either without inspection or by overstaying a visa, and making them undocumented. The desire to migrate to the United States is shaped by existing transnational family ties, but it has also resulted in a sharp uptick in mixed-status families, with many fewer opportunities for legal relief than in the past. As a result, entire families are subject to the powerful negative effects of illegality, including limited economic opportunities and life "in the shadows." Poverty disproportionately affects their children, and fear of law enforcement fosters crime in neighborhoods where no one wants to call the police.

However, there are also strategies in response to these limitations. Family resilience is exemplified by stories of crossing the border and risking everything to reunify with loved ones. Community activism is robust, as people organize in their neighborhoods to invoke change and to contest anti-immigrant legislation and practices. Agency is also evident in the often unexpected and contested forms of identity that people choose for themselves. Undocumented Mexicans may feel like citizens because of their high levels of incorporation in the United States, even as natural-born U.S. citizens more readily identify as Mexican because they witness their own family's exclusion from the nation, in addition to feeling like "suspect citizens" themselves due to ethnoracial criteria attached to ideas of belonging.

These social processes are a product of the spatial uniqueness of the region. The complex and often violent history of U.S.–Mexican relations has split apart communities on both banks of the Rio Grande and produced complex ethnic and political identities. Local practices of resistance and transnational ties have also fostered a strong sense of regionalism. Family members often live right across the border, and may cross easily and frequently using the Border Crossing Card. This upholds kinship ties and fosters a shared sense of binational space. At the same time, proximity to Mexico brings with it a relentless and normalized environment of surveillance and militarization. The presence of Border Patrol agents is part of everyday life, and the checkpoints limit mobility, trapping people within this distinct geopolitical buffer zone.

After arriving in this unique regional landscape, both recent immigrants and the children of those who arrived decades ago remain in constant dialogue with bordering processes and their social implications. Those who became undocumented upon their arrival are forever set apart from their U.S.-born family members and must negotiate the implications. The next chapter turns inward to focus on the household, examining the dynamics between parents and their children, as well as between siblings, that result from discordant legal statuses within the same family.

CHAPTER 2

UNITED YET DIVIDED

MIXED-STATUS FAMILY DYNAMICS

SIXTEEN-YEAR-OLD JESSICA was a straight-A student in her high school, a sophomore with ambitions of studying psychology upon graduating. She lived with her mother and younger sisters in a well-maintained, bright yellow-and-white home in an unpaved, rural *colonia* located just off a major road. Live oaks and huisache trees, branches swaying gently in the coastal winds, bordered the front yard. Her mother had planted colorful aloes and scarlet sage along the walkway.

Jessica and her younger sisters are U.S. citizens. Their brother, John, is also a citizen and serves in the Marines; he had recently returned from deployment abroad. He frequently sends money to support his undocumented mother, who watches children and works part-time for a local community organization. Jessica's older sister, Mary, was born in Mexico and grew up undocumented in the United States. She was a Deferred Action for Childhood Arrivals (DACA) recipient, and was working as a teacher at a local elementary school. Mary lived with her husband, a U.S. citizen, and their two daughters just a few miles down the road.

The ceiling fan humming in the background, I asked Jessica to describe what it's like growing up in a mixed-status family. Without hesitating, she said, "Well, I do feel undocumented too, just because I live with them. So everything that they go through, I go through. It makes me feel like I don't have papers either. I don't get to have everything that other people do. I see the struggle that they go through, and it's a struggle for me too. Honestly, it hurts."

She continued, "It is hard sometimes, knowing that something could happen. Knowing that I could lose my mom. She's a big part of my life, so you live with that fear. And a lot of people think that it's only undocumented people who live with the fear, but I live with that fear too, even if I'm from here. I live with the fear of losing my mom." How did she first find out her mom and older sister were undocumented, I asked her? "When I started kindergarten, I was like, *my family is not like everyone else's family.* I knew what was going on. I knew, but only really understood by second grade. That is when my fear started, just seeing a police car I would get scared. I didn't know how not to be scared. How can you not be afraid?'

Scholars have long been interested in how migration changes familial dynamics, exploring how practices, roles, and attitudes related to parent–child relationships, child rearing, and gender become transformed.[1] Studies of immigrant families have historically focused on the integration experiences of the second generation, born and raised in the host country.[2] There has been a particularly heavy focus on how the children of immigrants assimilate to norms of the receiving country, including, more recently, those who arrived in the United States as children or adolescents.[3] However, because the growth in mixed-status families has been fairly recent, there has been little examination of the roles and experiences of U.S. citizens living in these families, like Jessica. And because most studies have focused on parent-child relationships—since the primary interest has been the adaptation or incorporation of subsequent generations—the dynamics between siblings with different legal status remains underexplored. However, sibling relationships have the potential to reveal so much more about the effect of legal status precisely because they are peers in the same household: there are no generational differences, and they were raised in the same environment.

This chapter discusses mixed-status family patterns, including shared norms, interpersonal tensions, and systems of mutual support. Family relationships necessarily challenge simplistic distinctions between citizens and immigrants, and underscore the impossibility of assigning rigid juridical categories to entangled social lives. Juxtaposing the perspectives of various members within the same family illustrates how those experiences play out in complex ways. Members share in each other's daily lives, willingly or unwillingly, and these patterns only become evident by examining the family as a whole; that is, these experiences are relational. This chapter shows how parents and siblings communicate the meanings of illegality as well as the range of responses.

We will see that tensions within the family result from the differential opportunities that stratify family members, sometimes leading to feelings of resentment, jealousy, and anger. Because of limitations associated with parental legal status, poverty is a common feature of mixed-status households, and parents express regrets about how their own illegality resulted in low incomes, heavy work schedules, and mobility restrictions. Some parents felt as if they had "robbed" their children of a "real childhood." However, despite the disadvantages and occasional friction within families, unity is the overwhelmingly dominant theme, and mutual support is critical. Young adults provide "internal remittances," or financial contributions to the parental household. Certain family members take on specific roles, interfacing with institutions or using their legal status, name, or Social Security number to assist others. "Identity loan" between family members is commonplace and functions as a mode of reciprocity in resource- and document-poor communities and is complexly interwoven with kinship relationships.[4] U.S. citizens also serve as the family representative, traveling to Mexico when others cannot, or serving as a link to extended family or those who have been deported, thus lending their mobility privileges to support others. Christina Getrich refers to children in mixed-status families as "border brokers" because of their role assisting others with navigating daily life.[5] Citizens often grow up with an awareness that they can help legalize their parents' status, which also shapes household power dynamics. Finally, the progress of the entire family and social mobility of subsequent generations is viewed as linked to children's educational success. Education is seen as the ticket out of poverty and the lingering effects of undocumentedness, and is thus an underlying but important focus of household dynamics.

Teaching Children What Illegality Means

More than 2.5 million undocumented young people have been living in the United States since childhood, and a significant body of literature has emerged in recent years on their incorporation patterns and subjectivity.[6] These individuals are often referred to as the "1.5 generation," because while they share the same legal status as their parents and often retain some characteristics of their home country (such as linguistic proficiency), their orientation is primarily toward the United States, the country in which they have grown up. Sometimes called "DREAMers," there have been several attempts to regularize their status—through the DREAM Act, legislation which has been introduced several times but has stalled in Congress—or to lessen the impacts of their illegality, most notably through the creation of the DACA program in 2012.

Undocumented adolescents and young adults experience, and learn to cope with, distinct challenges. As they begin to grasp the magnitude of the implications of their status, they may lose trust in their social and material environments. They must, as Roberto Gonzales has explored, "learn to be illegal,"[7] which involves a complete retooling of social patterns, daily routines, and aspirations for the future.[8] This often means avoiding activities from which they might be excluded and reconsidering their educational trajectories and career goals. They may be confronted with challenges that impact their emotional well-being as they experience the erosion of "ontological security," or their confidence in the reliability and constancy of their social environment.[9] This can result in positive coping strategies—political organizing, listening to music, exercising, playing sports, attending church, and turning to close family members or friends for advice—as well as negative coping mechanisms, including behaviors that result in self-harm, including eating disorders, using drugs or alcohol, and even ideating or attempting suicide.[10]

Illegality touches the entire family unit, as Jessica's story at the beginning of this chapter shows. However, the experiences of citizen siblings and other family members, and the interpersonal dynamics that accompany those experiences, are often left out of discussions about immigrant families. Citizens, too, must cope with the situation and "learn to be illegal" in their own ways.

How do parents communicate the meaning of illegality to their children? When and how do they find out, and what do they make of the situation? There is, of course, a range of practices and responses. Some parents were forthright with their children from the beginning, such as Herminia and Felipe. The couple came to the United States in 2002, overstaying a visa (B1/B2, Border Crossing Card). "We were escaping the violence," Felipe, who had owned a business in Reynosa, explained. "Mexico is our country, and it hurt us to leave, but that was the sad reality. I had hoped that things would change, but they never did. It was so bad over there when we left." Herminia emphasized that they never hid anything about the situation from their children, who were five and nine years old at the time. She said,

> Since they were very little, they were always aware. I would tell them, "Sons, this was the reason, our motivation for coming here. But we are a team and let's always be united. Let's be a team and pull ourselves up, together. We did this so

that you all can have advantages, that you can realize your dreams, your goals, so that all the bad things happening in Mexico don't affect you. We want you to triumph in life. And that is why we have to stay united."

In other cases, children began to find out on their own, usually through interactions with peers or at school. Oftentimes, they had never considered where they had been born or questioned their family's legal status. At the same time, they had picked up enough clues from their social environment—through the media, in their neighborhoods, at school—to know that illegality was something that is stigmatized. This often resulted in difficult conversations for parents. Mayra, for example, was confronted by her son after an incident in school. She said,

> They were going around the room in his freshman year, saying, "Where were *you* born? And where were *you* born?" And since he had never asked me before, he just said, "I was born here." Then he came home and asked, so I told him he was born in Mexico. He said, "So I'm from Mexico?" And then that's when he told me, "Well, up until now I was going to go to college, but I can't if I don't have a Social Security number."

This surprise and disappointment was echoed in other conversations with parents. Another mother, Juana, recalled a similar story in which her son "started asking why we didn't come here to have him born as well. He says he can't have the same freedom." Like Mayra's son, her son became angry after this revelation. "Even though he studies a lot and brings home good grades, he says he can't go to college because he doesn't have a Social Security number. Or he says, why study if he can't work in the field that he gets his degree in? Now he's just always very negative." Juana's son has even used situation this against his mother during arguments: "If I scold him for something," she says, "he blames it on that. He says, 'You don't like me because I don't have papers!' He became rebellious." Her relationship with her son deteriorated because of the status revelation. However, when I spoke to Juana again a year later, she told me that the family tension and his negative outlook had all changed when her son received DACA. He had applied and was approved within four months, and now had a work permit and driver's license. "Everything changed," she said. "He went back to school and is at the university now. He can go out and work and he doesn't have to hide from anyone." Importantly, he and his mother had a good relationship once again. Indeed, the DACA program offered abundant tangible and intangible benefits for young adults, in addition to generally positively impacting their family lives.

Juana's U.S.-citizen daughter Jennifer had a much different reaction when she found out about her status. Jennifer knew that her parents were undocumented—she told me it really sunk in when the family couldn't travel to Mexico for her great-grandmother's funeral—and had become involved in immigrant rights activism as a teen. Living in a mixed-status family, she identified with their experience, to the extent that she didn't realize her own U.S. citizenship status and the advantages that came with it. Her mother told me,

> Jennifer always thought she was undocumented, too, until she got to high school and realized she was actually a citizen. There was a school field trip, and she told me she couldn't go because she didn't have papers. And I said, "What? Why not? You're a citizen." She was shocked, and instead of being happy that she could go, it made her sad that she wasn't Mexican. She always thought she was Mexican and undocumented like the rest of us.

When she discovered that she was a U.S. citizen, Jennifer was confused and upset because her status set her apart—she wished she were undocumented, too. In one of several interviews over coffee, Jennifer laughed when I asked her to recall that experience. She shrugged, a little embarrassed, saying, "Well, most of our friends, most of our community is undocumented." To her, it was simply the status quo. But more than that, it represented her own sense of belonging, as illegality had become intertwined with her sense of self and personal identity through innumerable social interactions. In high school and college, she advocated for immigrant rights, an issue that she cared deeply about. Now twenty-four years old, she worked for a law firm specializing in immigration cases.

But Jennifer recalled that it was at this point in her life—when she discovered she was actually a citizen—that the differences in opportunities between her and her brother started to become abundantly clear. While her brother was the eldest, he was unable to take on expected social roles because of his undocumented status. Jennifer explained, "I know my brother is the older one, but I'm the one who has to keep things under control. My mom has been in the hospital several times, so I've had to step up at home. I'm the one that drives them around when they need to go somewhere. If we need to go to Mexico to be with our family, I'm the one that represents everyone." As is discussed below, Jennifer would also play an important role as the legal representative for the family because of her ability to take out loans and mortgages and put various bills in her name.

One aspect of disclosure unique to mixed-status families relates to the interaction between U.S.-born siblings and their generally older undocumented brothers or sisters. This shifts the usual dynamics of birth order, making the younger children of the family ostensibly the most powerful in terms of rights, opportunities, and resources. At the same time, older siblings remained protective of younger ones. In many cases, they moderated what their younger brother or sisters knew regarding the family's legal status, or wanted to prepare them even before the parents disclosed anything. In some cases, children instinctively figured it out even though it was never explicitly discussed. Brittany, an eighteen-year-old U.S. citizen, described her seven-year-old brother's knowledge of the impact of illegality, noting, "My little brother knows what it means. I guess it just comes naturally. When he sees the *migra* he tells my dad, '*Papá, allí viene la migra* [Dad, here comes Border Patrol].' Yeah, he knows, he understands." The fear of law enforcement, and of Border Patrol in particular, is instilled in family members from an early age, often inadvertently as they observe their parents' patterns of response.

Twenty-three-year-old Melanie is the only U.S. citizen in her family and claims that she's "always known in a way" about her parents' and siblings' status. Because U.S. citizens can petition for the status regularization of their family members once they turn twenty-one, she recalled feeling both privileged and guilty at a very young age. She said, "I remember crying when I was five years old, because it really sucked that I was the only one that could help the situation, but I also had to be the youngest one. The only citizen in the family had to be the one that couldn't do anything to fix the situation right now." Melanie felt powerless as a child, given her realization about the family's legal status. Like many other citizen children, she grew up acutely aware of her particular role in the family as a future petitioner for regularization of status.

In other cases, young children were kept in a "bubble" of secrecy and protection, and not expected to know about their family's status until they grew older. Carmen talked about her younger sister, who is thirteen years old and the only U.S. citizen in the family. She says, "Up until a few months ago I hadn't realized that we had kept my little sister in this protective bubble, where she doesn't have to know because she would get worried. We wouldn't mention it to her, and didn't let her know that we could get deported. But then I got DACA, and she asked me, 'What's that?'" At that point, Carmen explained to her about the family's legal status, and the little sister was let in on the family secret. In the months to follow, I frequently saw her alongside Carmen at immigration rights events and rallies, excited to represent her family.

Within mixed-status families there is a range of disclosure practices regarding undocumented status. In some cases, parents saw no utility in keeping their or their children's status a secret; they explained why they had come to the United States and spelled out the limitations associated with it. In other cases, children found out on their own because of household discussions about possibilities for regularization, an entrenched fear of police and Border Patrol, parents' employment restrictions, or the detention of a family member. And some discovered their own status limitations in jarring and upsetting ways, as they realized they faced restrictions on college and employment opportunities. This often created tensions within the family, including lashing out in anger or responding with sadness or resentment.

Resentment Within the Family

For some families, jealousy among siblings—as well as anger toward parents—emerged as legal status began to stratify opportunities in life. This was a difficult topic to elicit during interviews; families preferred to emphasize their unity and play down any conflicts in the home. However, for many families, these stories of differences and the stratification they produced were an important part of their collective narrative.

Evelyn and Alfredo are a married couple who arrived from the state of Michoacán in 1993. The couple themselves was mixed-status. While Evelyn remained undocumented, Alfredo was able to gain permanent residency status through a little-known process called derivation.[11] Evelyn noted, "As a resident, he always has the doors open wide, whereas I don't. *Me siento como vedada* [I feel like I've been banned]." Though their two sons—one undocumented and one a citizen—were both adults now, the parents still had vivid memories of differential access to resources and the resentments this generated. For instance, their younger son Eric, who is a U.S. citizen, grew up with Medicaid coverage, while his brother Manuel had to go without medical and dental care. As Evelyn explained,

> Manuel always asked, "Why don't I get the same treatment?" Like when we got his brother's teeth cleaned and check-ups every six months. I would take him,

but not his brother. I would tell him, "It's because you don't have the same benefits as him. He was born here, and you are from Mexico. You came when you were very little." I would try to explain, but it was so difficult. It would break my heart.

The father, Alfredo, interjected, "Manuel noticed the differences a lot. This one has something and the other doesn't. He noticed the distinction, how the government distinguishes because people are from Mexico."

In a later conversation, Manuel, their eldest son, now twenty-five, recounted how these incidents and conversations affected his outlook on life:

> Yes, I remember. I was in fourth grade when I figured it all out. I remember losing all interest in school, how everything just fell apart. I thought, "If I'm not from here, I can't go to college, I can't work." After that, I was always aware that I was not from here. Eventually, I dropped out of school. It breaks your heart, because you want to keep at it and move ahead. But without papers, it's hard to find a job. They can work in the A/C [air conditioning], but not me. People without papers have to work in the blazing sun [*solazo*].

This distinction between working outside "in the blazing sun" versus in the air-conditioning came up repeatedly in conversations. Eric, two years younger, didn't recall such a stark impact on his brother because of their different statuses. He said that when he found out, "I was small. At first it didn't make sense. I was confused because of the difference that if you don't have papers, the benefits are really, really different." Instead, he says, as a young child he was preoccupied with the possibility of his parents being taken away. "I was thinking a lot about what would happen if they were deported. Am I going to go over to Mexico? What will happen to me?"

Today, brothers Eric and Manuel are not particularly close, in part because they are in different life stages—stages that in large part were determined by their differences in legal status and the trajectories they were set out upon. Eric is planning to start college. Manuel, on the other hand, dropped out of high school and had a baby with his girlfriend when he was sixteen. They got married, and now live in another city. Manuel works in construction—outside in the blazing sun, as he emphasized. Because he has been deported once in the past, Manuel's prospects for legalizing his status through his U.S.-citizen wife have all but disappeared.

Claudia is another U.S. citizen who became alienated from her brother over time. She discussed how discovering their different statuses—and the opportunities and limitations associated with them—affected their sibling relationship, and how they became ever more distant:

> When my brother tried to apply for a job, he found out he didn't have a Social Security number. So, he asked my parents and they said, "Well, we don't have legal status here, so you can't really work." And he was like, "Well, what about my sister?" "She was born here, so it's different." And that was when everything just fell apart for my brother. He felt stumped. This was around his junior year of high school, and he started to be like, "Oh, I don't care anymore." And I just kept going because I had the opportunity. I've gone my own way and continued my education. I know my brother is proud of my accomplishments, but I also know that he wishes that he had the same opportunity. We're definitely not as close as we used to be.

Like the brothers of Manuel and Claudia, many people described the discovery of their undocumented status as "everything falling apart." As their siblings' worlds crashed in, U.S. citizens in the family often experienced feelings of guilt. Legal status stratification often also reversed hierarchies of birth order, with the youngest sibling(s) being more likely to be born in the United States and so to have access to citizenship and its associated legal, educational, economic, and health benefits. Pecking orders intensified as some had more access to resources and opportunities compared to their brothers and sisters. Many wondered aloud, "How did I get so lucky?" The disconnect between place of birth—something they had no decision in or power over—and life opportunities appeared random, disconnected, and, most of all, unfair.

The interpersonal tensions between U.S.-citizen children and their siblings often took the form of a mixture of support and resentment. Similar to Claudia's experience, Jennifer said her brother was "not jealous to my face, but he'll be like, 'You know I didn't have that opportunity and you do. If I were in your shoes I would do it.' It's like he pushes me to do better because he knows if he had the opportunity, he would have taken it." However, some encounters were more negative. Twenty-three-year-old Melanie, the only U.S. citizen in her family, experienced firsthand how differences in legal status generated resentments. While all three siblings went to college at the same time, she was the only one to receive federal financial aid, since her siblings were ineligible because of their undocumented status. She said, "I always paid for my brother and sister's tuition, because I had grants and my parents don't really have the money. Whatever was left over from my financial aid was used for them." However, she was also resentful that this was expected of her, and believed her family did not recognize the hard work she had put into her academic achievements: "I remember I told my brother once that eventually he'd have to pay me back, and he's like, 'I don't have to pay you back. Why do I need to? This is money you're getting from the government. You didn't earn this.' I was like, but I did! Some of these grants are because I was in the top of my class!"

Melanie continued: "My brother holds this really big resentment towards my parents because they brought him here at the wrong time. I would always hear them argue. He would get mad at my parents, saying, 'Why did you bring us here? You screwed me over!' There might be some resentment towards me too, just the fact that I'm the U.S. citizen and he's not." For U.S.-citizen siblings, their privilege was not lost on them, and often created inner turmoil and conflicting feelings for them. Miguel said, "I was pretty much the star of the family because I had papers." Raised alongside his sister by a single mother—both undocumented—he described feeling responsible for them while simultaneously being the target of their jealousy:

> You get treated different. You get to go to the doctor and have medication and you get more help. And then you see your sister. When she would get sick, I would have to say I was sick to get the medicine for her. It brought us together, but at the same time it was separating us. It's like the system is separating two human beings. Even though we're still family, it's putting a barrier between us, because I'm a citizen and she's not. I never felt guilty, but I do believe there was some jealousy on her part. I was accomplishing all my dreams and my goals and she wasn't, because she was limited by the fact that she was undocumented. I think about it a lot. I feel like I'm responsible for her. In a way, it does bring you together, but not always in a good way.

It was not just U.S. citizens who experienced these forms of resentment. Twenty-three-year-old Adrian, whose parents and siblings are undocumented, said, "When I received my DACA, my parents and my siblings would joke and call me 'gringo.' Like they'd joke around, 'Oh, you're better than us now.' But joking, of course." This illustrates how, even though it was a temporary status, DACA conferred new opportunities to its recipients and in doing so produced new hierarchies and divisions within families. Some recipients experienced guilt because they had new prospects that their family members could not share. This, too, impacted intergenerational dynamics; as I discuss in Chapter 8, DACA created sharp distinctions between young adults and their parents. Advocacy for this program built approval around the idea that those brought to the U.S. as children are not responsible for their plight. Politicians and the broader public supported the program because of popular discourse about "innocent" children, brought to the United States by no choice of their own. By default, however, this implicated their parents as culpable, even criminal, because of their active choice to migrate with young children. This is one of the many ways in which policies draw lines between the "deserving" and "undeserving," and in doing so produce insidious hierarchies within families.

A Parent's Sorrow: "They Never Had a Real Childhood"

Parental guilt also came to the fore during our conversations. While children remembered the differential resources and opportunities afforded to those of different status, parents focused on the success of the family unit as a whole and how this was impacted by their illegality. Some parents talked about feeling like they had robbed their children of a "real childhood," or had made them grow up too fast, due to low incomes, heavy work schedules, and mobility restrictions. Maricela's story was emblematic of this. Throughout our multiple encounters over the years—including when I brought a group of undergraduate students from Florida to Texas during Spring Break to perform service work for an organization she was involved with—she was always an upbeat and energetic leader. But during one of our interviews in her home, she became introspective and melancholy.

Maricela and her husband, both undocumented, arrived in 1997 and raised all three of their children in the United States. She emphasized to me that they had instilled in them a strong work ethic. They owned an upholstery business and regularly expected the children to help out. On weekends, and when business was slow, the whole family was enlisted to do yard work to supplement the household's income. Her daughter Samantha remembered, "My parents never took us out to eat. I always wanted to go eat pizza, but they would say, 'No, we need to work. We don't have money.' So it was very hard to grow up like that, because I didn't have really many typical childhood things, like play or fun. It was just work, work, work, work." If any of the children wanted spending money, they had to find small jobs on their own—the girls babysat and helped out at a neighbor's store, and their son sold items at a local flea market.

All of this work left little time for the typical social and extracurricular events that teens crave. Maricela recalled, "No, my husband and I didn't let them participate in any of that. They would say, 'Please, I want to get involved in this club or that sport, basketball, football,' and we would tell them, 'No, we don't have time for any of that. And we only have one car, so we can't be driving you around.'" Reflecting on this, she began to weep and said, "You know, they were never allowed to be children, because of the circumstances. We were poor, and we didn't have papers, so work was all we had. Looking back, they never had a childhood." This display of emotion was uncharacteristic for Maricela, who was usually a confident and pragmatic woman.

Like Maricela, undocumented parents generally found themselves in low-paying jobs and had little free time to spend with their children. Poverty—as linked to an inability to get better jobs because they didn't have papers—was a frequent theme in many of the interviews. Sixteen-year-old Jessica, introduced at the start of this chapter, recalled, "Growing up, money was always a big problem. We always had a bunch of different cars. We would get a car, and it would last for a little bit. One car sounded like a motorcycle, but it got you places. I've learned that, as long as something gets me somewhere, I don't care how it looks, I don't care what it sounds like." Eva, a DACA recipient, recalled that, growing up, "the condos where we lived looked really poor. But in front of them was this real pretty house. Every time my oldest brother was dropped off by friends, he would ask to be let out in front of that house, so they would think that he lived there. He was so ashamed of our status."

In these examples, poverty and undocumented status are intertwined. Parents' inability to work in the formal sector meant that they worked in irregular and low-paying jobs; even those who owned their own businesses experienced heightened economic anxiety. Felipe, a fifty-three-year-old father, summarized his perspective: "We are accustomed to suffering, to struggling. It's as if you have one egg, but you have to split it to feed the entire family."

"We Are More United"

Despite the disadvantages and occasional friction, unity was the overwhelmingly dominant theme when families discussed how differences in status impacted their interpersonal dynamics. Most scholarship on mixed-status families has focused on the negative implications of parental undocumented status and the ways it disadvantages their children. While this is certainly true—and a major focus of this book, which argues that anti-immigrant policies produce ripple effects on others—it would be unfair to portray them as simply passive victims of legal exclusion. Instead, their lives are filled with a multitude of identities, experiences, and triumphs beyond illegality, and family unity emerged as a major foundation of these daily lives. While stratified access to resources may lead to resentment or preferential treatment, supportive attitudes were just as common.

An issue that frequently arose, due to the geographic context of this study, was families' inability to travel together outside the region because of the Border Patrol checkpoints set up along the major highways leading into the state's interior. Undocumented persons lamented that they would never travel, and so missed opportunities to attend important family events in other parts of the United States or to visit theme parks like Six Flags or Sea World in other parts of Texas. This prevented them from growing and experiencing adventures together, and from solidifying shared ties to the United States. DACA recipients recounted with excitement the first time they were able to leave the Rio Grande Valley, as the change in their status opened new mobilities for them. But, overwhelmingly, these discussions of mobility always led people to reflect back on the family unit, and on how important it was to experience things together.

Perhaps surprisingly, many people who could travel outside the region limited themselves because their family members lacked the same mobility. They avoided "showing off," in the words of one person, in order to enhance family unity and prevent differences from becoming too stark. Miguel, a U.S. citizen, emphasized, "You don't travel yourself. Let's say I have the chance and the money—I would still not go, because I would feel bad. I would be like, 'Wow, they can't go, and I'm going over here.' It puts a limit on the citizen in the family, too." Similarly, Justin was concerned about his sister's feelings. He had just been approved for DACA, but his sister was not, despite their identical migration circumstances, illustrating the discretionary nature of these administrative decisions. As Justin noted,

> Because my sister is still undocumented, I try to be understanding. I don't think she has resentment; we just try to help each other out. Sometimes I hide things from her because I'm like, "Oh, here I am, showing off." Like traveling. She is still stuck here. I actually try not to travel, because I don't want her to feel bad that she can't do that. So I've actually limited myself to not traveling much. I still feel bad because we have the same history, the same life that we both lived through, and I have this privilege that she doesn't, you know?

As a result of these actual and proxy mobility restrictions, leisure time to-gether as a family was often highly cherished through activities such as back-yard barbeques and going to the beach together. Almost every participant mentioned family outings to "the Island"—that is, to the beaches of South Padre Island, at the eastern end of the Rio Grande Valley. As Marisol noted, "We would go to the Island, all the time. It all revolved around the beach and fishing. During the summers, we all go together and just have a good family time. That's pretty much the only place we can go for vacation. Those are the most memorable times with the family. The best thing of the summer." Mel-anie pointed out that one important consideration was that extended family members from Mexico could join them during those times: "Every year we go to the beach for a week. It's still within the U.S., you don't have to pass the checkpoint, and your family from Mexico can come over and spend time with everyone because they have visas."

In another pattern that displays family unity, financial resources were shared. Mutual support is critical in mixed-status families, and is best illustrated in the "internal remittances," or financial contributions to the household by U.S.-born or DACA young adults.[12] While this occasionally involved turning over cash from one's earnings, it usually meant dividing up the household bills (often even if the person had moved out on their own). Edgar, a twenty-two-year-old DACA recipient, provided a fairly typical explanation of how this worked: "I pay the car insurance, the electricity, and the internet." Maricela's three children, now adults, still live with her. Her eldest daughter reviewed their arrangement for me, saying, "We divide all the bills. My mom pays the house and my brother pays the light. I pay the water, and divide the cable and the internet with my sister. For other things, we divide the whole bill by five. Everybody pitches in."

Family unity was also expressed through an explicit commitment to not leaving any member behind. Mayra described it in the following way: "Being in a mixed-status family has made us more united. It's like, 'I am going to pro-tect you because you need more help.' My youngest son is always there for his brother and sisters, because he knows they don't have papers, even though he's still so small." In another example, Juan and his wife, Irma, came to the United States from Veracruz, Mexico, in 1997, bringing their oldest son, Jesse, with them. Juan had given his youngest children a directive:

I tell my children who are citizens, "When your mother and I are not around anymore, do not leave your older brother alone. He doesn't have papers. Always help him out, because you are from here and have more benefits. The doors open more easily for you. Just because he wasn't able to be here legally, do not leave him alone." And I do think they will obey, because we always taught them to be united, to always help one another, to not look at the differences about who is a citizen and who isn't. No, we told them, "You are all equal, all three of you."

Roles for Citizen and DACAmented Family Members

Family members who are U.S. citizens or who had DACA take on particular roles and responsibilities, such as translating, interfacing with institutions, and using their name and documentation for family bills, loans, and auto and home titles. Twenty-three-year-old Jesse, whose parents and siblings jokingly called him "gringo" when he received DACA, recognized his new role: "So now you're different because you can help. You have more responsibility now, right? Because you can do more things for your family, like utility bills or loans that might need a Social Security number or credit." These individuals also frequently served as cultural brokers for their parents, as well as for their undocumented siblings.[13]

Jennifer—the U.S. citizen who thought she was undocumented until she got to high school—was able to help out her family by putting real estate titles in her name. This was important because they had watched as neighbors were defrauded by unscrupulous investors taking advantage of people's undocumented status. "There was this thing going on," she told me. "When families finished paying off their lot, and the owner knew they were undocumented, they wouldn't give them the title. They told them, 'You don't own it, we're not going to give it to you.'" In order to protect her family's investments, Jennifer had been made the legal owner on both properties they owned. "It was a way for that to not happen to us, to the house that is already paid for. We've since bought a second lot and built a second house. My parents worked hard to pay for that house. So those are both under my name, under my Social [Security number], because we don't want to risk that happening."

However, sometimes family members used citizens' personal information without their knowledge. A number of young adults told similar stories of finding out they had debts or a poor credit score because their parents had used their names for bills or lines of credit. For instance, Claudia said, "When I got my first credit card and started building my credit, I got a bill from Direct TV [satellite service] stating I owed money. I had to call my dad and he said, 'I'll fix it. Don't worry. I'll fix it.' I was like, 'Okay. You better fix it.' I don't say any-thing mean to him, though, because I know that we needed to do that. They depended on me." Of course, these uses of someone else's personal credit are not always easily "fixed," and can ruin their credit rating and ability to borrow in the future. In another instance, an undocumented mother used her U.S.-citizen daughter's Social Security number to obtain a driver's license a decade prior. When the daughter tried to get her own license at age sixteen, she was put in the awkward position of having to first formally acknowledge the use of her identity by her own mother. This would have exposed her to charges of iden-tity theft and/or impersonating a U.S. citizen, with deportation the probable result. Instead of doing so, Melanie decided to obtain her driver's license by going to a neighboring state that had more lax residency and documentation requirements than Texas.

Sarah Horton distinguishes between "identity loan" and "identity theft," arguing that the former is a voluntary, reciprocal exchange in which citizens or legal permanent residents allow undocumented persons to use their identi-fication or Social Security numbers.[14] In the cases described above, citizens were unaware that their information was being used, and it shared the same characteristics and implications of identity theft. However, because it was their own parents using them, it simultaneously takes on the character of an iden-tity loan: hurt feelings are quickly overcome, parents work hard to rectify any negative consequences, and although their role as "identity donors" occurred without their consent, children are not willing to report the issue to authori-ties. The practice thus resembles identity loan more than identity theft because of its function as a mode of reciprocal gift-giving in resource- and document-poor migrant communities, as well as its complex interweaving with kinship and family relationships. Nonetheless, precisely because of these kin obliga-tions, U.S. citizens really had no choice in the matter.

U.S. citizens often filled the unique role of family representative by travel-ing to Mexico to visit relatives. In this way, they lent their mobility privileges to emotionally support their parents and extended family. As Claudia noted, "I was the ambassador for my family. My summers were always cut a little short because I had to go represent them in Mexico. There was a point where I would be like, 'I don't want to go this year. I've been there every year.' But they would tell me, 'No. You have to go see your grandma. No. You have to do this.'" Her parents' insistence that she return Mexico each year helped to uphold af-fective transnational connections in the family, including across generations.

By far the most frequently discussed way in which U.S.-born citizen children supported their families is through their (future) role in regularizing their parents' status. They can generally regularize their parents' status by petitioning for them when they turn twenty-one years of age. As sixteen-year-old Carmen recalled, "My parents always reminded me that I would be the one to turn twenty-one first. I remember, growing up, my mom saying, 'When you're older you'll be able to help your dad.'" Similarly, twenty-two-year-old Melanie recalled, "My parents always talked about it, getting citizenship through me. I mean it was never like they directly asked, 'Will you help us?' It was just kind of like assumed that it was going to happen. But I never had any opposition to it." As a result, citizen children grow up with a keen awareness that they will take on this role someday, and this effectively shifted the power dynamics between parent and child. As children came to recognize that they had an opportunity to assist their parents, they also established a greater sense of control and level of authority within the household compared to their undocumented siblings and parents.

Carmen's little sister, who had been kept in a "bubble" about the family's status, was expected to help out her mother someday. Carmen noted,

> My little sister might not be aware yet, but when she is old enough to grant my mother legal status, she is bound to do it. It's something that we don't really talk about much, but I feel like that's her responsibility. I shouldn't see it like that, but it's just something that she has to do. I don't think she sees yet that she's the opportunity, but that is going to be her job.

While in many ways this was their "job" or "responsibility," it was also clear that it occurred within the context of familial and parental devotion. As Mayra's youngest daughter told her, "Mom, when I am able, I will fix your papers. And I will fix dad's papers so he doesn't have to work out in the sun anymore." The family was saving up money for the long and expensive petitioning process. As Mayra saw it, "It's not a responsibility, it's not a burden, helping us is something that she wants in her heart."

"My Children Won't Be Working in the Sun": Educational Success as Family Value

Parents felt it was of highest importance to foster their children's education because education is seen as the ticket out of poverty and the lingering effects

of undocumentedness. Encouraging children to do well in school and removing as many obstacles as possible to educational success were an important
aspect of household dynamics. Three years after my first interview with Jessica, she was enrolled in a psychology program at a local branch of the state
university. She told me, "I need one more class to be a junior. So that's really
exciting, because I'm trying to get ahead, and that means I'm going to graduate
two years earlier." She was already planning to apply for a master's program
and was starting a clinical internship the following semester. When I asked
Monica, Jessica's mother, what she thought of her daughter's progress, she
laughed and said,

> I always told my kids, "I have this big wall and five children. I want a degree
> from each and every one of you. I have room on this wall for at least those five.
> And if I run out of walls, that's OK, I can hang your diplomas here on the door-
> frame and over here and over there [pointing and laughing]." Every day I
> say, "See these walls? They're still so empty, I need to put something on
> them" [laughs].

Across the board, families emphasized the importance of their children's
education. It was often cited as the main reason that parents decided to migrate in the first place, as they sought a better life for their children in the United
States. As seventeen-year-old Michael noted, "They came for us so we could
have a better future, which is coming to fruition because I graduated distinguished. I'm going to college, which is what they came here for, right? So we
could succeed. My brothers are doing okay too, A/B honor roll, all of us."
Michael's mother offered her perspective on the issue:

> We always told them that there are more opportunities to study here than in
> Mexico. Over there you have to walk to school, you get rained on, you sweat
> because of the heat. Over here, the schools are covered and have air-conditioning.
> When it's cold, they have heaters. Coming here was our sacrifice. We left our
> families, our mothers and fathers behind for them. They need to know and ap-
> preciate that. We want them to go to school and have a better career than we
> have—with good pay, inside with air-conditioning, a nice house, and a car. That
> way they don't have to struggle outside in the fields. We came here for them, so
> they need to put some effort into studying.

One way in which parents' desire for their children's class mobility was expressed was in the hope that they would not have to work "in the sun." This is

perhaps unsurprising, given the blistering South Texas heat. The subtropical climate of the Rio Grande Valley features daytime temperatures in the high 90s and into the 100s from May through October. Many parents worked in construction or the fields, picking produce (colloquially, *el labor*). As Enrique told me, "My dad doesn't want me to go work in construction. He doesn't want me to be in the sun all day, because he always has problems. A few months ago, one of my uncles died from being in the sun too much." Beyond the very real risk of heatstroke and chronic illness among farmworkers, outdoor work was perceived to be associated with low social class.[15] It is historically tied to numerous ethno-racial stereotypes about labor niches in the United States. A job "in the air-conditioning" was seen as a marker of upward mobility, especially in this region, where many rural poor—including some of the families in this book—live in dwellings that lack air-conditioning, relying on fans and outdoor spaces during parts of the year.[16] Enrique's father, Adolfo, who worked in the fields alongside his wife for two decades, explained that he tells his children: "You need to go to school. You need to get that degree. I don't want you working out in the sun doing what your parents did. We want a better life for you." Samantha is Maricela's daughter, part of the family of five in which the mother reflected on the lack of a "real childhood" they had had due to her having worked all the time. As the daughter told it,

> My dad would tell us almost every day, "You need to go to school, go to college." He would take us to work, to cut grass in the hot sun, to work in the flea market, to show us that it's hard to not have a degree. He's like, "*Estás cansada?* You're tired? You're hot? Well, that's your future if you don't go to school." So I guess I always knew the meaning of that and the consequences.

Similarly, twenty-two-year-old Brian, who was a DACA recipient, described the enormous pressure his parents put on him regarding school: "It's this huge load that you're here to go to college. That's it. No less than college, period." College represents a major accomplishment and source of pride for the entire family. It offers young adults a chance to distance themselves from an everyday life of illegality, including poverty and working outside in the sun. It also underscores why the DACA program was so significant; it not only temporarily improved legal status but also positively affected larger familial aspirations related to education and class mobility.

United Yet Divided in Mixed-Status Families

The illegality of some family members influences opportunities, limitations, and resources for everyone in a household. For citizens in mixed-status families, this shapes individual subjectivity in particular ways. They become accustomed to the norms of their families so that those norms become a part of their own identity and they may even feel like they are undocumented themselves. Children pick up on these limitations and challenges early in life, and learn to fear separation from their parents through deportation. Citizen children may also grow up avoiding law enforcement agents and institutions. Meanwhile, undocumented parents live with guilt because they perceive that their legal status causes their children to grow up too fast and to never have a real childhood. In some cases, children became angry and begin to resent their parents. But jealousy may also be directed toward siblings with different statuses, as exemplified by nearly all the siblings throughout this chapter. On the flip side, U.S. citizens may feel guilty for having more opportunities and resources than others in the family. They may also restrict their own travels to avoid "showing off" in light of their family members' limitations. Stratification by legal status also often leads to a stratification of everyday responsibilities. Citizens in the family may step up to drive, representing the family as the "ambassador" in visits with kin in Mexico, or may assist others with everyday tasks or contracts where a Social Security number is needed. They may be expected to provide more internal remittances than other family members because of their ability to work legally, or to share college financial aid for which their undocumented siblings cannot qualify. While many gladly assist others, sharing is not always a benign or altruistic activity; family members may use their information or credit without their knowledge, leading to future problems. Power dynamics in the family take new twists and turns, as U.S.-citizen children grow up with the knowledge that they have the ability to regularize their parents.

Families demonstrate resilience first and foremost by staying united. The experiences presented here highlight both cooperation and conflict; they are, as many people told me, divided but still united. Despite friction in the family, mutual support is the most durable feature of these relationships. They share resources, pool income and other supplies, and split costs to lessen the burden. Citizens pitch in more when they can, aware of the increased opportunities they have, and help out their parents by putting utility bills and loans in their names. Parents spend enormous amounts of resources—time, money, and encouragement—fostering their children's education because it is viewed as the ticket out of poverty and lingering effects of undocumentedness. Some people used the formative experiences growing up in a mixed-status family as a motivator to advocate for the wider immigrant community or as the impetus to choose careers in law, education, or social services.

The uniqueness of the Rio Grande Valley shapes experiences, even in social interactions within intimate household spaces. Because their mobility is hampered by border enforcement practices such as checkpoints, families are unable to travel places together, negatively affecting shared experience and cohesion. This lack of shared mobility impedes their ability to experience new things and develop together as a family. But it also fosters other kinds of togetherness. Because of cheap and plentiful land in South Texas, many undocumented persons are able to purchase property and settle down, which fosters an experience of place that is much different from other parts of the United States. This creates a sense of home for mixed-status families as they put down roots in the community, and shapes their identities as more oriented toward the geographic region in which they live. Proximity to the international border means that kin networks in northern Mexico are easily maintained, with relatives regularly crossing over for short visits and to reinforce social bonds.

Several of the issues introduced in this chapter—educational trajectories, the journeys of citizens who legalize their parents' status once they become adults—are revisited in subsequent ones. The next chapter first turns to external interactions, extending beyond the family unit to explore how being part of a mixed-status family affects relationships with the broader community.

CHAPTER 3

"LITTLE LIES"

DISCLOSURE AND RELATIONSHIPS

BEYOND THE FAMILY

"IT'S A LOT OF, 'What do I tell people? How can I say it?' I feel like I'm living a double life, having to tell little lies. It really bothers me. I have never told anybody that my family is undocumented, because I don't know how they would act." Jessica paused and let out a long sigh. "I always think about consequences. I've never told anybody." Tears welled up in her eyes, and I quietly asked, "Am I the first person you are telling?" She nodded, and I felt a knot in my stomach, a mixture of sadness and great responsibility.

These "little lies," told to people outside her family, even extended to Jessica's relationship with her best friend, whom she had known since fourth grade. Her best friend's family invited Jessica to join them on trips to California, to Six Flags amusement park in San Antonio, and on a weekend trip to Las Vegas. All of these are beyond the Border Patrol highway checkpoint or require a flight out of the Valley, places that Jessica's own family can't go because of their undocumented status. Sitting on her bed, she wept openly as she revealed:

> My best friend doesn't even know. When I'm with her family on a trip, I secretly wish it were my family. Sometimes she asks, "Why don't you travel with your parents?" and I'm like, "Oh, we don't have money." That's my excuse for everything. I've known her for six years. Her mom sees me as her second daughter. But, I don't want her parents to say anything, or criticize my mom because of her status. I'd rather just keep it to myself. What happens if one day

we have a falling out? I don't want to risk any of that. I should be able to tell her anything—I mean, it's my best friend, you know?—and I can't tell her that.

This secrecy, as it turned out, also extended to her romantic life. She hid her family's status from her boyfriend: "The guy I'm dating, I haven't told him anything about it either. I tell him the same thing that I tell my best friend—that we are just poor, and that's why my family doesn't go places. It hurts me that I can't tell them. They're such a big part of my life, and you know, it hurts that I lie to them."

A year and a half after this conversation, I asked Jessica if she had told anyone about her family's undocumented status in the meantime. She was more upbeat and confidently told me, "Actually, yes, since last time I have been thinking about it a lot. You know, these are people that I trust." So how did it go, I asked?

> I told my best friend, "I need to tell you something. But it's like—it's a big deal."
> To me, it was like the hugest secret anyone could ever have. And so I told her,
> and she's like, "That's it? You made it sound like it was something huge." And
> I was like, this *is* something huge, but, okay, well, that was easy. We kept watch-
> ing TV, and then later she had questions: "So then how did this happen? And
> what about your sister? She's not from here?" And I said, "Look, I'm sorry that
> it took me so many years to tell you," and she said, "No, I totally get it, it's ok."
> But it was funny the way that she reacted towards it at first, like, "*That's* your
> secret? I kind of already knew that though." And I'm like, "You did?!"

Jessica's best friend was unsurprised about her family's status. Being undocumented is often an "open secret" in the Rio Grande Valley. This is a region where at least one in ten persons is undocumented.[1] A person's legal status is not immediately evident, and everyone here seems to know someone who is undocumented. While race and ethnicity play an important role in the popular imagination about who is undocumented in the United States, this conflation is problematic. In regions of the country comprised predominantly of Latino citizens, geography and sociopolitical history readily betray these assumptions. At the same time, discourse imposed from the outside often constructs the border region as filled with people characterized as dangerously noncompliant with American normative ideas of citizenship, prosperity, and security.[2]

What information do those living in a mixed-status family opt to share with others? Why, when, and how do they choose to disclose legal status? Roberto

Gonzales describes a "brutal disruption" that occurs in adolescence, as undocumented youth undergo a cruel rite of passage.[3] As they "learn to be illegal," they may become more guarded about their status, background, and family lives when interacting with peers.[4] This chapter reveals how other members of a mixed-status family must also "learn to be illegal" in their own unique ways. Even for U.S. citizens and lawful permanent residents, there comes a time when they must decide which secrets to tell and which to keep to themselves. While the reasons are clear for those who were undocumented, the impact on citizens is less obvious but often equally troubling for them. They, too, lived with a big secret as they interacted at school, with friends, and in romantic relationships. Their hesitation is exacerbated by the condition of deportability, which makes undocumented persons highly vulnerable and exploitable precisely because of the constant threat of being apprehended at any time. It is this *possibility* of deportation of family members, not the actual event, that instills fear.[5]

Anthropologist Sarah Horton has noted that migrant "denounce-ability" has joined migrant "deportability" as a powerful new tool of subordination.[6] People must carefully guard information about their own or their family members' status to avoid consequences. Sociologist Jason Orne has proposed a model for examining disclosure management strategies that includes direct disclosure, clues, speculation, and active concealment, all of which are touched upon in this chapter.[7] However, the "little lies" that come with concealment can impact interpersonal relationships in serious ways. Positive emotional well-being and emotional capital is fostered through the development of meaningful social connections, and interconnectedness with others can help to restore security for those who are undocumented as well as their family members.[8] For those individuals who feel they cannot be sincere and open to others, another layer of discord is created that affects their sense of being in the world.

This chapter explores the relationships between people in mixed-status families and the wider communities in which they live. Whereas Chapter 2 examined interactions between family members, this chapter turns outward and focuses on the disclosure management process in other relationships— that is, to whom, when, and why people talk about their family's status or not. Both undocumented persons and U.S. citizens describe living with "little lies," or acts of concealment, and of feeling as if they live a double life. Disclosure is weighed against the possible repercussions, including stigmatization, discrimination, ridicule, and fear of denunciation by friends, lovers, neighbors, coworkers, and even other family members. Even the closest friendships and most intimate romantic relationships are not immune from secrecy. As in Jessica's case, this often extends beyond undocumented persons themselves, affecting others in the family, including U.S. citizens and lawful permanent residents. People in mixed-status families face difficulties in adhering to normative expectations of dating and courtship, especially because marriage looms large as a potential pathway to citizenship and future stability. This chapter also explores empowered disclosure, or strategic "coming out" as undocumented, or as someone with undocumented family members, and its role in creating new identities and political subjectivities.

Disclosure Management in School

During childhood and early adolescence, the importance of one's own legal status is largely suspended, even while children may experience significant stress related to their parent's deportability. Undocumented children navigate schools and other institutions in similar ways as their peers, largely because of the 1982 Supreme Court case of *Plyler v. Doe*, which ruled that all children can assert claims to public elementary and secondary education regardless of legal status. Public schools function as important equalizers, especially during elementary school years, even as they simultaneously become sites of stratification reflecting larger social inequalities.[9]

It has been estimated that, across the United States, 7.3 percent of all children enrolled in K–12 public and private schools have at least one undocumented parent, reflecting an marked increase in recent years.[10] In Texas, that percentage rises to 13 percent and is estimated to be 25 percent in the Rio Grande Valley, or one-quarter of children in the region's classrooms.[11] Children make deliberate choices about when, why, and to whom they talk to about their own or their family's legal status. In school, these decisions may begin early, with children as young as ten and eleven years old engaging in decisions about whether they should disclose or disguise legal status, often prompted by activities in the classroom.[12] While the *Plyler v. Doe* decision ensured the right to a K–12 education, on the ground, it has been interpreted as a kind of "Don't ask, don't tell" policy, in which school districts "don't ask" questions about families' immigration status, and children "don't tell," because of socialization practices learned at home. Undocumented parents may explicitly warn their children not to provide information at school.[13] Sometimes this results in unintended consequences. In mixed-status families, parents may not respond to school outreach efforts to enlist their participation if correspondence utilizes words like "citizenship"—for instance, invitations to attend ceremonies where "good citizenship" awards are given—as this may seem to imply immigration enforcement.[14] Teachers may also create conflicts for children through assignments that generate anxiety about legal status or that inadvertently prompt disclosure. In one study, teachers noted that elementary school students struggled to answer assignments related to family history because they elicited information about migration.[15] In these ways, schools may appear bureaucratically hostile to parents, even when that is not the intention.

In the school setting, active concealment of status was the most common pattern. Parents often coached children to conceal their origins in order to protect them. For example, Daniela, a twenty-three-year-old college student with Deferred Action for Childhood Arrivals (DACA) status who arrived from Mexico at the age of nine, was told to tell strangers that she was born in the United States: "I remember when we first got here, our parents told us that if anyone asked us, we're from here. So growing up we knew that. If someone was like, 'Oh, where are you from?' the answer was, 'I was born here in Texas.'" Samantha, another DACA recipient, added, "My dad would always say, 'Don't be saying that you're not from here. If they ask you, just say you were born here.'" Samantha was reminded of the reality that she was not "from here" in other ways: "In school I remember they would ask, 'What did everyone do on summer vacation?' It was kind of embarrassing because my classmates were like, 'Oh I went to San Antonio. I went to Mexico.' Then when it was my turn, it was like, 'I just stayed at home.' I wanted to be able to travel, to go to places. But I couldn't." Indeed, for many young adults, their ability to travel and, for instance, visit theme parks located in cities on the other side of the U.S. Customs and Border Protection checkpoint functioned as a proxy for legal status.

However, when undocumented children and youth claim to be born in the United States rather than in Mexico, they are not just hiding their status from others. This often feels closer to the truth for many of them. Many like Daniela and Samantha, who were coached to say they were "from here," arrived at a very young age and grew up in Texas, developing a strong sense of belonging to the region. Especially in contrast to their parents, who might maintain ties to Mexico and have felt the exclusionary effects of illegality for longer periods, undocumented youth are much more connected to the United States, where they grow up. Many parents are aware of the 1986 amnesty, in which people were able to adjust their immigration status, and many undocumented youth were raised expecting that a similar form of relief would be possible for them as well someday. All of this fosters their commitment to the country where they were raised. However, as Gonzales notes, it also means that parents relay a false sense of security, expecting that by the time their children were grown, their immigration situation would have resolved itself in some fashion.[16] As he notes, "Parents' efforts to enforce secrecy were a rational strategy to avoid trouble and to keep themselves and their children safe. But for adolescent children, keeping these secrets meant concealing large parts of their everyday lives and telling lies that were often hard to keep track of."[17]

Avoiding the truth was not limited to undocumented youth. Jennifer, a citizen born in the United States, had similar experiences because she was part of a mixed-status family. Her parents could not take the family anywhere past the checkpoint. "I never told my friends I couldn't go to amusement parks because my parents are undocumented. I would just say, 'Oh, I'm scared of rollercoasters,' or 'We went to the beach instead.' Since we live in an area where there's a lot of people who can't afford it, I think my friends thought, 'Oh, she's one of the people that can't afford it because she's poor.'" She was able to deflect questions about her parents' legal status and embrace "being poor," a less stigmatizing identity than being undocumented.

Bullying

Bullying is another reason for active concealment of status in school settings. Sociologist Joanna Dreby examines this issue in Ohio and New Jersey, pointing to interracial tensions and the usage of slurs regarding country of origin.[18] However, in this overwhelmingly Latino region, the fault line is legal status. Rather than ethnicity or country of origin, in the borderlands children may be picked on because of their own or their family's illegality. Abusive language and actions hit close to home for those whose parents were undocumented. Sarah is a forty-two-year-old undocumented mother of two U.S.-citizen children. She recalled an incident at her son's school:

> There are often boys or girls who bully other kids. They will say, "Your dad is a *mojado* ['wetback,' a derogatory term for Mexicans who enter the United States illegally]." I was called to my son's school because he had gotten into a fight. One boy told another, "Your momma is illegal," and my son tried to defend him. He was trying to stand up for parents like me. They use "illegal" as a form of

racism. I went to the school and told the principal, "I want you to respect us. We never get in trouble with anyone." And we sat down with the counselor and had a serious conversation with the boys who were bullying. My son already has his head full of ideas that I am going to leave, ever since his dad was deported when he was three. He's just scared.

This illustrates how family legal status, rather than race or ethnicity, becomes a primary site of division for children in school. As Sarah notes, the term "illegal" functions "as a form of racism." In another poignant example, Rosa recalled an instance when she went to school to confront a teacher who had called her daughter names. She said,

My daughter's teacher called her a *mojada*, and she came home crying. She's never been late or lazy in school, and this teacher picked a fight with her . . . I went and discussed it with him and demanded he respect her. I said, "I just want to set things straight. Yes, my daughter is in this country, but it's not her fault. She didn't come voluntarily, but because I brought her." . . . She had already fallen into a depression. She was so saddened by her teacher's words. She had never done anything wrong, she always tried her best. That teacher forgot that we are all humans, and that we should not treat people differently just because of legal status.

Although this was a disturbing and memorable example of inappropriate behavior by a teacher, in almost every other conversation with parents, teachers were portrayed as highly supportive of children in mixed-status families. Parents credited teachers for treating everyone in their classrooms equally and for not calling attention to differences in legal status, approving of the supportive atmosphere in local schools.

Vanessa, a forty-year-old undocumented mother of four U.S. citizens, shared a cautionary tale. She and her husband lived with their children in one of the semi-rural *colonias*, where many families are mixed-status. As we were having coffee in her kitchen one morning, she spoke of an incident that had happened to a neighbor who lived down the street:

I want to tell you about the case of my friend, who brought her children over from Mexico when they were very young. I think she made a mistake by not telling them they didn't have papers. I have always told my children the truth—that I didn't have papers—so that they wouldn't grow up ashamed of that. My friend should have told her kids, "Look, I don't have papers, and neither do you, but that doesn't make you different from other people." But, instead, she hid it from them.

One day they were in school, and the funny thing is they started bullying other kids, saying mean things, like calling them "Mexicans" and "illegals." They got into a fistfight, and the police took them in. And at the police station the kids discovered that they didn't have papers either, that they were undocumented. I mean, it was the sons' fault that they got into a fight, but it was also the parents' fault for not teaching them values and to not say those things to other kids. They should have said, "Sons, don't treat people like they are less than you." You have to teach them to not discriminate or mistreat others because they don't have papers, when they are in the exact same position. You know what I mean? They were harassing other kids with those mean words, and all the while they were the same. But they realized it when they went to jail. They could have been good kids, but now they are in jail.

One particular form of teasing related to state of origin in Mexico. Since the population in this region is almost entirely made up of Mexican-origin persons, most—regardless of legal status—had family ties to specific parts of that country. This meant that regional and class stereotypes carried over through the migration process and via extended family dynamics.[19] For instance, being from Nuevo Leon (and especially its capital city, Monterrey, known as a metropolitan commercial and banking center) was seen as more prestigious than having ties to the much poorer, rural, and higher crime state of Tamaulipas. As a result, people from Nuevo Leon (often simply abbreviated to "NL" in conversations) were seen as coming from a higher social class—and thus less likely to be considered undocumented—by their peers.

As twenty-year-old Selena described it, "In middle and high school a lot of people were like, 'Oh, I'm from NL—Nuevo Leon,' that was like the thing. Everybody wanted to be from NL, all the cool kids." She laughed. "They would dress nicer. But I wasn't ashamed. I was like, 'Your *parents* are from Nuevo Leon, not you. You were born here; you're U.S. citizens.' They go over there on vacations, were partially raised over there, so they'll say they're from over there." For those undocumented persons with ties to Nuevo Leon, the messages and markers of social class were communicated clearly to them. Martha, twenty-six years old, recounted, "I have cousins in Monterrey that are higher economic class, but I don't really talk to them. When I was over there I would go to family gatherings, but my mom's side is lower economic class, so they didn't like us. *Fresas*, upper class, that's the people that usually come from Monterrey."[20] These examples demonstrate the complex and intersectional nature of migration and illegality, in which regional stereotypes persist in the migration process but where race, class, and legal status do not always neatly match up.

The Everyday Threat of Denunciation

The threat that someone will call Border Patrol or Immigration and Customs Enforcement (ICE) is part of everyday life for undocumented persons and can carry over into various relationships. This threat represents a form of social control that neighbors may use to harm people they don't like, that employers may utilize to exploit workers and prevent them from receiving proper working conditions and adequate wages, and that may keep individuals from leaving abusive relationships. Daniel, a twenty-five-year-old DACA recipient, recounted, "The Border Patrol are everywhere. That is why it is also an unwritten rule that you try to keep the secret to yourself, the secret that you are undocumented. There are a lot of people out there that are willing to call the Border Patrol, just because they don't like you or because they had some kind of conflict with you."

Street-level bureaucrats in a number of settings—local law enforcement, schools, health care, municipal services—often find themselves "cross-deputized" by laws and policies that require them to utilize their roles to cooperate directly or indirectly with immigration enforcement agencies. Cross-deputization is the hallmark of legislation such as Arizona's Senate Bill 1070 (2010) and other copycat legislation around the nation, which has sought to involve local law enforcement in immigration activities. In recent years, laws targeting sanctuary cities have dominated, with the reverse strategy but the same effect—by punishing local governments that actively refuse to enforce federal immigration laws.[21]

In 2017, Texas passed Senate Bill 4 (SB4), often dubbed a "show me your papers" law, which allowed police to ask people about their immigration status during routine traffic stops, threatened elected officials with removal from office if they did not cooperate with immigration authorities, and mandated that local entities pass on immigration information they obtain to federal officials. It sought to punish sanctuary cities and fine local officials who were uncooperative with federal agencies. Like similar legislation in other states, many elements of the law were quickly tied up in an appeals court after major cities and counties filed lawsuits to stop its implementation. Nonetheless, the primary component of SB4 was allowed to go into effect, which meant that local law enforcement officers in Texas can ask about immigration status during a lawful stop or arrest, and can provide that information to ICE. Effects of SB4 have included increased fear, allegations of racial discrimination, and strained relations between local police and immigrant communities with damaging effects on public safety.

In fact, the trend toward cross-deputization has increasingly extended beyond authorities themselves and sought to turn all of civil society into collaborators with immigration authorities.[22] In this way, enforcement practices have crept into other social institutions and civic life. As Patrisia Macía-Rojas notes, border residents "are at once regulators and regulated. As law enforcement agents, suspected smugglers, immigrants, or long-term residents, they have become directly and indirectly involved in policing even as they themselves are policed."[23] Sarah Horton has illustrated how labor supervisors in California's Central Valley used knowledge about a person's undocumented status—and their use of fraudulent documents or borrowed identities—against them.[24] Even beyond the workplace, the threat of denunciation is an everyday reality for people in mixed-status families. Hiding one's status remains an important strategy, as the threat of denunciation by others is always present. Forty-eight-year-old Herminia described fibbing—telling harmless little lies— to deflect her neighbors' questions. She said,

> I don't share my status with friends or neighbors. You never know the intentions of another person, so you don't tell anyone. Sometimes people ask, "Why don't you work, since you went to college?" And I say, "Oh, I prefer to stay home." But it is a lie. I would like to work. Or the neighbors say, "Why don't you go with your son when he visits family in San Antonio?" And I say, "I had a headache." I always have to look for a pretext to not say I don't have papers.

Others may use information about a person's status to extort or harass. Selena recalled a time when a landlord sexually harassed her mother after the family fell one month behind on the rent: "He decided to take advantage of the situation and told her, 'Now you have to sleep with me.' My mom refused, and he threatened to deport her. I know that was really hard for her. Because of her status, he wanted to take advantage of her." Selena's mother was too afraid to call the police and report the incident, illustrating how this type of threat effectively silences victims. There are even cases where someone's own family member has threatened to call ICE out of rage or jealousy, or to extort money.

Fifteen-year-old Jaime told me: "Somebody from our own family from Reynosa, my aunt's children, threatened to call immigration on my dad. Why? They were planning to get money out of him. It's always about money. It's crazy."

Like deportability, denounce-ability functions as a powerful and remarkably efficient technique of governance precisely because everyone knows someone who has experienced it.[25] There were many actual cases where people were reported to immigration authorities, and this heightens fear for everyone who is vulnerable. Michelle was in fifth grade when she, her sister, and their father were deported after an angry neighbor called immigration following a dispute. The neighbor didn't want the family to use a side yard that was part of the space they were renting, because she used to park her car there before they moved in. After months of arguments over the space, the neighbor reported the family to ICE, leading to their deportation.

In another example of how fear operates to limit people's livelihoods, a rival business owner threatened Rosa, a hairdresser who works out of her home. Like several entrepreneurial women I met, she had a room in her home set aside as a beauty salon—in her case, it was the living room, just inside the front door—with an adjustable salon stool, mirrors, and prices on the wall. "I cut hair out of my house, but people get jealous," she told me. "This lady down the street who owns a salon heard about me, so she said 'I'm going to call Border Patrol, that is against the law and I'm going to stop her.' She was going to snitch on me. We would see cars come back and forth, and the lady's family was taking pictures of people coming in and out of my house." As a result of this intimidation, Rosa told her clients, "I'm going to stop cutting hair. I can't risk everything that I have, even if it's something that I love doing."

In some cases people were threated during bureaucratic encounters. Following a visit to a local health clinic, Juana was advised by a social worker that she should apply for Medicaid for her citizen daughter Lisa. She told the following story about the encounter:

> I went to the office to fill out the paperwork, and she asked me for my Social Security number. First I said I didn't have one, but she said I had to have one to apply. So I gave her the number my husband was working under. She came back and said, "Do you know this is a fake number?" and I said I did. She said she could call immigration or end the application process right now, that it was up to me. "Whatever you prefer," she told me. I told her to cancel the application.

This is an example of bureaucratic disentitlement, in which staff acted in ways—requiring documentation that was unnecessary for the application—that essentially led to the child being deprived of their statutory entitlements.[26] Despite their eligibility for benefits such as Medicaid and the Children's Health Insurance Program (CHIP), children in mixed-status families access these programs at lower rates than those with citizen parents.[27] Given experiences like this, it is easy to see why. After the incident, one of Juana's friends told her that a Social Security number was actually not needed and encouraged her that she had every right to apply for her daughter. She suggested going to a different office, where Juana had a more supportive experience: "The person there guided me, thank God, and said, 'Your daughter can receive these benefits because they are for her. She's already six years old. She should have gotten them since she was born. She is entitled to Medicaid. I am going to enroll you in this program, and it will not affect you in the future when you try to fix your papers.'" This example illustrates that beyond everyday threats and fear of denunciation, families are structurally vulnerable because fear can lead them to hold off applying for programs for which they are eligible. It's an insidious trade-off: by accessing resources intended for their children, undocumented parents make themselves visible to state authorities, putting them at risk of being deported.[28]

Concealment and Disclosure in Friendships

Concealment of status and feeling like one is living a double life can strain friendships. Eva, a twenty-three-year-old day care worker who had DACA, said that when it came to social situations, "I felt sad, heartbroken. I wasn't ashamed of where I came from, but I was ashamed that I didn't have papers. I was afraid if I told one of my friends, they would make fun or just not hang out with me anymore. I'm fearful and a little ashamed." Often, because of their status, it took a while for people to feel comfortable with others and establish friendships. Daniel explained that he finally felt able to open up to friends when he was in college:

> I found a group of people I clicked with. So I told one of my best friends about my legal status. Over time I told a few more people within that circle. It was pretty much the same situation for everybody. They would say, "Oh, I have a friend or a family member who is dealing with the same thing." It's something you hear about often around here, so they weren't biased. The only thing that

they would say is that they were surprised because I have a light complexion and light eyes. They would say, "I have difficulty assuming that you're Latino, let alone that you're undocumented."

Reactions to Daniel's disclosure were met with understanding and awareness. His friends all seemed to know someone undocumented and in the same situation. This empathy and understanding represents another possible outcome (other than stigmatization or denunciation) in a region where encountering undocumented persons is rarely a surprise.

However, the embarrassment of being undocumented still leads people to hide their status from friends. Sometimes this can have devastating consequences. Leticia, now a permanent resident, told a story that highlighted the consequences of secrecy and the social pressures of being a teenager. Her brother, a high school student, had been reluctant to tell his friends about his status and that he couldn't legally cross the border for a birthday weekend they had planned for him. She said, "His friends invited him to celebrate his birthday by partying in Reynosa. But he was embarrassed to tell them he was undocumented, so he used somebody else's papers to go over there. When he was coming back, it was the day of his eighteenth birthday. He got caught and was punished for it." Sadly, when an opportunity to regularize their status emerged through a relative, Leticia's brother was left out. "Because of that," she said, "he wasn't able to get citizenship, like we were." Charged with impersonating a U.S. citizen, he became permanently inadmissible and could not apply for residency status. The consequences for attempting to hide his status from his peers were severe and permanent.

Since this is a region with heavy law enforcement, many people live in neighborhoods with Border Patrol agents, police officers, and other officials, and count them among their neighbors, friends, and even family. The decision to hide one's status takes on a new urgency in these cases. Jennifer talked about a friend of her mother's who lived next door:

> Our neighbor is really good friends with my mom, but her son was a Border Patrol agent. She had another son who was a state trooper, and then the other one worked for the Constable's office. So, that was the only person who it was like, "We're not telling you we're undocumented." [laughs] I guess they always thought that we were documented because we have a nice house and a brick fence—but that's because my dad is working in construction and his boss gave him leftover material. We have no money to pay for an expensive brick fence.

So my mom was talking to her friend, and her sons had just lost their jobs because of the government shutdown. They were laid off. She was talking to my mom about undocumented people, and then my mom was like, "Well, we're not all that bad," and the neighbor was like, "You're undocumented?" because she had this image from what her sons told her. So I was like, well at least you waited till her sons got laid off to tell her. [laughs]

Jennifer's mother eventually disclosed her status to the neighbor because she wanted to set the record straight about the character of undocumented people. In this region, undocumented people and law enforcement officers live side by side. José described the irony of having grown up with friends who aspired to be in immigration enforcement—Border Patrol and ICE offer arguably some of the most well-paying jobs in the region—but who didn't know that he was undocumented. "Even now, my best friend still doesn't know. The funny thing is that my friends are all studying criminal justice to be ICE, Border Patrol, customs agents. Ironic though: One day they will find out, hey, you know what? It was right under your nose this whole time." Like Jennifer's mother, José did not discuss his status with friends who had direct ties to law enforcement, but neither was too afraid to continue investing in those friendships. This was a fine line to navigate and required an unusual level of trust.

"Me daba mucha vergüenza": Romantic Relationships and Dating

Being in a mixed-status family also impacts romantic relationships, and the full range of disclosure management options appeared to be on the table—direct disclosure, clues, speculation, and (initially) active concealment. Sociologist Daniela Pila has noted that legal status negatively colors the trajectories of intimacy and partnership for undocumented young adults, and that this plays out in particularly gendered ways.[29] Undocumented young adults are often inhibited when trying to adhere to normative expectations of dating and courtship, especially because marriage looms large as a potential pathway to citizenship and future stability. For undocumented persons, marriage means so much more than simply part of the transition to adulthood (and there are certainly plenty of young adults with no plans to get married). Legal status is an important factor at all stages of family formation, and those who are undocumented have unique concerns and experiences compared to their citizen peers. At the same time, DACA changed some of these implications and opened new avenues for dating and for forming relationships. Of note, parents in this study were less likely to be legal status-discordant, which is why this section focuses primarily on disclosure in young adults' romantic relationships.

One Sunday afternoon, I interviewed Armando at his older brother's house. The whole family had gathered there, as they did every weekend. Armando's girlfriend, Selena, and her brother joined them, and everyone was busying themselves between the kitchen and the backyard, where they were grilling and enjoying beers on an unusually pleasant June afternoon. As Milena interviewed Selena's brother at the kitchen table, Armando and I sat in the living room. He told me about what it was like when he first started dating Selena:

> *Me daba mucha vergüenza.* I was so ashamed. I felt so worthless. Like, you don't deserve to go out with me, because there is no future with me. I can't be like a normal boyfriend. They have cars and take their girlfriends out everywhere. For me to have a car, I need a better job. So at the beginning of our relationship, I was so embarrassed. So ashamed of being undocumented.

Selena had been helping in the kitchen and overheard some of our conversation. Later, she confided in me that, "When I was hearing him just now, it hurt me, because he's very emotional. Sometimes he cries. He cried when he told me that he's not from here. It hurt." Selena herself had DACA, so understood well the implications. Neither of them could provide the other with papers through marriage: "We can't help each other. But we decided to stay together. It's hard. He was so embarrassed because he felt I was going to reject him. But we're supporting each other for the moment. I don't know what's going to happen." She noted that he now had a better job in roofing, so made enough money to support both of them and to buy a car.

From their mutual perspective, the relationship was doomed in the long run because neither could legalize on their own or obtain residency status through the other if they decided to marry. As Selena continued, "Unfortunately, it's something that I do have to consider. We've talked about it. Unless something happens, we're going to have to separate. Because we need to think about our futures." She teared up and sighed. "It's just a subject that we get very emotional about." Selena recalled that, growing up, people would always tell her that "the only way you can be here is if you marry a U.S. citizen." But she was not interested in that. She said, "I don't want to marry someone just for citizenship. I want to marry because I love him." Selena and Armando's story had all the elements of a tragic, Shakespearean star-crossed lover's tale.

Twenty-six-year-old Olivia always felt the same way about her relationship with her husband. Even though she had DACA and had already been married to a U.S. citizen for several years when I met her, she has adamantly refused to get papers through him. She recounted dating him in the following way:

> He goes, "So how can you get your papers?" "I would have to get married, to a U.S. citizen," I tell him. And he's like, "I'm a U.S. citizen!" [laughing]. I'm like, "Noooo, that's not how it works." He says, "Well yes, we should do it." I'm like, "No, if we get married, it's because we love each other, not because I need a legal status." So when I met his mother, the first thing she thought is that, "*Esta quiere papeles* [That one, she wants papers]," you know. His mother was very hesitant and very cold towards me. I was very ashamed knowing that she thought I wanted a relationship with her son just because of that.
>
> Until this day everybody, says, "He's a U.S. citizen, why don't you just get your papers?" But I feel like that's something that I'm going to be judged on by his family. I feel like they think, "As soon as you get your papers, you're going to leave him." So I told him when we got married, "I'm not marrying you because I want a legal status; I married you because you are the love of my life, because I want a family." So to this day, even though it could be so easy to just get a lawyer and do the paperwork, I don't feel like that's the way.

Most participants emphasized they would only marry "the right person," with whom they were truly in love.[30] Even though legalization would bring better opportunities for socioeconomic mobility, undocumented young adults were opposed to marrying strictly for papers. They did not want to establish new relationships or transform existing ones strictly for strategic, economic reasons. This refusal to "marry for papers" stands in stark contrast to public discourse and anxieties around marriage fraud. Like their American peers, many 1.5-generation young adults were also simply not interested in marrying in their twenties. Romanticized notions of love and finding the "right person" are important values and moral undertones in these discourses; many rejected the idea of utilitarian or instrumental relationships. However, those who decide to marry enter into a legal partnership that often creates new mixed-status families.

The consideration of legal status came up frequently while dating. Sitting in the kitchen in their newly built home, Adriana (who is undocumented) and Eddie (a U.S. citizen) recounted how it played out in their case. Adriana started by saying, "My husband always said he wouldn't date someone who was undocumented. That was his mentality because he saw how his brother and sister-in-law were struggling with the process because she didn't have papers. He always said he would never do that." Eddie chimed in: "They can't travel together; there are always things that are off-limits. You can only vacation in the Island; that's all there is here at the border." Adriana stood up and walked to the refrigerator to pour her young son, who had been tugging at her shirt, a glass of apple juice. She continued, "So when the topic came up, he would always tell me, 'I won't marry someone who doesn't have papers. I don't want to go through all that.' And now look," she laughed. "He married someone who doesn't have papers. Here we are." Both chuckled at the outcome. As people fall in love and decide to stay together, their initial calculations, intentions, and perceptions may shift.

Most relationships are impacted to some degree by the decision to disclose one's status or not, and when. The stigma of being undocumented still negatively impacted dating opportunities. Olivia recounted: "One time I had a boyfriend, and the topic of legal status came up. He broke up with me the next day. I think he was in the same situation and wanted someone who was a citizen, so that he could fix his papers. It's like he said, 'Why would I want you? You're no good to me.'" She could laugh about this now, but of course the rejection hurt deeply at the time. While legal status doomed some relationships before they even started—with some people opting to break up rather than disclose and make themselves vulnerable—in others, the sincerity of the relationship was cast into doubt. The specter of hidden intentions lingered, as people worried their partners believed they were only in the relationship to gain legal status. Brian, who came to the United States at age fourteen, had such an experience. "I didn't tell my girlfriend I was undocumented at first. It's scary because you don't know what someone is going to say. Is it going to be like, 'Oh no, undocumented, we can't date?' So you're nervous. I ended up finding out that actually her mom and her sisters were also undocumented. But then I had that fear that because I'm dating her, a U.S. citizen, is she going to mind?" The moment of disclosure is hard enough, but even afterwards a loved one may suspect the partner is calculating the risks and benefits of the relationship.

On the far end of risks associated with disclosure in intimate relationships lies the possibility of threats and intimidation. Martha shared a frightening breakup story that highlighted this: "My mom always says, 'Be careful who you tell; they might turn you in,' and there's always that fear in the back of your head. A few years ago, I had a boyfriend who wanted to do just that. He was really jealous and possessive, and when I broke up with him, he threatened to call ICE on me. For months after that I was afraid, just never knowing if they would come." Disclosure produces vulnerability, even (and often especially) in the most intimate relationships. Like many of the participants in this study, Martha's parents taught her to disclose her legal status to as few people as possible.

The gendered intersections of violence and trust in relationships are complex. Having immigration authorities summoned is both an ongoing fear and a very real threat, and denounce-ability is a powerful and efficient tool for subordination. Martha learned this when her boyfriend claimed he would call immigration authorities in retaliation for the breakup, showing just how easily these threats can become an abusive power play in personal relationships. Several participants mentioned intimate partner violence during interviews, in which the threat of deportation was used to drive fear into the victims. Indeed, other studies have shown that women experience barriers to seeking help when their legal status is used against them, especially if they rely economically on their partner.[31] How many undocumented women—and men—cannot leave, especially when they are economically dependent on their partner? Without additional social support networks, people feel that they have no ability to exit the situation. At the same time, other families reported that the cycle of violence had been broken for them precisely because authorities were called and the abuser was detained and/or deported.

While fear of disclosure is prevalent, because there are so many undocumented persons in this region, it is not uncommon for people to know already or to be in similar situations themselves. Eva, the day care worker with DACA, told me, "I actually didn't have a real date until I was seventeen years old, because I was scared, ashamed that they would find out. I had to tell my girlfriend I was undocumented, because my brother was about to be deported." The disruption this event caused in her life had become difficult to hide, and she yearned for the comfort of a loved one. Still, she says, "I was afraid she would break up with me. But when I told her, it turns out she had the same status! It was hard for me: 'I'm undocumented, I don't have papers.' But she's like, 'Don't worry about it, I'm the same.'" In fact, the girlfriend was secretly afraid to tell Eva for the same reason. "At first, I didn't believe her," she recalled, laughing, "because I thought she was just trying to be nice, so I wouldn't feel bad."

The heavily gendered and heteronormative aspects of conventional ideas of dating further complicated experiences. Traditional dating script norms make it difficult for undocumented persons to participate.[32] Hegemonic gender roles often attribute more responsibility to men, who are expected to finance dating activities and have a car. Undocumented women had an advantage in these situations because normative dating practices did not require them to have such resources. This was evident in Daniel's commentary on how his experience differed from his sister's:

> My older sister is dating a citizen. We were talking about the possibility that one day they might get married, since that's one way that people get legal residency. But it was a situation where I felt like gender roles were limiting me, because it's easy for an undocumented female to meet a citizen who is a male, in terms of courtship or dating. In traditional dating rituals females aren't expected to pay; they're expecting to be picked up in a car, and the gentleman will pay for everything. Eventually, if it's the right person, they may marry them. But in my situation it's very difficult. I didn't have a vehicle. I didn't have a means of income. So I felt like I was already at a huge disadvantage because I wouldn't be able to provide the very bare necessities to even date someone, because of gender role expectations.

Distinct gender expectations for men meant that they were disadvantaged over women, and they worried more about normative practices if they were undocumented. For men, lack of money or a car—along with a general lack of confidence with meeting new people—greatly impacted their dating lives. Additionally, for all genders, the inability to obtain a government-issued identification card represented another barrier to dating—since without one, undocumented persons cannot enter bars or clubs. DACA changed this for many, since they were suddenly allowed to obtain driver's licenses, for the first time in their lives and often well into their mid- to late twenties.

During the course of this study, two landmark U.S. Supreme Court decisions changed the prospects for same-sex relationships, with profound effects on the ability to adjust legal status based on marriage. A 2013 ruling determined that the Defense of Marriage Act (DOMA) was unconstitutional, thus opening the door for same-sex spouses to receive the same immigration benefits under federal law that "traditional" marriages had long received. However, Texas had passed a statewide ban on same-sex marriage in 2005, making it difficult, if not impossible, for this to benefit residents of that state. This changed in 2015 when the U.S. Supreme Court confirmed in the case of *Obergefell v. Hodges* that the fundamental right to marry is guaranteed to same-sex couples by the Fourteenth Amendment to the Constitution. These rulings opened the opportunity for LGBTQ immigrants to adjust their status if they are in a bona fide marriage to a U.S. citizen, thus allowing same-sex spouses to receive the same benefits under federal law that "traditional marriages" had long received.

A number of participants in the study identified as LGBTQ, but few were considering marriage at the time I spoke with them. One exception was Justin, a twenty-five-year-old DACA recipient. In our first interview, he told me, "I'm gay. So, it's not legal to get married. I've been dating someone for three years. He is a U.S. citizen, and we have talked about it. His family is also mixed-status, so he understands what it's like to have your mom be undocumented. His mom and brothers are, too. So he can relate." A little over a year later, following the 2015 Supreme Court decision, we met up again in the same coffee shop. Justin started the conversation with a surprising bit of good news: he and his partner had gotten married and started the process for Justin's permanent residency. The Supreme Court's decision had opened a new door for the couple.

Empowered Disclosure: Coming Out as Undocumented

For many young adults, "coming out" as undocumented was a critical part of their disclosure management process and autobiographical construction. This was facilitated by changes in policies and opportunities in recent years, most notably DACA, but also tuition equity laws and other inclusive efforts at institutions of higher education. These shifts in the social and political landscape have encouraged many undocumented immigrants to come "out of the shadows." Many initiated these vulnerable conversations and disclosed their legal status only when some degree of control and trust was evident. However, their decisions were also sharply informed by the presence or absence of a climate of fear resulting from the institutionalization of anti-immigrant sentiments, which vary greatly by place.[33] As people "come out" as undocumented or as citizens with undocumented parents, they create new and complex identities and political subjectivities (see figure 2).

Figure 2. Mixed-status family defending DACA in front of the Texas Attorney General's office. Source: Nathan Lambrecht/*The Monitor* (McAllen, TX).

Empowered disclosure, or "strategic outness" enabled many to view their legal status as an asset, reframe its meaning, and even challenge others.[34] Camila, for example, recalled a confrontation in school. After a classmate made an anti-immigration comment during class discussion, she jumped in:

> I told the guy in my class, "You know what? I don't have my papers." And he's like, "Oh, you're like a *mojada*?" He didn't say it in a mean way. I couldn't blame someone that is ignorant about it. Even when people are mean about it, I don't get mad. I feel like I need to teach them. Being undocumented, to an extent, it does hurt. But at the same time, it really empowers you to make a change. When you're oppressed, you want to make the change. But when you're not affected by anything, it's hard to recognize you have a privilege. It's understandable. If they haven't faced it, how can they understand?

Brian, who had DACA, illustrated how his personal biographical construction was intimately tied to this form of strategic disclosure and the greater connections he was able to develop with others in the same position. During college, he had become active with an immigrant rights organization and began to present in front of large crowds. As he explained,

> I started presenting, giving my story, the story of my family. It started getting to the point where it wasn't me. It was just a huge story of people who are connected to so many people around me. It was like I was telling my story, but I'm also telling your story. It got so comfortable to the point where now I can tell my story in peace without having that fear, without being nervous or scared.

Some participants experienced a second "coming out" if they identified as LGBTQ in addition to being undocumented, which has also been referred to as the "double closet."[35] Some found it more difficult to disclose their undocumented identity than their sexual identity based on perceived social acceptance. Justin, for example, had been active with an LGBTQ organization in college and thus had been out as gay for many years, but he still hesitated to tell his friends about his legal status:

> As a gay man, I had just gone through one identity crisis, through my own self-exploration and self-identification. I am a lot more comfortable saying that I am queer than saying that I'm undocumented. Just because ever since *Lawrence v. Texas*, it's not illegal to be gay.[36] It's not something that you can go to jail or be deported for, or be branded as a criminal. But it's that fear, that rhetoric in our nation, that holds me back from telling people I am undocumented.

Justin told me he identified strongly with the work of Gloria Anzaldúa, a queer Chicana poet, writer, and feminist theorist from the Rio Grande Valley: "She's a very famous writer, from here, from the Valley. She graduated from the same university I did. Gloria Anzaldúa was also lesbian, she was gay, so she understood. Her work resonates because I am LGBT, I'm Hispanic, I'm undocumented." Anzaldúa's work focuses on the borderlands, which she takes both literally and metaphorically to explore issues of marginalization, alienation, and the oppression of those who are culturally and sexually different.[37]

Living with "Little Lies" in Mixed-Status Families

In exploring interactions with the broader community, it is evident that the condition of illegality influences opportunities and resources for many people in a mixed-status family. U.S. citizens may feel like they are living a double life and must formulate "little lies" in order to deflect questions from friends and romantic partners. In school, children avoid discussing their parents' legal status, because in addition to the fear of someone reporting them, it opens the door for bullying. U.S. citizens and permanent residents are affected in other ways as well. Parents may be hesitant to sign their children up for programs to which they are entitled. When they do, they may face denunciation and bureaucratic disentitlement, for instance when enrolling children in Medicaid. Legal status can also hinder the development of friendships and romantic relationships. In cases where partners have discordant legal status, people may hesitate to forge intimate ties. Others find that potential or current partners outright reject them when they disclose their status. Even following marriage, undocumented people in mixed-status relationships often continue to worry that others believe they are simply in it for the papers.

However, families and individuals develop a set of strategies in response to these situations, situations that are often full of anxiety and mistrust. To protect their children, some parents downplay or hide their legal status from them, or coach them to tell others that they are "from here." As we have seen, U.S.-citizen children also stick up to bullies who call their parents or other children names. Parents also made sure to intercede, meeting with school officials to demand respect and protection for their children. Resistance and agency are also evident in other ways. After facing difficulties enrolling in services or programs to which they are entitled, parents turn to their peers for advice and support. And some undocumented persons choose to disclose their status in the classroom or at public events, outing themselves to counter stigma and educate others as a form of personal empowerment.

Through all of this, the uniqueness of the region frames their experiences. In the Rio Grande Valley, being undocumented is an open secret; when people disclose their status to others, this is frequently met not by surprise but with understanding and even nonchalance, as Jessica at the start of the chapter discovered. Nonetheless, legal status does represent a major line of social division in the region, and disclosure creates vulnerability and must be weighed against possible stigmatization, ridicule, and fear. While bullying and discrimination in other parts of the United States often reflects interracial or class tensions, in this overwhelmingly Latino area, people's own or their parent's illegality is often a reason for harassment. In addition, proximity to Mexico means that regional differences and stereotypes are carried over. As noted in prior chapters, the Border Patrol has a heavy presence in the region, so that many people count them among their neighbors, teachers, friends, and even extended family. This further complicates issues of trust, concealment, and disclosure.

The next chapter examines larger issues of physical mobility, which I analyze as a stratified resource. It illustrates how the cultural, political, and economic features of the region result in spatial restrictions. Practices related to the policing of their mobility, it argues, affects people of different legal statuses and produces racializations that impact the dynamics in mixed-status families.

CHAPTER 4

ESTAMOS ENCERRADOS

IM/MOBILITIES IN THE BORDERLANDS

ONE MORNING I RECEIVED a call from Rafael, inviting me to an event he was organizing. We had first met in 2013, and stayed in close touch over the years. Rafael came to the United States at the age of ten and was undocumented. He was now a community organizer in the Rio Grande Valley. Because of his undocumented status, he could not travel to the state capitol or other major cities for events, since these were beyond the U.S. Customs and Border Protection (CBP) checkpoints set up along major highways. Neither had he been able to pursue his dream of attending law school after he graduated from the local branch of a state university. Growing up in a mixed-status family, he watched as his U.S.-born siblings experienced a wider range of social and spatial mobility: they had driver's licenses, frequently traveled out of state with their friends, and could apply to any college they wanted to. Near the end of our conversation, he paused and said,

> I wanted to tell you about a dream I had last night. I was driving, I don't know to where exactly, but trying to go up north. Out of the Valley. In the dream, I kept having to turn around and go back because I had forgotten something. I would get started again, and the same thing would happen. Each time there were different people in the car, but each time I kept having to turn around. It was frustrating, like, "Ahh! I just want to get on the road already!" [We both laughed a little.] And then finally, I got to the checkpoint and crossed. I was on my way. Suddenly it was like Narnia—you remember that book? I was pushing

through to the other side. It was snowing, all white and crystals and beautiful, the minute I crossed.

Young undocumented adults like Rafael define their lives by the distance they can travel before reaching a permanent checkpoint or other spatial boundary: two hours to the west, through sparsely populated brushland and cattle ranches; thirty minutes to the south, until stopped by the international border; an hour and a half to the east, until stopped by the ocean; and only forty-five minutes to the north, where they end up facing the fixed highway checkpoints. In a decade and a half living in this country, this is the only United States Rafael has ever seen. In his dream, he manages to leave the Rio Grande Valley only after enormous frustration and difficulty. He pushes through the portal and enters what seems like the fantasy realm of Narnia, where animals can talk and mythical beasts abound.[1] It snows and glitters and offers relief and a sense of freedom, a contradiction to the subtropical, heavily militarized South Texas landscape in which he grew up.

For mixed-status families along the U.S.–Mexico border, mobility is a stratified resource and a contradictory process. Rafael is one of 1.7 million undocumented immigrants living in Texas concentrated within a 100-mile-wide strip along the border that forms a secondary boundary to the interior of the United States. Over the past decade, CBP has doubled the number of agents and operates some thirty-four permanent interior checkpoints like the one referenced in Rafael's dream. The permanent checkpoints are visible from miles away, along lanes of all highways that lead away from Mexico and into the interior of the United States. While the Rio Grande serves as a geographical marker of the first barrier to be crossed into the United States, these checkpoints represent a "second river," further impeding mobility into the interior.[2] These checkpoints are supplemented by random roadblocks placed along major roads where people live and work, where police or state troopers inspect drivers' documents. These enforcement practices each impact the mobility of persons in the borderlands, but with different effects. While the permanent checkpoints trap people within a distinct space, the temporary roadblocks— combined with random traffic stops and driver's license restrictions—fuel fear and uncertainty within that space. This spatial containment results in immobility and a particular experience of "stuckness," in which people's movement is constrained by a stillness imposed through larger bordering processes.[3] The containment of immigrants along the U.S.–Mexico border is an example of the complex spatial effects of the securitization of migration management and the ways in which it produces marginalized spaces with particular consequences for the people that inhabit them.[4] Over the past two decades, this securitization has led to increased reliance on border enforcement, detention, and deportation as strategies to control unauthorized movements, as highlighted by the current "defense in depth" strategy of CBP that creates layers of entrapment.

To explore the sense of confinement that Rafael and others like him experience on a daily basis, it is important to understand the competing logics of containment and mobility that are part of contemporary migration management.[5] Starting in the 1990s, securitization discourse and practices have dominated, especially through an internalization of border controls. This has expanded surveillance beyond the physical international border and toward the interior of the United States, and has been accompanied by a proliferation of inspection checkpoints, technologies, and detention practices. Inspection and policing practices have expanded both within and beyond territorial boundaries, making life increasingly uncertain for immigrants in interior communities.[6] Nonetheless, the physical U.S.–Mexico border continues to feature prominently in the regulation of mobility and is an important reminder of the enduring territorial authority of the state. These extraordinary spatial tactics have produced particular political geographies, leading to the transformation of national spaces and rendering certain locations ambiguous.

This is particularly evident in the Rio Grande Valley, where people described feeling "trapped" or "locked up" within an uncertain territorial space. Particular groups experience a stuckness, in which their movement is constrained by a stillness—or as Rafael describes it, a ricocheting in place—produced and imposed through larger bordering processes.[7] Others, like those who were Deferred Action for Childhood Arrivals (DACA) recipients, experienced an augmentation of their social and physical mobility and the opportunity to leave their positions of stuckness to cross new frontiers. These differential possibilities occur within families and communities, producing new hierarchies based on mobility. These legally differentiated internal spaces may not be apparent to residents, unless they are in mixed-status families or undocumented themselves. As mobility itself has become an important stratifying factor, it is useful to distinguish between those who are mobile versus those who have aspirations they cannot actualize.[8] Through interior enforcement practices, migrants are confined to subnational spaces, where they must remain to avoid detection or harassment. The spatial violence resulting from checkpoints and policing practices leads to a hierarchy of experiences, producing mobility for some while leaving others feeling *encerrados*, locked in or locked up. The increased securitization of immigration control has made some national spaces resemble, in certain respects, detention centers.[9] As a result, entire regions have become zones of confinement.[10] Dorsey and Díaz-Barriga argue that the presence of the checkpoints, combined with mass incarceration and everyday surveillance, creates a "state of carcelment" for the Rio Grande Valley.[11] This highlights the intersection of racial and spatial dynamics that emerge from legal precedents as well as the actual effects on people's everyday lives, as a way to understand how an entire region becomes interred.

Enforcement tactics that treat all residents as potentially suspect have important implications for the nature of citizenship. These practices have spillover effects, in that everyone—including U.S. citizens—must pass through inspection points and demonstrate proof of identity and legal residency. As Susan Coutin argues, "Treating residents, legal or otherwise, as potentially undocumented thus transforms the nature of citizenship itself."[12] However, even as these practices target the broader population, they produce different racialized experiences, so that those with a "phenotypic passport" are more likely to move about unchallenged.[13] This "passport" may include features like light skin, eye and hair color, and accent-free English, but it also extends to how people dress, what music they play, and what car they drive; these characteristics allow some individuals to pass more easily and to cross spaces unrestricted. Guillermina Gina Núñez and Josiah McC. Heyman note that these dynamic "processes of entrapment," through which Border Patrol, police officers, and other state agencies impose significant risk on movement of undocumented people, are also met with various forms of agency as people both forgo travel and covertly defy their containment.[14]

This chapter focuses on spatial restrictions to mobility, including through the various kinds of checkpoints; the fear of driving that exposes people to apprehension; and the racialization of illegality through policing and inspection practices. It illustrates how differences in legal status within the family become embodied as stratified forms of mobility. Due to shifting legal terrains and requirements, a range of legal driving opportunities often coexist within a single family. For everyday driving practices and during inspection at one of the many checkpoints, racial and ethnic profiling is a recurring theme. The geographies of policing mobility in the border region are distinct from those in other parts of the country, by virtue of the constraints of the international border, the 100-mile-wide buffer zone, and specific enforcement practices. As this chapter shows, fear, anxiety, and pressure are all part of the affective nature of the borderlands. A rethinking of borders as dynamic and inhabited places[15] allows us to shift our focus from the stillness of border walls to the stuckness of people, and specifically the ways in which they become immobile.[16]

The Checkpoint

The fixed, tollbooth-like checkpoints are routine for anyone driving near the border, separating the region from the rest of the United States. These permanent checkpoints are located far from the actual international boundary (with its own formalized inspection practices), and stretch along all lanes of highways leading away from Mexico into the interior of the United States. They are operational 24/7 and visible from miles away and cannot be circumvented. As cars approach, they are corralled by cones and organized into neat lines to await inspection. A white sign declares year-to-date seizures of "drugs" (by pound) and "undocumented aliens" (by number of people), in a particularly dehumanizing manner, as people are equated with contraband. As cars slow toward the checkpoint, a dozen cameras are trained on them. Agents and drug-sniffing dogs approach to inspect the vehicles (see figure 3). Upon stopping, the driver and each of the passengers are quizzed: "Are you a U.S. citizen?" "Where are you headed?" The whole affair takes between ten minutes to half an hour; if a secondary inspection is called, many more hours may pass.

As part of its layered approach, known as the "defense in depth" strategy, CBP deploys agents up to 100 miles from the border and utilizes about 140 immigration checkpoints along all highways between 25 and 100 miles from the Mexican border, although not all are continuously operational.[17] There are two types of checkpoints—permanent and tactical—that differ in terms of location, size, and infrastructure. While tactical checkpoints are intended to be set up for short-term or intermittent use, permanent checkpoints are generally intended to be operational all of the time. Permanent interior checkpoints, of which there are currently thirty-four, are further characterized by their brick-and-mortar structures, including covered lanes for vehicle inspection, administration buildings, detention areas, storage, and canine kennels. In the Rio Grande Valley Sector, there are two permanent checkpoints; the largest, on U.S. Highway 281 south of Falfurrias and 70 miles north of the Mexican border, is

Figure 3. U.S. Customs and Border Protection highway checkpoint leading out of the Rio Grande Valley, located approximately seventy miles inland of the Mexican border. Source: AP Photo/Eric Gay.

the busiest in the country and being expanded to eight, rather than the current five, lanes.

Legal Antecedents: The "Second River"

Court rulings have confirmed that the Fourth Amendment of the Constitution, which provides protection from unreasonable searches and seizures, does not apply at spaces up to 100 miles away from the U.S. border. 8 U.S.C. § 1357(a)(3) addresses CBP officials' authority to stop and conduct searches on vessels, trains, aircraft, or other vehicles anywhere within "a reasonable distance from any external boundary of the United States." Without further statutory guidance, regulations alone expansively define this "reasonable distance" as 100 air miles from any external boundary.[18] Notably, however, roughly two-thirds of the U.S. population (about 200 million people) lives within 100 miles of a land or coastal border, including the nation's largest metropolitan areas such as New York City, Los Angeles, Houston, and Miami, along with entire states including Connecticut, Delaware, Florida, Hawaii, Maine, Massachusetts, New

Hampshire, New Jersey, Rhode Island, and Vermont.[19] However, because it is almost solely invoked to defend practices along the U.S.–Mexico border, it can be concluded that the "100-mile" rule utilized by CBP is arbitrary and leads to discriminatory practices. It has never been subjected to serious scrutiny by federal lawmakers.

The basis of this authority to stop and conduct searches is rooted in judicial interpretations at the U.S.–Mexico border in cases primarily related to the "war on drugs," and not the movement of undocumented individuals. Beginning in the 1960s, judicial opinions began to paint the U.S.–Mexico border as "elastic" rather than static, opening the way for a relaxation of the standard of probable cause.[20] The 1965 case of *Marsh v. United States*—involving a car searched sixty-three miles north of the official port of entry—exemplified this shift in interpretation. In 1961, Reynaldo Guerra Garza was the first Mexican American appointed to a federal district court. He utilized his knowledge of the Rio Grande Valley—his home—to argue that the checkpoints constituted only a "very minor intrusion" on daily life and in effect would constitute a "second river" for smugglers and those entering illegally to have to cross.[21] This had the effect of justifying checkpoints in a number of legal cases from the 1970s onward. In 1972, judicial opinions in the case of *United States v. McDaniel*, which related to marijuana possession, agreed that a "reasonable stretch" of the Fourth Amendment is allowed at permanent immigration checkpoints. However, the minority opinion of Justice Goldberg, Fifth Circuit of the U.S. Court of Appeals, also argued that "proximity to the frontier does not automatically place a 100-mile strip of citizenry within a deconstitutionalized zone."

Legal precedents provide a basis by which agents may "stretch" Fourth Amendment rights without a warrant or probable cause. Today, while some refer to South Texas—and other border regions like it—as a "Constitution free zone,"[22] it is in fact not literally devoid of constitutional protection. Border Patrol agents have legal authority to stop a vehicle at checkpoints for brief questioning of its occupants even without reason to believe that there are illegal occupants or drugs, nor do they need a judicial warrant (*United States v. Martinez-Fuerte*, 428 U.S. 543, 545 [1976]). The Supreme Court has held that, provided the intrusion is sufficiently minimal, agents "have wide discretion" to refer motorists to secondary inspection. The constitutional threshold for searching a vehicle, however, must be supported by either consent or probable cause (e.g., a trained canine detecting concealed people or narcotics, *U.S. v. Ortiz*, 422 U.S. 891,

896–898 [1975]). Notably, what are viewed as roughshod abuses of civil liberties mostly occur in border settings, in regions where people of color make up the majority of inhabitants.

Checkpoint inspections have increased in recent years and drawn the ire of many residents, with U.S. citizens arguing that this violates their right against arbitrary searches. However, the resistance has not been primarily from communities of color. Anti-checkpoint movements have not emerged precisely because of the precarity that these Latino communities face due to racial profiling and the high proportion of undocumented persons and mixed-status families at risk of being separated. As Dorsey and Díaz-Barriga note, "many border residents recognize that they are not required to respond to the citizenship question; in practice, however, few are as bold."[23]

"Trapped in a Cage": The Permanent Checkpoint and Experiences of Containment

In this study, the single most commonly mentioned feature of the Valley was the permanent checkpoint. Large numbers of undocumented persons in the region are relegated to life within this small strip along the border; unable to reenter the United States if they cross back into Mexico, they are also unable to travel north to other parts of Texas or to other parts of the United States. Several participants thus described feeling "trapped in a cage" by these physical limitations on their mobility, and many had not left the Valley for decades.[24] Gerardo, a forty-five-year old father of two, told me, "I always say, we are in a prison here. It's just a large prison, and it has a beach. We can only travel to the beach and along the banks of the [Rio Grande] River, and that's it. We can only exist between here and the checkpoint. It's like we are locked up [*estamos encerrados*]. It affects us completely, totally, and you feel like a prisoner." Some other comments during interviews included:

> "The Valley is its own place. Because you have so many people here, thousands of people, who can't cross that checkpoint."
> "We are stuck on an island. Can't go south, can't go north."
> "It's easier to enter the United States from Mexico than it is for someone to travel within the United States."

For undocumented persons, multiple tiers of containment operate simultaneously. While these spatial limitations represent a form of social inequality,

for undocumented persons there is the additional, very real threat of detention and imprisonment associated with this lack of mobility.

Yet mobility is a necessity for those living in South Texas, where even densely
populated areas are separated by wide open spaces. Many people work as migrant laborers and must travel to farms across the United States as growing sea-
sons shift. High school sports teams, bands, and extracurricular organizations
travel by bus to other parts of the state for competitions. Most colleges and universities are beyond the checkpoint, an issue that young applicants are keenly
aware of as they make decisions about their futures. Business professionals regularly travel to major cities in the rest of the state, such as Houston, San Antonio, Austin, and Dallas. The Rio Grande Valley has a long history of military
service and is home to tens of thousands of veterans, who must travel four hours
north to San Antonio, where the nearest Veteran Affairs hospital is located. Recreational and tourism destinations are also on the other side of the checkpoint.
Finally, most people have relatives living in other parts of the United States. For
undocumented persons, the fixed CBP checkpoint impacts their ability to attend
important events such as weddings, birthdays, baptisms, and funerals, even
though they are in the United States, leading to a weakening of family ties.

Many undocumented young adults reminisced about field trips while in
elementary, middle, and high school, when they were not scrutinized in the
same way as when they became adults. Twenty-one-year-old Betty, who is undocumented, noted: "I was in cross-country [running team], and we made it
to regionals in San Antonio and then to state finals in Austin. And I was president of two clubs, and we got to go to Dallas. I got to go to places without being inspected at the checkpoint." Similarly, Michelle told me, "That was the only
way I could travel, so I would go for high school football games whenever I
could, even though I didn't care at all about the games." I asked, "And they
didn't check who was going?" "Nah, they didn't," she replied. "The bus just goes
right through. So I miss school now because I don't get to travel." Indeed, this
shift to immobility and greater surveillance was a key part in the transition to
adulthood for many.

U.S. citizens in mixed-status families also feel the effects of this immobility produced by the checkpoint. Elizabeth, Gerardo's daughter, described the
limitations she felt about going to college:

> Because my parents can't go out of state, I have to limit myself so it's a reason-
> able distance and I can still come and see them often. I don't want to go out too

far and something important happens or there's an emergency. So, I did have to consider my college choices because of my parents. Especially like now they're building a new part of the border wall, in addition to the drones and all the state troopers.

Camouflaged in South Texas

Crossing the checkpoint is difficult and dangerous because it can result in deportation, a risk that very few are willing to take. However, some noted that they could mislead agents about their status. Twenty-two-year-old Andres described his tactic for crossing the checkpoint before he received DACA:

> I would lie and say that I was a U.S. citizen. It was really scary, really scary. But once I get to a checkpoint, adrenaline kicks in, and I am like ready, so I look them straight in the eye. I mean, I watch *Border Wars* [a TV show] a lot. They tell you a lot of the secrets they look for, so I came prepared. They have never asked me for identification, but there I would have been screwed.

Because he had grown up in the United States, Andres's mannerisms, speech, and dress would have made him indistinguishable from a citizen. In addition to some tips learned from a television program, he relied on the fact that the vast majority of Latino youth in the state of Texas are U.S. citizens—for agents, they are indistinguishable until their papers are scrutinized.

On the other hand, another young adult, Justin, recalled with horror a friend's suggestion that he lie to cross. He told me,

> I have a friend who was undocumented, and she would cross all the time. She's like "Oh, it's not a big deal, you just say you're a citizen." I'm like what? No! But she has green eyes. She's white. The way she looks and the way she speaks, you would never guess she's undocumented, but some people don't have that privilege to be able to do that. I'm not going to risk it.

Again, those with "phenotypic passports" and accent-free English are afforded fewer threats of being stopped for inspection. Angelica similarly noted, "Because of the way I look and the way I sound—I don't have much of an accent—I learned that it's easier for me to blend in. With encounters with Border Patrol, when I eat at a restaurant or see them at the grocery story, I say hi. So you're at risk, but if you know you're camouflaged and have an advantage, you're not so afraid."

In addition to the highway checkpoints set up within 45 miles of these border towns, access to air travel is restricted. In cities further north, such as San Antonio or Houston, a valid Mexican passport is generally sufficient to pass Transportation and Security Administration (TSA) security at airports. However, at airports in border regions, CBP officers are always a conspicuous presence alongside TSA agents. They monitor and often check the documents of passengers traveling out of the region and into other parts of the United States, rather than simply those entering. In other words, their purpose is to prevent people from leaving the border zone to enter the interior. Angelica, who arrived in the United States at the age of eight, was a DACA recipient. She described her experience at the airport:

> People who don't have documents try to cross the checkpoint and fly out of San Antonio. They don't have Border Patrol there, so they just need a picture ID when you fly out of other airports. But here, they make sure you have your DACA paperwork and everything. Some people are afraid, like my mom says, "Oh I can't go to the airport because there's Border Patrol." I think it's sad, though, because people are afraid of going to see their loved ones go away or to pick them up. Sometimes I would like for my mom to be there. Especially the first time I flew out. I don't think my mom has even seen an airplane up close. It's just sad that the airport here is like that, because it keeps a lot of people from seeing their family.

The experience of Pulitzer Prize–winning journalist, filmmaker, and immigration activist Jose Antonio Vargas corroborates these stories. In July 2014, Vargas was taken into custody at McAllen-Miller International Airport before boarding a flight. He had gained prominence following a 2011 essay, in which he revealed his status as an undocumented immigrant to promote dialogue and advocate for the DREAM Act.[25] Prior to his arrest, Vargas had been in the Rio Grande Valley to attend a vigil organized by the group United We Dream. He says that he did not realize that he would have to cross through a CBP checkpoint to leave, even though following his arrival many local activists wondered aloud how he would.[26] Vargas was released later that day, but the event cast an immediate spotlight on deportations of immigrant youth in the region.

The event also revealed the patchwork of immigration enforcement that had allowed Vargas to travel freely to forty-three states over the preceding three years, since domestic airport security officials did not check his immigration status.[27] Though he had flown frequently to promote his film *Documented*, once he arrived to this heavily patrolled border region he had to pass through a checkpoint to leave. Writing just before his arrest, he said,

> In the last 24 hours I realize that for an undocumented immigrant like me, getting out of a border town in Texas—by plane or by land—won't be easy. It might, in fact, be impossible. . . . I'd heard about checkpoints and border patrol agents, but I didn't realize just how much a militarized zone the Texas border is. I didn't know that border patrol agents check IDs with airport security agents. I've spoken with a few undocumented people who live in the McAllen area, and they feel trapped. I don't think the American public at large understands that reality for undocumented people in the border.[28]

New Mobilities: Crossing with DACA

Crossing the checkpoint legally for the first time was groundbreaking for those who had received DACA. Many participants excitedly relayed their stories, like José and his sister Carla. José laughed and said, "Actually, they didn't even ask me for anything." Carla explained, "He was really mad!" She laughed and continued, "He called me, and said, 'You know what? They didn't even ask for my papers. I wanted to show them!'" Aaron similarly described the experience as legitimizing and satisfying, saying, "After I got my DACA, the first time I went through the checkpoint, more than anything it was very empowering. I was afraid, but inside I felt confident. I had something legal, an ID that I could pass through with and they couldn't do anything to me." But he emphasized that agents were still very careful to check the validity of paperwork and work permit. Carolina, who was brought to the United States when she was nine, described the following experience:

> That day as I was leaving the house, I said, "Mom, I'm going to go to San Antonio." And she was like, "What?!" And I said, "I know, calm down." She was so worried, scared all day, like, "Why haven't you texted me in the past five minutes!?" And like, "Mom . . ." That was the first time I crossed the checkpoint with DACA. I was so nervous. I had handed the officer my papers, and we drove away, no big deal, and my world was like shattered. It was just like, "This just happened to me." I just crossed, and I was alright! I was like bawling, "Oh my God, I'm free!" And I cried thinking about the kids who go through this, the frustration that they carry driving past this place, thinking of all those who are not eligible for some reason. And my mom, who can't leave this place. She

saved me from a world of poverty and violence in Mexico, but she also let her dreams go so I would have even an opportunity.

Twenty-two-year-old Brian felt dissociated from the entire experience of crossing the checkpoint legally. Like Rafael's dream about Narnia at the start of this chapter, Brian felt as if his sense of reality had been skewed through his lifelong immobility. Unlike Rafael, he had received DACA and could now travel more freely, but described the conflicted emotions that he felt in the following way: "We're so traumatized from not traveling when we grow up, that now it almost feels like traveling isn't real. I feel like it's fake. I feel like I'm in this virtual reality, where people are just driving me in a circle and it's just the pictures outside the window are changing." Although he could now travel more freely, he still experienced an internal struggle when it came to contextualizing this new freedom.[29] For many residents of this region, their mobility is akin to "driving in circles" or ricocheting back and forth; this is a particular form of "stuckness" that is also simultaneously imbued with activity and movement within a confined area.

Illegality, Automobility, and Fear of Driving

While the permanent checkpoints are unique to border regions, immigrant mobility is more commonly contained through restrictions on driving. Angela Stuesse and Mathew Coleman use the concept of "automobility" to explore the dialectic of freeing and fixing movement for undocumented persons in the United States.[30] Automobility refers to the assemblage of cars, roads, and other physical infrastructures that permits people to extend their lives through space and time.[31] It is a highly stratified resource. For undocumented persons, the otherwise mundane act of driving quickly becomes the activity of highest risk.[32] In many regions, driving is simultaneously necessary and prohibited. Vehicles thus become mobile sites of power and contestation in their own right.

Driving and traffic enforcement rest at the very core of initiatives like 287(g), Secure Communities, the Priority Enforcement Program (PEP), and Texas's Senate Bill 4, which encourage coordination between local law enforcement agencies and U.S. Immigration and Customs Enforcement (ICE).[33] Under section 287(g) of the Immigration and Nationality Act, ICE delegated federal immigration authority to state and local law enforcement agencies. Under

President Obama, this and the Secure Communities program were replaced with PEP, which essentially worked in the same way, tracking fingerprints and helping ICE agents issue detainers and retrieve people from local jails. Then, despite its troubled history—including the high cost to localities, racial profiling, and trail of pretextual arrests—287(g) was resurrected in 2017 under the Trump administration. This means that with any traffic stop in a 287(g)/S-Comm jurisdiction, undocumented drivers risk detention and deportation.[34] These efforts have not been without pushback, however, and the Department of Homeland Security's own Southwest Border Task Force recommended that 287(g) be strictly limited. The vice chairman of the task force, Sheriff Lupe Treviño of Hidalgo County, argued that enforcing federal immigration law distracts local authorities from their primary duties, in addition to fostering fear in immigrant communities.

Another major concern for undocumented persons is their ability to obtain a driver's license. A driver's license may be simply a small card, usually tucked away, but it holds enormous meaning and potential for undocumented persons. It represents belonging, movement, and social reproduction, and is a required resource for getting to and from work, school, health services, religious events, and leisure activities. Regulation of licenses occurs at the state level, and in recent years legislative activity around this issue has markedly increased. Until the 1990s, undocumented persons' access to driver's licenses anywhere in the United States was unrestricted. Then, starting with California in 1993, states began to alter their laws to require that applicants prove legal immigration status. By 2011, undocumented persons could only obtain licenses in three states: New Mexico, Utah, and Washington. However, an opposite trend emerged in 2013, as legislative debates about issuing driver's licenses focused on the impact on public safety and on insurance and accident rates. The federal REAL ID Act also set the context in which states began to reconsider their legislation. This law, enacted in 2005, created national standards for all state driver's licenses that can be used for federal identification purposes (such as entering a federal building or boarding a commercial aircraft). For this reason, the REAL ID law requires that states extending driving privileges to unauthorized immigrants issue a document that can be used only for this purpose and is distinct from regular driver's licenses in specific ways. As a result, states established new eligibility requirements allowing many unauthorized immigrants to obtain "driving privilege cards," "driver authorization cards," or other alternative licenses. In many states, there was considerable debate over the design of these cards, which frequently were a different color, or contained phrases like "LEGAL PRESENCE NO LAWFUL STATUS" in bold red font.[35] While DACA recipients were eventually able to obtain driver's licenses in every state, most also had to provide proof of an employment authorization document and a Social Security number.

The State of Texas is among the most restrictive when it comes to driver's licenses, and the Department of Public Safety (DPS) now verifies applicants' legal status with the U.S. Department of Homeland Security. However, this lawful presence requirement was not always in place. The change in the Texas law was initially enacted in 2008, with an important modification in 2011 that allowed U.S. citizens with a Social Security number on file to renew online, while all others who hadn't renewed in person in the past six years had to present proof of lawful presence.[36] All of this means that, at the time of the study, a variety of scenarios played out, often within a single family: some undocumented persons still held legally issued driver's licenses (if obtained before 2008); others faced the prospect of losing them entirely as the renewal date approached; some had never obtained one; those with DACA had just acquired their first licenses, though with questionable duration; and U.S.-citizen family members were unrestricted once they turned the minimum age. Thus, this range of legal driving opportunities was structured by legal status, generation, and age.

Driving is a necessity in this vast region, which has an underdeveloped public transit sector, few taxis (which generally only serve out-of-town business visitors on short trips from the airport to hotel; they are not oriented to serve local residents), and no ride-sharing services operating in the area until mid-2017. Not driving is not an option for families. For undocumented persons who did not have a relative or friend to drive them places, they simply drove without a license. However, this was not without fear. I asked Brian, "What about before you had DACA, did you drive?" "Yeah, I still drove," he responded. "But usually there's a lot of minors that don't have a driver's license. So I was thinking that's maybe an excuse if I got pulled over. It still put me in panic when Border Patrol or police passed by. I would panic—and I still do. Even though I have a license now, I still panic when I see police." This speaks to the entrenched fear that comes from a lifetime of avoiding police, of the anxiety associated with the ever-present possibility of separation from parents, and of the self-monitoring that goes along with undocumented status even after his legal situation had changed. As twenty-five-year-old Rafael told me, "Growing up undocumented, you have to be careful when you drive, not to go crazy partying like normal people do. You have to stay in line."

U.S. citizens are also impacted by the variable driver's license opportunities within their families. They, too, learned to fear law enforcement as part of a general sense of anxiety that came with "learning to be illegal" alongside their undocumented family members. Seventeen-year-old U.S. citizen Elizabeth noted she holds back from asking her parents for rides because of the threat of being stopped:

> I try not to ask them too much to let me go out with friends because I'm scared that they might stop us. They're both excellent drivers, they are really careful and they've learned how to avoid police. But it's still a fear of mine. What if I ask my mom to take me to the movies and on the way, they stop us and my life changes from there? It's kind of scary for me.

This example highlights the repercussions on others in the family, even if they are they are not themselves deportable. In Elizabeth's case, she restricted her own social activities as a result of her parents' inability to drive legally.

On the other hand, their influential role as an authorized driver created additional pressures on citizens to both assist and protect their family members. As twenty-four-year-old Leticia, a U.S. citizen, explained,

> I'm scared driving when I have my [undocumented] brother with me. I get nervous even if I'm taking him to the convenience store right here. You bump into a state trooper or something, they might stop you for a light, or because they think you're nervous, or because you look Mexican. I see one and I'm like, "Oh my God, *hay un policía* [there's the police]." It goes through my mind every time he asks me, "Take me to this place, take me over there?" because he doesn't drive. I don't want him to be on my conscience, like they stop you and they took your brother and deported him. You know what I mean?

Siblings feel responsibility for each other—especially in the case of their more vulnerable undocumented brothers and sisters—and are aware of the severe repercussions should they be pulled over with them in the car. This impacts larger family dynamics and becomes a delicate balance, provoking considerations such as: Should I drive my brother around? Will I get in trouble with my parents if something happens to him? Will it all be my fault if he is deported? Leticia also comments here on the fear of racial profiling. It was commonly agreed by participants that "looking Mexican" was a risk when driving; usually this referred to phenotypic features like skin and eye color, but it could also encompass drawing attention to oneself (e.g., by playing loud regional music or by having Mexican license plates). On the other hand, markers of belonging—proficiency in English or wearing a Dallas Cowboys hat, for instance—might have the opposite effect and lead to less scrutiny.

Another way in which citizens feel the effects of their family's status is in the process of obtaining the driver's license in the first place. In Texas, driver's ed classroom instruction is paired with thirty hours of behind-the-wheel training with a licensed driver over twenty-one years old. Seventeen-year-old Elizabeth was in the process of getting her license but was having trouble getting enough hours in with a licensed driver, since both of her parents were undocumented. Her parents have always driven, and when their licenses expired in 2013 and they couldn't renew them, they continued to drive to work and for errands out of necessity. She told me, "Actually, my dad drives a lot for work. As part of his job, he has to transport all this stuff. He's pretty brave out there, driving back and forth all the time!" At this point she and her father, Gerardo—who was sitting at the kitchen table with us—laughed heartily and made a few lighthearted and sarcastic jokes about how brave he is. When the laughter had stopped, she said quietly, "That is a fear of mine too, that they stop him someday." Gerardo weighed in:

> Well, the truth is, in construction we have to work everywhere, drive everywhere. We run into immigration all of the time. Last week we were working on one of the bridges right on the banks of the river, right at the border crossing. So I always wear my company uniform to look professional. The immigration people wave hello and greet me in the mornings when I arrive. But I have to drive. Of course I'm scared, but you have to work.

Nonetheless, Gerardo and his wife were unable to help their daughter practice her driving, since neither was a licensed driver. In this way, Elizabeth, a U.S. citizen, was hindered in her quest for her own first driver's license because of her parents' illegality. "I actually start driving school next week," Elizabeth told me. "But that is the impediment. To finish, you need thirty hours at home, and you need someone to be watching you that has a license. Both my parents don't have a valid license, which means I have to drive with someone that does. I don't know how I'm going to do that. Yeah, that's another barrier."

Roadblock Checkpoints: Racial Profiling and Phenotypic "Passports"

Checkpoints are one of the greatest threats to unlicensed, undocumented drivers. In addition to the permanent immigration checkpoints, there are irregular, unpredictable, and temporary roadblocks set up throughout the borderlands to inspect drivers along major roads where they live and work (similar to DUI checkpoints). They tend to emerge in response to specific political conditions, such as heightened anti-immigrant discourse, election cycles, and media reporting on "surges" of entrants in the border region. During the time of the study that forms the basis of this book, a particularly intense episode of checkpoints occurred, coinciding with widespread concern about the large numbers of unaccompanied minors crossing in southern Texas and bringing immigration to the fore of national public debate. The Texas DPS set up numerous temporary checkpoints, allegedly to check if drivers had a valid driver's license and auto insurance. While they assured the public that they would not check the immigrant status of drivers, there was evidence that this was not the case.[37] From the beginning, eyewitness reports and photographs and videos posted online showed Border Patrol vehicles at roadblock locations.

The practice of roadblock checkpoints is not limited to the border region, although they tend to be more effective there. The fixed checkpoints hemming populations in creates heightened fear in interaction with roadblocks to create an environment of entrapment.[38] While highway checkpoints are easy to avoid simply by restricting one's movement to the densely inhabited strip along the border, the temporary roadblocks are much more of a concern to everyday lives because they impact people's ability to go to work, school, shop, and socialize. Even short trips down the street become dangerous, and families rely on licensed drivers—usually U.S. citizens—to ferry members around town for daily activities.

Practices of racial profiling are more complex—and more insidious—when the majority population is Latino, as law-enforcement officers and agents attempt to parse out some undefined marker of "undocumentedness" or "Mexicanness" as part of surveillance and inspection processes. The components of today's immigration enforcement regime—including mobile checkpoints, as well as detention and deportation—arguably rely on racial profiling.[39] This practice is more complex in a region that is majority Latino, but it still highlights the role of race, class, and legal status in inhibiting free movement.

Certain types of people remain privileged over others due to social class or outward appearance. Even in a place where the majority of the population is Latino, outward appearance and "whiteness" allow some people to pass more easily. Their "phenotypic passport" may allow them to cross unchallenged.[40] This may include fair complexion, light eyes and hair, and accent-free English but also how they dress, what music they play, and what car they drive. Twenty-five-year-old Manuel told me that he was not afraid of language challenges when facing inspection at a roadblock checkpoint—he felt he could get along fine in his broken English—and his outward appearance gave law enforcement reason to leave him alone. "When they see me, with my fair hair and complexion [*güero*], they say, 'He's from here.' But they always ask my wife for her papers, because she looks darker [*morena*]. They pay more attention to her, not me." The irony here is that Manuel is undocumented, while his wife is a U.S. citizen.

The consequences of being caught as an undocumented person are more immediate in the borderlands, as deportation is swift due to processes like voluntary return and expedited removal, which can be invoked for anyone apprehended within 100 miles of the border and which deprives individuals of due process. Participants often referred to these tiers of containment as "*estamos encerrados*" or "we are locked up/in." This limited mobility produces social inequality, in addition to being linked with the very real threat of detention and imprisonment. People learn to police themselves, restricting their own actions and routines to avoid potential trouble.[41] They conduct themselves according to the law in hopes that a new pardon or relief program will emerge to provide a pathway to legal status, for which they must be able to claim "good moral character."

Forty-eight-year-old Herminia told me,

> We were very afraid to leave our homes during that time of the roadblocks [*retenes*], when there were a lot of them here. But you go anyway because you have things to do. You have to go to the store, to pick up the kids. But you are always in fear while in the streets, because we all know people who were picked up and sent back to Mexico. I've been here eleven years, my whole life is here, what would my children do without me?

Daniela, who was a DACA recipient, talked about the impact of these random roadblock checkpoints in the region:

> I remember that time, the random checkpoints. It shook the community a lot. My parents were very scared. We didn't let my mom drive, even though she had

a driver's license, because we didn't want her to get pulled over and asked about her papers. Friends of my dad just wouldn't go to work at all because of the random checkpoints because they didn't want to get deported. My dad has a white skin tone, green eyes. But he still gets discriminated [against], and he was afraid too.

While programs like 287(g) have not explicitly mandated the use of traffic enforcement to check the immigration status of individuals, traffic enforcement and roadblock policing are the primary ways in which immigrant drivers come into contact with local police and state troopers.[42] Under SB4, Texas's law that allows local law enforcement agencies to do the work of federal immigration agents, officers can ask about immigration status if they choose to. However, this can only occur during a lawful stop or arrest; they cannot stop someone solely to ask about immigration status. Roadblocks, along with roving stops based on moving violations and investigatory police stops—in which a driver is stopped not to enforce traffic laws or vehicle codes but to check out people or vehicles that appear suspicious—disproportionately impact minority populations, bringing issues of race and ethnicity to the fore. More than simply the errant judgment of individual officers, institutional structures and practices have been found to contribute to the racial discrimination that accompanies traffic stops.[43]

Notably, forms of "altermobility"—or strategies to resist and regain mobility[44]—are also present. In response to the roadblock checkpoints, information is shared within the larger community. In the face of intensified policing, social media became an important vehicle for warning people about the presence of temporary checkpoints. One Facebook group, "Alerta de Retenes 956," drew more than sixty-seven thousand users at one point and spawned several subgroups over time.[45] This does not appear to have been organized by any group in particular, but emerged spontaneously to help manage fear in the community. As Adrian noted, "We would avoid going out as much because there was more danger. There was a page on Facebook where they would be like, 'They're over here,' or, 'They're over there.' We would try to be very aware and avoid those places, kind of like evading obstacles." While these strategies allow for resistance and greater safety, they can also end up trapping immigrants within their homes—ultimately, increasing their spatial isolation and alienation.[46]

Im/mobility and Family Ties

Beyond the impacts described here already, immobility has several distinct re-percussions for mixed-status families as social units. It splits family members apart, dividing siblings' opportunities according to status. Norma is a U.S. citizen, while her sister is undocumented. As Norma explained,

> My sister used to play soccer; we were on the same team. She went with the team on a few out-of-town trips because it's less common to be stopped at the [fixed] checkpoint if you're with a group, like school or church. She wasn't afraid to travel, but my mother made her afraid. "What if they stop you? Or you have to get out of the bus?" So she got scared and stopped playing with the team.

The inability to travel together to other parts of the state or the United States also impedes cohesion with extended family members. Forty-three-year-old Juana said she feels

> *encerrada aquí*. It's very stressful, because this is supposed to be the land of the free, and you can't even move freely. We are supposed to attend my niece's wedding next month, and we can't go. We can't be together with family. My children really wanted to go places when they were younger, but we always had to stay here. They would say, "Let's go to Disneyland!" and we couldn't. I would tell them, "I'll wear the Mickey Mouse mask, don't worry." We always tried to downplay it, so it wasn't something upsetting for them.

Her daughter, Jennifer, a U.S. citizen, shared the guilt she felt when traveling without her family members. She said, "We had a road trip up north to see my uncles. But it kind of sucked to know that we're going to go see my dad's brothers, and my dad also hasn't seen them in a long time. So the road trip was bittersweet: we're going to get to see them, but what about my parents?" Similarly, Brian, a DACA recipient, reflected on his parents' limitations: "I'm still hoping for that day when I can at least take them to San Antonio and say, 'Hey, this is something outside the Valley.' The stories I tell them, they imagine them. I show them pictures. But they're still waiting for that day where they can go too." While different opportunities to travel emerge within families because of differential legal status, the barriers to mobility created by the checkpoints are extensions of those processes, manifested as spatial realities.

Equally disheartening, people are inhibited in their ability to travel in the other direction. For mixed-status families living near the border, maintaining ties in Mexico is simultaneously facilitated by its proximity and full of frustration because of their inability to actually visit there. Angela, who is undocumented but whose husband is a legal permanent resident, described how her young children are always saddened that she cannot join them:

> They go with their dad to go see my mom in Mexico, and they say, "*Mami*, we want you to come with us!" And I say, "No, I don't have papers, so I can't cross. If I go with you, I will have to stay there." And my middle son always says, "*Ay mami*, when I am big I am going to help you so that you can go over there too, to see grandma." So that always makes me sad, but at the same time I am happy that at least they can go over there to visit.

After decades in the United States, those family ties begin to loosen, and the immobility causes people to no longer be as close to family as they once were. Irma said, "People don't understand what it's like to leave everything, to leave your whole family over there. I have nieces that I just saw for the first time when my sister came here. They are twelve years old now, and I had never met them." Sighing, she continued, "Your family changes, and you have changed because you live here. It especially affects you that you can't see your own parents as they are getting older. It affects us a lot, emotionally. We get depressed. Currently my husband is very sad; he puts on music that reminds him of his family and cries." Most poignantly, there were numerous stories about being unable to attend funerals, especially of parents or grandparents. Michelle told the following one:

> My grandma, my dad's mom, recently passed away, and it was hard because my dad really wanted to go, but if he went he wasn't going to be able to come back. It happened when my own mom passed away, too. So my dad didn't go to his own wife's funeral [in Mexico]. I never got to see her when she passed away. Now that I am an adult, I am thinking about it—I'm like, oh my God, they took her to Mexico and I never saw my mom. They sent her over there and buried her. So, I missed my mom's funeral and then I couldn't go to my grandma's funeral either. It was hard.
>
> One of my aunts had a grave plot that she gave to my dad. When we were finally able to go over there, we went to my mother's grave. But since we're not there, our family doesn't really keep up with the maintenance. She didn't have a stone marker. It was just dirt. So, they told us that they were going to take her [body] out if it stayed like that. They were going to just go throw her in a hole

or something! So, my dad saved up and sent the money to get the marker. They sent us a picture, and that's when we saw they misspelled her last name. And we're like, oh my God!

This misspelling underscored how little control Michelle had over the memory of her mother. Today, Michelle is the mother of two children. She is also sad that they were unable to meet their grandmother while she was alive, noting, "If I had papers, I would be able to go see my family over there more often and my baby would've been able to meet her grandma before she passed away. Because now she will only ever know her by pictures."

Estamos Encerrados: Im/mobilities and the Mixed-Status Family

Border policing affects the physical movement of mixed-status families, and differences in legal status become embodied as stratified forms of mobility. U.S. citizens may limit their own mobility because they want to remain close to family members who do not share the same ability to relocate. Many young adults reported being scared of driving, even if they themselves were not undocumented, rooted in a fear of police that is often subconsciously instilled in them. Others reported being anxious that, when driving around undocumented family members, they would become responsible for them if they were detained during a traffic stop. U.S. citizens may have trouble obtaining a driver's license because there is no one in the family to accompany them in order to complete their training. In addition to legal status, age and generation shape opportunities for mobility: young people can more easily move through the spaces of the borderlands, with their various checkpoints and roadblocks. School trips on buses, which are less likely to be thoroughly inspected at checkpoints, are a specific opportunity available only to children and youth. Indeed, part of becoming an adult is transitioning from the relative freedom of one's school days to a state of immobility. Through these poignant examples, the chapter demonstrates how the construction of illegality for some members in a family influences possibilities for everyone.

On the other hand, people develop a set of strategies to combat the limitations to their mobility. Some forms of resistance are dangerous, such as being dishonest about one's citizenship status in order to cross a checkpoint, or driving without a license. Other people employ tricks to remain inconspicuous. Gerardo, who is undocumented, must drive to work without a license, but he wears his company uniform to look "professional" and greets Border Patrol agents with a friendly wave each morning. Finally, large-scale resistance emerged through use of social media to warn about random checkpoint locations.

Local context impacts the everyday experience of illegality when it comes to mobility. The geographic boundedness of life in the Rio Grande Valley—with Mexico to the south, checkpoints to the north and west, and ocean to the east, not to mention the patchwork of temporary roadblocks throughout—creates a unique landscape impacting the "policeability" of immigrants compared to communities in interior parts of the United States.[47] While the permanent checkpoints trap people within a distinct space, the temporary roadblocks fuel fear and uncertainty within that space. They synergistically produce a sense of entrapment. Like those in the interior of the United States, temporary roadblocks affect everyday spaces of labor and circuits of social reproduction in immigrant communities.[48] Many people are unable to travel out of airports, even if they have a valid form of identification, since Border Patrol works alongside TSA in border sites, preventing people from leaving. In the border region, there is a unique interplay between space and the expediency of enforcement practice: the consequences are more immediate, as processes like voluntary return and expedited removal can be invoked for apprehensions within 100 miles of the border. As a result, undocumented persons experience legally differentiated internal spaces that may rarely be apparent to legal residents, unless they are in mixed-status families.[49] Many people described feeling as if they are trapped in a cage, or stuck on an island, or *encerrados* (locked up/locked in), or living in a jail that happens to also have a beach. This immobility skews their sense of reality; travel begins to feel like "virtual reality." The containment in or confinement to the region also impedes family cohesion and prevents families from traveling to experience new things together. Finally, racialized policing practices play out differently in this region of the border. While mobile checkpoints, detention, and deportation rely on racial profiling, these practices are more complex in a region that is majority Latino, since they treat all residents—including U.S. citizens and permanent residents—as potentially suspect. Residents of South Texas appear to live in a state of legal exception due to the policing practices that affect everyday life.[50]

Physical and social mobility are intimately tied to one another. This chapter focused on the first, but with implications for the latter. The next chapter extends the idea of boundaries and mobilities to social spaces and life opportunities, examining the secondary borders that individuals in mixed-status families encounter in attending college or pursuing their chosen careers. There are numerous tertiary borders, such as the emotional toll on individuals and families, but also strategies to overcome them.

CHAPTER 5

ADDITIONAL BORDERS

EDUCATION, WORK, AND SOCIAL MOBILITY

THE DAY AFTER THANKSGIVING in 2011, Joaquín Luna, an eighteen-year-old senior at Juarez-Lincoln High School in Mission, Texas, wrote letters of goodbye to relatives, friends, and teachers in the pages of a spiral notebook.[1] He asked his brother to take good care of his nephews and his niece. He let a friend know that he had left a memento for her in his Bible.[2] He helped his diabetic mother to bed, kissed her goodnight, and told her that he loved her and needed her forgiveness. Then he put on a suit and tie, went into the bathroom, and shot himself in the head with a .38 revolver. He died instantly.

Joaquín was born right across the border in Tamaulipas, Mexico, and was brought to the United States at the age of six months. His mother and older siblings worked as migrant farmworkers, and he traveled alongside them to Arkansas, Indiana, and Minnesota, where they worked in the asparagus, cotton, jalapeño, melon, and tomato fields. They eventually settled back in the Rio Grande Valley. Joaquín had a natural affinity for math and science, bringing home report cards with nothing but A and B grades. He aced the college credit classes offered at his high school. But he was undocumented and knew that this would limit his future.

After the suicide, his brother (see figure 4) said Joaquín had been distraught over his legal status, which left him with little hope of ever fulfilling his dream of becoming a civil engineer. Joaquín had already been accepted into several prestigious universities but found out his immigration status made him ineligible for scholarships. He knew that his family could not afford the tuition, and

Figure 4. A photo of Joaquín Luna, who died by suicide, hangs on the wall as his older brother stands in the background. Source: AP Photo/Gabe Hernandez, *The Monitor* (McAllen, TX).

he also knew that, as an undocumented person, he would not qualify for federal financial aid. He also knew he would risk deportation if he tried to cross the checkpoint to attend college outside the Rio Grande Valley. And even if he did complete a college degree, he knew a career as an engineer afterwards would be out of reach.

His mother, Santa Mendoza, buried her son on her own birthday. "I think I buried myself with him," she said a few months later.[3] His funeral card, which still rests in an alcove in her living room, depicts a confident Joaquín in a white shirt and black tie. The message reads, *"Para llegar al cielo NO se necesitan papeles* [To get to heaven, you DON'T need papers]."

More than 2.5 million undocumented young people like Joaquín have lived in the United States since childhood; of these, more than a million are now adults.[4] They often face secondary borders related to social mobility after having crossed the physical border, especially hurdles to accessing higher education and entering the workforce. The death of Joaquín Luna energized efforts to find solutions for DREAMers at the national level. College students around the country held vigils and painted posters reading, "I am Joaquín," as protests strengthened and rallied for legislative change.[5]

In the Rio Grande Valley, Joaquín's death was instrumental in galvanizing the DREAMer movement. Many participants in the study that forms the basis of this book described his suicide as "devastating"; some had known him personally, while others sympathized and identified with him even though they had not. Twenty-year-old Selena was a founding member of a student organization established at the local university in the wake of his death. She recounted:

> Joaquín was here from the Valley. He committed suicide because he lost hope. He thought that because he was undocumented he was not going to be able to attend college. It happens. People lose hope. When his story came out, that's when our organization started. I never met him in person, but I know his family. He was very handsome, very smart. So it motivated us, like, "Don't lose hope. Joaquín did this, but you have to learn from it, for his death not to be in vain."

Representative Rubén Hinojosa told Joaquín's story on the floor of the U.S. House of Representatives shortly after the suicide, urging his colleagues to pass the Development, Relief, and Education for Alien Minors Act, or "DREAM Act." This proposed legislation, first introduced to Congress in 2001 and then again in 2009, 2011, 2012, and 2017, has enjoyed broad bipartisan support over the years. The Act sought to offer a path to citizenship for qualifying young undocumented immigrants who grew up in the United States. While the Act was never passed, the debates around it kept alive the discussion about the future of undocumented youth and ultimately resulted, seven months later, in President Obama's announcement of the Deferred Action for Childhood Arrivals (DACA) program. Joaquín would have been eligible for DACA and could have pursed his higher education dreams, had he still been alive.

This chapter examines the social mobility of children who grow up in mixed-status families, including the barriers and secondary borders they encounter as they try to go to college, obtain jobs, and become independent, as well as the ways in which they overcome these obstacles. Here, social mobility refers to opportunities for (generally upward) movement in location within a highly stratified society, especially as it relates to social status, class, and occupation. While these issues are perhaps most obvious to tease out among those who are undocumented, this chapter also explores how U.S. citizens experience secondary borders by virtue of being part of a mixed-status family. While early experiences in schools are generally inclusive and positive, this shifts in high school and with the pressures of applying for college. One major issue for undocumented youth living in the border regions is their inability to attend colleges in the nation's interior, past the U.S. Customs and Border Protection checkpoints. High-performing students may be severely limited in their higher education options, including U.S. citizens who restrict themselves from moving away from undocumented family members, thus affecting their own social mobility. Once accepted into college, financial barriers, discrimination, and feelings of alienation coexist alongside educational success. But not everyone wants to go to college; this chapter will also explore young adults' desire to enlist in the U.S. military or Border Patrol, an issue that is rarely explored elsewhere. Both are common career paths and often a local "tradition" in this region, which has few alternative well-paying jobs. This chapter follows the disappointment encountered by those who did not have the opportunity to pursue those dreams because of their legal status, as well as the experiences of citizens who did. Because of the longitudinal nature of the study, it was possible to follow young adults as they finished high school or college and went on to the next stage of their lives—ranging from low-paying jobs similar to those of their parents to attending prestigious universities in other parts of the country.

Social Mobility, Assimilation, and Legal Status

A key theoretical concern related to mixed-status families is the social adaptation of the second generation, whether they are citizens or part of the "1.5 generation" of undocumented youth. Traditional segmented assimilation frameworks have argued that the trajectory of the second generation depends on a particular group's "mode of incorporation"—a concept largely based on how particular nationalities fare under U.S. immigration policy and the contextual features of the communities in which they are raised.[6] There is also a common assumption that intergenerational mobility and social assimilation are unidirectional and positive; while their parents are stuck in undesirable, poorly paid, and often dangerous jobs, the children of immigrants are expected to surpass their parents in education levels, English proficiency, career opportunities, and social capital.

However, as Roberto Gonzales shows in his book, *Lives in Limbo: Undocumented and Coming of Age in America,* the opposite is true for undocumented youth, who challenge traditional assumptions about the incorporation patterns of the second generation. Their exclusions are often multiplied, forcing them to live shadowed lives. These limitations often become evident in the transition to adulthood, and many end up only a small step ahead of their parents in terms of social mobility, if at all. As they age, they are pushed even further to the margins. Blocked mobility due to undocumented status breaks down the assumed link between educational attainment and material and psychological outcomes, disrupting traditional ideas about the role of education in intergenerational mobility.[7] Even after completing postsecondary education, undocumented youth are often left with as few options as those available to their parents.[8] After a while, Gonzales argues, their "deferred dreams begin to die" and fade into the realm of impossibility, as illegality becomes a "master status"—much like race and gender—by the time they reach adulthood.[9]

The children of Mexican immigrants, including U.S. citizens in mixed-status families, often grow up in households characterized by high levels of poverty because of their parents' labor market limitations. As a result, they inherit conditions including cramped dwellings, neighborhood violence, and low-performing schools.[10] Studying may be difficult in their home environment. After school, they may need to care for siblings or work in the family business, while parents are often unable to drive them around for extracurricular events like clubs, sports, and social gatherings. Nonetheless, children's orientation to U.S. society is markedly more positive than their parents'. Their English skills quickly surpass that of their parents, and they feel at home in the society in which they have grown up. Public primary schools offer them the opportunity to learn civic participation and feel included; their legal status is often irrelevant within the walls of the school, especially at the elementary and middle-school levels. Because of this fairly level playing field, during this stage of life they typically navigate these institutions in ways similar to their peers.[11]

However, as those peers begin to move through important rites of passage—including entering their first jobs, obtaining their driver's licenses, and applying to college—undocumented youths' inability to join them sets off a series of discoveries about their limitations.[12] At the onset of their transition to adulthood, their status becomes achingly apparent, and they must "learn to be illegal," a process that involves an almost complete retooling of daily routines, survival skills, aspirations, and social patterns.[13] Many do not even know they are un-documented until they start applying for college. This results in shock, confu-sion, anger, frustration, and despair, followed by a greater realization of the adverse effects that will impact them the rest of their lives. Overnight, impen-etrable barriers emerge, which takes its toll on emotional and mental health and requires that undocumented youth reorganize, reformulate, and retell dis-courses about their lives as they are faced with a sense of dislocation and un-certainty.[14] Their emotional well-being is particularly affected as they enter adulthood and face expectations to go to college, form relationships, and par-ticipate in the labor market.[15] This is where Joaquín Luna found himself, with-out a path forward, that Thanksgiving night in 2011.

Everything changed on June 15, 2012, when President Obama introduced the DACA program. It temporarily deferred deportations for an estimated 1.9 million eligible undocumented youth and young adults, in addition to provid-ing temporary Social Security numbers and renewable two-year work per-mits. The program had an immense effect on the lives of almost 800,000 young adults in a relatively short amount of time. Unlike the proposed DREAM Act, it did not provide them a path to legal permanent residency or citizenship. None-theless, this relief program fostered social mobility not only for undocumented youth but also for their families. DACA was able to mitigate temporarily the condition of illegality for many. Even those who did not attend college or dropped out of high school now had the opportunity to join the regular workforce, es-sentially modifying the impact of illegality as master status by creating an-other axis of stratification that influenced their pathway of incorporation, until the program was rescinded in 2017.

High School and Applying for College

While *Plyler v. Doe* opened the doors for public elementary and secondary education, it did not address postsecondary opportunities. Of the estimated sixty-five thousand undocumented students who graduate from high school na-tionwide each year,[16] only between 5 and 10 percent eventually go on to pursue higher education.[17] A patchwork of state laws and higher education policies benefiting undocumented students has emerged across the country in response to DREAMers' activism. At least twenty states and the District of Columbia now allow undocumented students to pay in-state tuition, and a growing number—at least ten—of these also offer them state-based financial aid. In

2001, Texas became the first state to offer in-state tuition to residents without legal status when the legislature passed Senate Bill 1403, which also made these students eligible for state financial aid.

In their discussions about education, most participants in the study focused on experiences in and after high school, underscoring that their primary school experiences differed very little from other children. Most had very fond memories of elementary school. They remembered a welcoming environment, involvement with activities, field trips—including out of the Valley—and a strong sense of belonging.[18] However, in high school, academic sorting mechanisms begin—students are tracked into different curricula, some focused on college preparation and others not—and inequality rears its ugly head. Access to school-based resources and support is a major determinant predicting who will be going to college, and some students end up as part of a select group who are cultivated by teachers and counselors.[19] The role of mentors—in school and outside of it—is critical to their support system and, ultimately, to their educational success. In addition, personal and environmental protective factors increase individual resilience.

Because of the high numbers of undocumented children and mixed-status families in the region, schools in the Rio Grande Valley long ago adjusted to this reality and have instituted processes for handling students without Social Security numbers or assisting them with atypical college application processes. High schools regularly host workshops to assist families in applying for DACA or the TAFSA, the Texas state-level application for college financial aid, for which undocumented persons are eligible. A 2016 workshop on applying for DACA I attended at a high school was standing room only: every chair was occupied in the school's library, and many waited at the back of the room. In total, about sixty students and their parents attended this collaboration between community organizations and a public high school.

Nonetheless, getting to college remains a high hurdle for many in mixed-status families. Most undocumented participants described similar challenges during high school. Michelle, for instance, had a class that required her to apply for colleges and federal financial aid as part of the final semester grade. Feeling helpless, she spoke to the teacher about her status and inability to complete the applications. "Everything required a Social Security number, so I couldn't do the assignment. I had to get a paper notarized saying that I was undocumented. That's the only way I could pass the class." She found this experience humiliating and felt she should not have had to disclose her status to the teacher. Carmen, who was a DACA recipient, described a similar scenario, in which she had to reveal her status as part of a high school requirement to apply for college:

> I didn't know what undocumented meant until I hit high school. I was always like, "I want to be a lawyer, I want to do this, I want to do that." My mom would always say, "Yes, yes, you can do it!" But I went into this little depression in high school, because they call all the seniors to go the library and apply for colleges. And there I was on the computer, ready to apply for college, and then it asked me for a Social Security number, and then we started raising our hands, "Oh, I don't have one," or, "I don't know mine."
>
> And then the teacher made an announcement, "Okay, if you don't know your Social Security number, or if you don't have one, come to this table." So all of us went to that table, and they just left us there. Everyone else finished, and then, "Okay, go back to class." They didn't tell us anything. For me, it was a slap in the face, because I felt like, "What, am I not worth your fucking time?" to apply to college, or to tell me how I should do it? I knew I was going to have to try harder to find the resources, because I knew undocumented people who were in college. My mom told me that I had to go to school, and I would not disappoint her because of everything she went through. She's waiting tables, instead of working something decent in Mexico. The least I could do was make her proud. So I kept on going.

This incident demonstrates yet another example of disentitlement; Carmen and the other undocumented students were materially excluded from assistance with applying for college, even though they had every right to do so. Another young woman, Selena, found out about the limitations associated with her status when she applied for scholarships. She said, "I'm never going to forget that moment, because I realized that the opportunities are very limited for those of us who are undocumented. It really, really hurt. That was a moment it really clicked, and I cried. I told my mom like, 'Why didn't you have me here?' *Pero*, yeah, it was in high school. That's when you start doing applications and they start asking you those type of questions."

As part of this set of hurdles, undocumented youth—like many other first-generation college students—often had not learned a "college culture" through parents, older siblings, and friends. They often lacked information about how and when to apply—for example, not realizing that applications must be started almost a year prior to enrolling—as well as how to pay for college. Instead of four-year institutions, many enrolled in community colleges, which are affordable and often more convenient if they are working (which all were, at least part-time). However, they may view community college as lacking academic challenge, especially as their classmates go on to traditional four-year colleges across the country.[20] As a result, many drop out or may be deterred from transferring as originally planned; statistics show that only one in five students at community colleges end up transferring to a four-year institution.[21]

One major issue for students living in the border region that has remained largely unexplored to date is their inability to attend colleges in the nation's interior, past the Border Patrol checkpoints. This limits high-performing undocumented students as well as U.S. citizens with undocumented family members. Undocumented students who are accepted to and attend colleges further north, including in other parts of the state, have to first risk crossing the checkpoint to get there in addition to facing the prospect of not returning home for the full four years. They often had to make alternative arrangements to house and support themselves during semester breaks and during the summer, when other students leave campus to return home.

As a result of their inability to pass the checkpoint, many simply resigned themselves to staying in the Valley to attend college, such as Cesar, who had just graduated with his bachelor's degree when I interviewed him. He said, "When we started making plans to go to college, I knew that I wouldn't be able to get past the checkpoint. So I had to suck it up and say, 'Well, I'm going here [local state university branch in the Valley].'" Alan described a similar experience:

> I didn't have Social Security numbers that define who I was. So, it was sad. My parents saw my potential, my brothers saw my potential, and we couldn't do anything because they knew that I could either stop going to school or go here [local state university branch], which is not bad; I love it here. But I know that my parents expected me to go much higher. So living here within the border, I felt trapped. That limited the options that I had for school. I realized that I would be taking a big risk if I went to a university past the checkpoint. My parents didn't want to let me go over there and be at risk. So that basically eliminated all the other opportunities, any other universities outside of the Valley. So that's the only place where I applied.

Interestingly, even U.S. citizens restricted themselves from moving away from their undocumented family members, affecting their own social mobility. Jennifer is a U.S. citizen, but her decision about where to attend college was influenced by her family's status: "I got into so many universities up north, but my parents weren't going to be at my graduation ceremony anywhere past the checkpoints. So it's kind of—I don't want go if after all their hard work paid off, they can't even attend my graduation." While she was accepted to a prestigious flagship university in another part of the state, she turned down the offer and went to the local branch instead. Similarly, other citizens commented that they would worry about family members they left behind, wondering, for example, who would drive them around or assist with everyday activities like bills. Miguel, a U.S. citizen, told me that he wanted to avoid "showing off" and making his undocumented sister feel bad—after all, she was considered the high-performing scholar in the family—so he did not apply to any colleges outside the Valley.

Twenty-four-year-old Adrian and his parents shared a story about the moment the limitation associated with his undocumented status hurt the most. Adrian started out by saying,

> Honestly, because I've been here almost all of my life, I didn't feel different. The moment that changed was at the high school graduation ceremony. I graduated in the top 10 percent of my class, and I noticed during the ceremony that a lot of students were getting scholarships, they were getting financial aid real easy, and I knew that I had a better ranking than them. But I only received a small scholarship of $200. I guess that's when it hit, because I felt like all the work I had done was for nothing.

His father, Juan, continued the story:

> He was one of the best in the school, and we all thought he would earn a big scholarship. So the whole family went to this ceremony, all dressed up in our best clothes. And everyone crossed the stage to receive these big scholarships, but not my son. He was the last one they called. When we got home, he cried all night long. And we suffered, too, watching him like that. He studied so hard and deserved so much more.

His mother, Irma, recounted:

> We told him to pray and ask God for a miracle. But he fell into a depression. We had to take him to a psychologist because he wouldn't sleep. That was a difficult stage for the family. All because he wasn't a citizen. I think that was the saddest thing that ever happened to us. He couldn't achieve his dreams, even though he was accepted to so many colleges. But then God answered our prayers

and Obama announced this plan, DACA. Now he is almost finished with his studies. But it was the saddest thing that happened to us.

In interviews with undocumented and DACAmented youth, as well as with U.S. citizens from mixed-status families, there were often underlying narratives of "wasted talent."[22] These thoughts only added to existing psychological and emotional burdens, including frustrations and feelings of hopelessness. Melanie, a U.S. citizen, was in a similar situation as Jennifer—she decided to stay with her family and attend a university in the Valley, despite being accepted elsewhere—but was left feeling angry and cheated:

> I had a friend who was going to Cornell, an Ivy League school, and he would always tell me all this awesome stuff about it. I remember I went into a depression my freshman year, because I was just thinking like, "My friend's at Cornell, and I'm fucking here." I'm here in the Valley, and this isn't regarded as a good school. I just felt like I kind of wasted my own potential, but it was just my own fear of leaving my family.

Students' relationships with teachers, counselors, coaches, and other adults sometimes helped to mitigate the impacts of legal status. The school environment fundamentally shapes opportunities for undocumented youth—which is why the study incorporated interviews with teachers, administrators, and school counselors—and efforts have increased in recent years to catch students before this confusion or frustration sets in. For example, RGV FOCUS is a "collective impact initiative" that was launched in 2012 to transform college readiness, access, and success. The group brings together school district superintendents, higher education presidents, philanthropic partners, and business and community leaders with the goal to "transform the lives of the region's more than 415,000 students by aligning systems across the cradle-to-career pipeline to make sure each student is college ready, has access to and achieves postsecondary success, and pursues a meaningful career in the Rio Grande Valley and beyond."[23] A member of their leadership team explained to me:

> In serving undocumented students, we've got the universities helping with financial aid. We've got the community-based organizations providing direct support. You've got the school districts identifying students that need assistance—everybody knows what their role is. It's almost like a relay race, where everybody knows when the handoff needs to happen, right? There is this moment where if you hold on too long, you slow down the race. If you hand it

off too quick, you drop it. A lot of what has happened is we kind of just hand off people, and it's not a really good transition. And so through collective impact, our role is to bring all the partners together to help them rethink the work that they do.

Experiences in Higher Education

Once those who are from mixed-status families are accepted into college, the primary barrier for them is financial. Undocumented youth generally come from low-income families but do not qualify for federal financial aid or any other form of financing (e.g., bank loans, because they have no credit history or cosigner available); they also cannot work legally to cover the costs of education. Few private scholarships and fellowships exist for them. This is one area where DACA played an important indirect role in ensuring college access: recipients were better able to support their studies because they received a work permit. However, students who work full-time in college have less time to devote to studying and are at greater risk of delaying graduation or of dropping out altogether.

While U.S. citizens in mixed-status families are eligible for federal aid on the other hand, their ability to apply via the Free Application for Federal Student Aid (FAFSA) may be hampered by their parents' lack of Social Security number, tax returns, or documented formal work history, all of which are needed to establish the Expected Family Contribution rate. As a result, they also require tailored assistance. For instance, they can add the parental Social Security number as "000-00-000," but they are then not able to utilize the Internal Revenue Service (IRS) Data Retrieval Tool and must request any tax transcripts separately. This unwieldy process is another way in which they are affected by the undocumented status of a family member. Some colleges— particularly those with a College Assistance Migrant Program (CAMP)[24]—have support systems in place to assist these prospective students who are U.S. citizens or lawful permanent residents; however, they must first be willing to disclose their parents' status. The threat of denounceability means that they must weigh closely the potential risks and benefits.

Since the 1980s, a number of state legislatures have addressed the gap in educational access for undocumented students, especially as it relates to affordability. Texas was the first state to pass an in-state tuition bill in 2001, allowing undocumented students to pay in-state rates and providing access to many cohorts since then, including at the graduate level. The local branch of a state university has earned a reputation for being "undocumented-friendly," and has a dedicated financial aid counselor just for undocumented students, who advises on need- and merit-based opportunities not linked to citizenship status. Undocumented students in Texas may also apply for and receive publicly funded state assistance through the TEXAS grant;[25] this fairly unique opportunity has resulted in quite different experiences compared to other states. Nonetheless, some participants described the financial challenges they faced after admission to a university. For instance, Robert emphasized, "I got the TEXAS grant. But I still needed to pay for things. That is one of the challenges—I have to work twice as hard keeping up my grades. People from here, they have it super easy. I mean they don't need to do anything, basically. My friends, they use financial aid for stupid things. I get mad at them [laughs]. It's real frustrating."

While the inability to secure financial resources for college is one piece of the puzzle, undocumented students often encounter a great deal of misinformation on college campuses. Staff in admissions offices may not know that undocumented students have a right to a college education, much less how to process those applicants without Social Security numbers. They may ask bluntly, for instance, "Are you even allowed to be here?" The experiences with these frontline staff are important, and an initial rejection, or misinformation, can seriously discourage students from persisting. Many staff do not have good knowledge of the policies that apply to undocumented students, resulting in those students being shuffled back and forth between different offices on campus. Other limitations may arise in the course of getting a degree: some internships (most notably those with federal funding or that include security clearances) require a valid Social Security number, and study-abroad opportunities remain off-limits. While seemingly minor, these represent secondary borders and barriers to social mobility, especially as potential employers have increasingly come to expect resumes with these kinds of extracurricular experiences and additional training.

Colleges and universities can be spaces of inclusion and safety, and many of the students in the study were involved in advocacy groups and clubs on their campus. They also became involved in leading workshops and organizing protests and marches. They became "out" about their status, risking visibility to assert claims of belonging on campus and, by extension, within the broader community. The university is often an inclusive space in which they can feel buffered from the immediate effects of their illegality, but at the same time it forces them to eventually confront their limitations. As a result, many undocumented students face difficulty in the years after graduating—especially if they must return home—after experiencing this freedom and being exposed to new ways of living.[26]

Camila's College Journey: Alienation, Loneliness, and Trapped Far Away from Home

As undocumented students have been welcomed into colleges and universities around the nation, a largely celebratory narrative has emerged about them and their successes. However, this has also had the effect of erasing the difficulties they face, including discrimination, feelings of alienation, and—for those from border regions—an inability to return home. When I first met seventeen-year-old Camila, she was a senior in high school waiting to hear back about her college applications. "I applied to eleven schools, some out of state, hoping maybe I can make it. But I know the statistics, and I know there will still be challenges. I know that if I leave, I might not be able to come back," she said, referring to the checkpoints she would need to cross to leave the Rio Grande Valley to attend college in another part of the country. "But it gives me hope, just knowing that even if I get in and I don't go, I had the potential."

A few months later, Camila told me she had been accepted into a prestigious private liberal arts university in the Northeast, one of the so-called Little Ivies. She had been awarded a full ride—with tuition, room, and board covered in the value of over $72,000 per year—through a collaboration between the university and a nonprofit organization that helps to expand educational and career opportunities for high-performing undocumented students. Rooted in its values of inclusion and access, the university had made an explicit commitment to recruit undocumented students and treat them identically to domestic applicants, such as U.S. citizens or permanent residents. Camila was part of the first cohort, to whom the university provided a number of special resources—ranging from translation assistance, academic support, and linkages to private legal services—and housed in dorms in a nearby sanctuary city.

Camila's transition to the Northeast as part of this inaugural cohort was an exciting one. However, despite being surrounded by undocumented peers and new friends, she still felt misunderstood. Like the others in the group who did not have DACA, she was quickly confronted by her limitations, such as not being able to work and living with a more precarious status than the others.

Furthermore, in this diverse group of undocumented students from multiple continents, Camila was the only Mexican. Living in a metropolitan area that already lacked a robust Latino community, this proved isolating. In consultation with private lawyers, many others in the cohort had started applying for various forms of legal relief, options of which they had previously been unaware. But Camila's discussions with her lawyer confirmed what she already knew: "There's no hope for me."

Finally, she was the only one of these students to hail from the U.S.–Mexico border region, and the implications of this quickly became apparent. As one of Camila's professors who came to know her well (and who Camila later gave me permission to speak with directly) explained,

> Her experience is unique. She can't go home—not that traveling is entirely without risk for the other students here who are also undocumented, of course—but in her case the circumstances are even harder. The fact she can't see her family for the whole four years she is here is just cruel—to quote directly what another administrator here told me when I alerted him to how much she was struggling.

There was a tragic irony to the fact that Camila had grown up feeling "trapped" in the Rio Grande Valley, only to experience being trapped *out* of the same region once she left for college. As her professor explained, "She's trapped out. She can't go home. She tells me she is so grateful for all the university has provided, but at the same time, she feels like she's always here and can't leave. Now, she's trapped *here!*"

After the 2016 election, the entire undocumented cohort struggled to come to grips with its implications, including the fate of the DACA program. Camila struggled more than most, worried about her family in the increased anti-immigrant environment and unable to be with them as the holidays approached. Camila's sister, with whom she is very close, is also undocumented and could not visit her because of the checkpoint; while their grandmother, who adopted them, is a permanent resident, she was too infirm to travel. And of course, Camila herself could not return home. The university had agreed to accommodate her over the semester breaks. She told me, "They allowed me to stay as much as I want and provided me housing and meal money. They're not going to bring my family, but at least they're giving me that economic support to stay on campus. Over the Christmas break it was really lonely, but I worked through it."

Her support networks at the university—undocumented peers, student success staff, caring professors—all urged her to remain there for the next four years to wait it out. "Hold on to these four years, do not give up," her professor reported urging her, knowing that these would be four years at least of guaranteed physical safety, being at the university, even if they would not be enough to solve her larger problems. Nonetheless, Camila longed to return home; if she did, she knew that she could be detained and deported, but she began to feel that it was a risk she was willing to take in order to see her family back in South Texas. If she went, she knew she wouldn't be able to return to finish her degree. And yet, she also felt caged in at the university, the very place that supported her. But that material support was simply not equal to the kind of emotional sustenance her family could give her. Camila wondered aloud whether "all this was even worth it if it means you can't be with your family. I mean, what is life if you don't have your family?"

When I checked in with Camila the next semester to see how she was doing, she was enjoying her college experience but still clearly missed her family. I asked how her relationship with her sister was now. While they continued to talk on a daily basis, she said, "We ended up in such different places, and yet our feelings are so much the same. She feels stuck in that place. I feel caged in here, too, because I can't go home. Sometimes I feel like I can't breathe here, and I'm just so tired." Following our conversation, Camila sent me one of the poems she had written about life in college, which also referenced her feelings about the 2016 election. Used with her permission here, it reads:

> To those that told me "it would be okay"
> Or "You'll survive for the next four years"
> All I want to say is "fuck you"
> Because I hope that the weight of this country does not crush you
> Because I hope you don't wake up with panic attacks
> Not knowing what happens to your family
> Nor your body
> I hope you don't go through mental breakdowns
> or cry each night out of fear
> I hope you are not afraid of deportation
> Or of someone grabbing your pussy
> I hope you don't go through constant depression
> thinking of the uncertainty of your future

I hope you are not afraid of going to the doctor
or reporting a crime
I hope you don't have to call your parents everyday
because you are unsure of when you will see them again
I hope that when you sleep you are not undocumented even in your
    dreams
I hope that every class and conversation about the political climate
    does not make you wanna cry
I hope that you can have the privilege to study abroad and forget
    about this country
I hope you have the resources to just "move to Canada" . . .
At times, I no longer feel like I can continue.
So stop telling me "it will be okay" . . .
By saying to just "get over it"
you fail to acknowledge my fears
You fail to acknowledge my history
My value
So next time don't tell me "it will be okay"
please tell me
"I am here"
"I'll fight with you"
"We can take turns"

Camila's story illustrates well the counter-story to the successes of undocumented students: many experience college as a place of alienation and loneliness. The poem beautifully highlights the mental stressors these students experience (panic attacks, mental breakdowns, depression), all of which are compounded by their new college environment. Her fear of deportation looms large, as does the feeling of losing the family support that is so important for her. In this poem, Camila describes struggling to survive the "next four years," which refers both to her college experience and also to the decidedly anti-immigrant new presidential administration. The fear of sexual assault also reveals the anxieties of a young woman in her freshman year of college, as well as referencing a quote made famous by then–presidential candidate Donald J. Trump about his repugnant treatment of women.[27]

Perhaps most tellingly, her poem references the special challenges she faces at the university, despite its wealth of support, because her situation coming from the U.S.–Mexico border is so different from that of other undocumented students. On a daily basis, Camila was provided with access to academic, mental health, and external legal resources by the university, along with opportunities to debrief and discuss her experiences with other undocumented students. Yet she also resents the insensitive comments she hears that reflect privilege at this private institution, like when her peers said they wanted to "move to Canada" after the election—an option unavailable to her. She told me, "I've given several talks, and did an orientation for freshmen in which we talk about these issues. This school talks so much about privilege, like say, gender and race, but what about the intersectionality of it? I'm a brown woman that is also undocumented. You don't think of citizenship as a privilege, but I feel like there has to be so much more conversation about that." In the poem she tells us how she wants allies to treat her and what they should say: I am here; I will fight with you; we can take turns.

Joining the Military, Law Enforcement, and Border Patrol

Rather than college, several young adults in this study had their sights set on joining the military. This is a common career path in the region, where enlisting in the military is highly valued and often a family tradition. The Rio Grande Valley has a long history of military service and is home to tens of thousands of veterans.[28] Other scholars have commented on the deep patriotism of Mexican Americans in this region.[29] At a time when the U.S. military has found it difficult to find new members, recruiters in South Texas consistently meet their target among the largely Hispanic, bilingual population.[30] Indeed, recruitment practices have historically targeted enlistees from economically disadvantaged backgrounds. With a reliance on an all-volunteer force since 1973, this has created what is commonly referred to as the "poverty draft."[31] This is especially successful in this region, where there are few well-paying alternative careers for young adults.

John is a U.S. citizen with undocumented parents and two older sisters who were recipients of DACA. Married with two children, he had been serving in the Marines for four years when I met him, having recently returned from a deployment overseas. He explained that wanderlust motivated him to join the service:

> During high school, the recruiter just came up and asked me. I thought it would be a chance to just get away. I didn't know if I was going to be able to do that

otherwise. I hadn't seen anything outside of Texas. So that pushed me to do it, to just see something else. And it did open up a lot of opportunities for me. I mean, I've been to all the states, and I've been to Kuwait and Iraq. It does expand your horizons, leaving the Valley.

The career choice also had benefits for his mixed-status family. He acknowledged, "I knew a few people who joined the military to gain citizenship and to help their families out." After turning twenty-one, John petitioned for his undocumented mother to receive permanent residency status through a special expedited process available to active duty military members (discussed further in Chapter 8).

For those who were not U.S. citizens, their military service aspirations were cut short. Alan said that this was in fact how he discovered he was undocumented: "I never really understood the situation. I just knew that we couldn't travel north or south of the Valley. It wasn't until September 11th, after the attacks, when we were going to war. I wanted to join the Marines because I felt the call, and I couldn't because I didn't have a Social Security number." Noncitizens can enlist in the military if they have a valid alien registration card (green card); however, undocumented persons and deferred action recipients generally cannot. Unfortunately, even some recruiters misunderstand the military's stance on immigrants' eligibility for service.[32] Participants reported being given false information by recruiters, especially the promise that joining the military would provide them a green card or even citizenship.

One unique opportunity existed until recently. A Department of Defense policy allowed some noncitizens with specialized skills, including recipients of deferred action, to enlist in the military through a program known as Military Accessions Vital to National Interest (MAVNI).[33] The program allowed applicants to bypass the green card process entirely, fast-tracking them for citizenship while also providing money for college.[34] The MAVNI program specifically recruited health-care professionals and persons who spoke strategic languages (which does not include Spanish). It was limited to 1,500 persons a year, and with more than 5,000 on the waiting list, only a very small number benefited from the program. Since the program's inception in 2009, it has brought some 10,400 troops into the military. Some 141 DACA recipients had enlisted as part of the program.[35] With the end of DACA, the MAVNI program was also cancelled in September 2017.[36] This not only took away their military careers, but effectively exposed those servicemen and servicewomen who enlisted to deportation.

In Alan's case, he didn't even realize his status at the time and was simply angry that he was not allowed to serve his country. In another example, Maria, who was raised in a coastal city in Mexico, where she had watched the Mexican Navy ships pull into port, had wanted to join the military ever since she was a young girl. She was devastated when she found out she was not allowed to, and attributed this to her depression and lack of ambition to continue with studies after high school:

> I have a friend from China. He came here with a student visa, and after a year, he was already in the [U.S.] military. And I've been here since I was twelve years old! And I can't join. I graduated high school here, and I can't join. I live here, you know? I want to protect my family here, I want to protect my friends because, you know, this is my country and you are all my people.

Similarly, Jose explained the impact of this rejection on his academic plans. After dropping out of high school (he later obtained a General Equivalency Diploma [GED] and then a work permit through DACA), he worked as a firefighter. However, his initial career plan was to join the service. He said,

> I didn't want to go to college. I wanted to go into the military. When my buddy passed away [in combat] in the Marines, I actually dropped out of school because I realized I couldn't join the military. They told me, "You know you can't even be here? Technically, we're supposed to call ICE." To me, that was heartbreaking, so I left school. When my friend passed away, because we were supposed to go together, it hurt me because we didn't go together.

Besides military service, a career option also rarely explored elsewhere is young adults' desire to join the Border Patrol; it is a particularly poignant, and presumably incongruous, choice for those living in mixed-status families, since on the surface it seems incompatible with their experiences of living with undocumented family members, who are the targets of this enforcement. This is another valued career path in a region with few alternative well-paying jobs. Because of its regional characteristics, many in the Rio Grande Valley know someone who is a Border Patrol agent, or are perhaps even related to one.

Michael is a seventeen-year-old U.S. citizen with undocumented parents. His mother, Vanessa, mentioned to me his goal of joining the Border Patrol during one of our conversations. When I looked incredulous—thinking it must be some type of adolescent rebellion—she assured me that it had always been his dream, and that she would support it. "His friend's father is a Border

Patrol agent. And he told me that's what he wants to be [laughs]. I told him about how I was treated when I was detained, and how sometimes people abuse their power, you know? And my brother was beat up by immigration; a Hispanic agent beat him very badly. And so my son says, 'No, *mami*, I will always treat people well.'" She paused pensively. "But I also worry because it's so dangerous. And then my other son wants to be a policeman. That's what they say they want to do." She shrugged and smiled.

When I later sat down to talk to Michael, I asked, "I want to hear about your plans to go into law enforcement, well specifically, to join the Border Patrol. How did that happen?" He answered: "I know, because it's like opposite, right? [laughs] Because my mom doesn't have papers, I know. I have always liked law enforcement since I was small. I like being outdoors and I felt that the Border Patrol would be a perfect option. I always play around, like, 'Well, if you want to cross, mom, I'll let you cross.' [laughs] I'm just kidding about that."

As it turned out, several of Michael's teachers at high school had been Border Patrol agents who retired in the region, opting for a second career as teachers. Two of his history teachers—in ninth and eleventh grade—and his Junior Reserve Officers' Training Corps (JROTC) instructor were all ex-Border Patrol. But, as Michael told me, his real motivation came from his mother's story of crossing:

> I remember my mom talking about when she was in detention. They weren't giving her food, right, and she was really hungry. There was this one Hispanic Border Patrol agent that was super nice to her. He brought her extra food sneakily, under the rail. He was really nice for doing that. I would do the same thing for people. There's like more compassion or more understanding if you come from that background.

Applying for a position with U.S. Customs and Border Protection requires a background investigation, which includes records checks to verify citizenship of family members, alongside credit and criminal history checks and verification of education and employment history. I asked Michael, "Don't they ask about your family's legal status and history?" He replied,

> They do, yes. But hopefully by that time my mom is fixed [that is, will have legal status]. When I was looking into my future career, it really affected me that my mom has to have a status. Are they just not going to let me work because of that? I was her main reason for coming—she wanted me to be a citizen so I can

pursue other jobs. And certain jobs, like law enforcement, you have to be a citizen. That's why it's like my destiny to do law enforcement. It's a sign, an opportunity for me.

"My Future Was Dark": Early Exiters

Other young adults in mixed-status families were discouraged from attending college or other forms of career training and decided to join the workforce directly from high school. However, a high school degree is no substitute for job experience, and many undocumented youth had little formal work history and thus thin resumes. Roberto Gonzales refers to these as "early exiters," noting that while the 1.5 generation are easily distinguishable from their parents early in life, over time they often become simply part of the larger pool of immigrant workers; this can be devastating as "most have internalized enough of the American dream ideology to leave them unprepared for their new, curtailed identities as outsiders."[37]

While early experiences with school are generally inclusive and positive, this shifts with the pressures of applying for and attending college. In many interviews, youth recounted the blocked opportunities they encountered once they discovered they were undocumented. As their limitations became starkly apparent, many described giving up in high school. Echoing the "wasted talent" narrative mentioned earlier, Andres stated, "I guess my future was just dark, you know. I didn't really see a point in trying, because I couldn't get into college." Andres, who worked odd jobs following high school, recently decided to continue his education at a local community college with a reputation for being affordable. Similarly, Maria, who was a DACA recipient, noted, "Being undocumented doesn't really affect you when you're a kid, because you're just going to school and that's it. When you start graduating high school and trying to get into colleges or maybe join the military, that's when it hits you." In some cases, young adults looked back at their trajectories and reflected on where things changed for them. Olivia talked about the positive influence of her favorite teacher in high school, who had recently passed away. She wept as she told me, "I was very blessed that I had this person that had gotten me through, knowing that a lot of us, being undocumented, weren't going to actually graduate and were not going to make it to a university or college at all. Most of us probably had potential and we stopped at some point. So actually, it's very sad."

Leticia is a U.S. citizen who helps care for her undocumented nephew, who is fourteen and was beginning to act out in anger about the limitations related to his status. After finding out he was undocumented when trying to apply for a summer job, he also lost interest in attending school. She told me she was struggling to keep him on the right path. She said,

> He's always like, "Why do I need papers? Who made that law? Why am I going to go to school? I'm not going to do anything anyway. I'll just go work with my dad." And I tell him, "No, one day, when you did everything you're supposed to do, they're going to give you a chance. Like that DREAM Act." I tell him just do whatever you can, but don't get in trouble.

Joaquín Luna did not live long enough to benefit from DACA. Others carry on his legacy and try to prevent despair in others. Selena was one of those who felt there was a message in his death, saying: "Unfortunately, sometimes our high school counselors don't know that we can go to college. Many of the parents didn't even know. I have friends who just ended up in a drive-thru or as a waitress. It's really sad because they had a lot of potential. It's like, you just throw it away because of one Social Security number. So many dreams and hopes wasted."

Traditional frameworks of immigrant incorporation have focused on the important role of educational success in providing upward mobility to the children of immigrants. However, because of the effects of illegality and impenetrable institutional barriers, even with a college education, it seemed unlikely that undocumented youth would surpass their parents in social and economic mobility. DACA changed all this. As Texas was the first state to grant in-state tuition in 2001, this means that many cohorts of students had already graduated with college degrees (including master's and doctoral degrees). When they received their work permits, they began to enter real professional positions, not just jobs in the low-wage sector. It remains to be seen what the long-term effects of DACA will be. When the program was rescinded, many people's lives were once again turned upside down. If they were in college, they contemplated: Should I finish? Is it worth it, given the fact that I may not be able to work in a career for which I am receiving training and education? For many, the hopelessness that Joaquín Luna felt that Thanksgiving evening had begun to creep back. Only this time, it was much worse because they had tasted a different life and now were expected to go back to being undocumented.

Additional Borders for Mixed-Status Families

Numerous borders related to social mobility are produced through the con-struction of "illegality," which young adults must transcend often after crossing the international border. As this chapter has highlighted, while it is undocu-mented status that creates limitations to social mobility, there are also effects on legal residents and U.S. citizens. When it comes to applying for college, mixed-status families—much like those of other first-generation students—may lack the experience to assist young adults with the application process and with locating financial support. For U.S. citizens, it may be hard to document parental income on federal applications for student aid. A lack of knowledge, coupled with the spatial limitations associated with the checkpoint, means that many end up attending community colleges. U.S. citizens from mixed-status families may also be unable or unwilling to attend college in other parts of the country—or even just on the other side of the checkpoint. They may feel a social obligation or financial need to stay close to family; however, this leaves them feeling they have wasted their potential. Others were discouraged from pur-suing higher education in the first place.

In response to these limitations, a number of strategies have emerged. At the community level, local schools held workshops for undocumented students and their parents to aid them in applying for college, while regional initiatives increased college readiness. Mentors in high schools and colleges helped stu-dents navigate confusing processes and encouraged them to continue with their academic plans. The state of Texas responded in 2001—the first in the nation to do so—by providing in-state tuition for undocumented students and funding to support their studies. Growing up in a mixed-status family can influence career choices in quite contradictory ways. For some U.S. citizens, intimate ex-periences with (in)justice and immigration left them with a desire to join law enforcement—including the Border Patrol—while others were keenly interested in attending law school. They used these formative experiences to pursue cer-tain kinds of careers. Youth mobilization around events such as Joaquín Luna's death helped mobilize support for DACA. In 2018, as Congress debated a per-manent solution for DREAMers following the rescindment of DACA, advocates in Washington once again invoked Joaquín's name, by holding signs that re-minded everyone of his story. Many years after his suicide, his memory lives on to inspire change.

As noted in prior chapters, the uniqueness of the region also structures experience. The checkpoints limit aspiring college students, and Camila's experience shows that the feeling of entrapment goes both ways: After growing up trapped in the Rio Grande Valley, she was now trapped at her prestigious East Coast college because she couldn't return home. Coming from the border region made her college experience very much unlike that of her undocumented peers, creating added stressors. All these issues multiplied the borders already present in the lives of youth in mixed-status families.

The next chapter describes another barrier encountered by mixed-status families—namely, the one created through unequal access to health care. As with education and career opportunities, different forms of access to medical care create stratification between individual members. Such inequalities have ripple effects not just for health; they also impact social mobility and the ability to succeed in life.

CHAPTER 6

UNEQUAL ACCESS

HEALTH AND WELL-BEING

IT WAS A WEDNESDAY morning on the kind of hot South Texas day where tasks are better accomplished early in the morning or after the sun sets. The heat was already starting to bear down at 9:30 A.M., and by mid-afternoon it would reach 96 degrees Fahrenheit, with a heat index of about 109 degrees. Veronica cut up fresh cantaloupe and honeydew melon to serve with our coffee. The children were in school, the rural neighborhood quiet except for mourning doves cooing in the backyard and the occasional dog barking. Veronica had just returned from her 8:00 A.M. Zumba fitness class, held at the local community center, and started off the conversation by emphasizing how she tried to keep everyone in her family healthy by serving lots of fruit—plentiful and inexpensive in the fertile Rio Grande Valley—and encouraging them to stay active. "We can't afford to get sick," she said. "So we eat lots of fruit and vegetables. We teach the kids to brush their teeth after every meal, floss every night. Dentists are just too expensive here."

Like many homes in her *colonia*, the family's house was a work in progress. From the outside, it was a run-down permanent wooden structure with a weathered mobile home connected to one side. The yard was full of debris— old broken patio furniture, buckets, deflated toys—and the grass had turned yellowish brown with the summer heat. But inside, a transformation was under way. The kitchen was being renovated. One wall to the outside was covered in nothing but plastic tarp, and the morning heat was beginning to seep in. Her husband was going to expand the dining area, Veronica explained, and they planned to pour the concrete slab this weekend. The remaining three walls had exposed two-by-fours and plywood sheathing, awaiting new drywall. Other parts of the house were in various states of completion. Since our last visit, the living room had been finished, with beautiful crown molding and recessed lighting installed and complemented with a fresh coat of mocha paint, bright white trim, and a new couch. They had also added a major upgrade: it now had air-conditioning via a window unit, the only room in the house to be cooled besides the two bedrooms. Although the family lived well below the federal poverty level—in fact, they lived off of less than half that amount—they continuously worked to improve their home, room by room.

Veronica is a thirty-eight-year-old mother of five children—three born in the United States and two in Mexico. She and her husband came to the United States eight years prior from nearby Tamaulipas, Mexico, leaving when the family's safety was threatened by the narco-violence. While they had been in the United States a shorter time than most participants in the study that forms the basis of this book (the average time was eighteen years), they were nonetheless a fairly typical mixed-status family. As we continued talking about health care, Veronica described the odyssey that ensues when her children get sick:

> Well, for the citizen children who have Medicaid, I call their pediatrician. If they are very sick, they will be seen the same day. But for the older two, I have to take them to El Milagro [a local charity clinic]. They are only open certain days and certain hours, and there is always a long line. And I don't have a car, so if my husband is working, then I have to ask a neighbor to take us. It's a lot of stress!

Different legal statuses result in divergent opportunities when it comes to medical care in mixed-status families. Parents like Veronica must cultivate the ability to take care of some health care needs at home, and seek services in multiple sites with distinct plans for individual members depending on their status. U.S.-born children who have Medicaid are able to visit private physician practices, while undocumented and/or uninsured individuals must avoid getting sick. When siblings with different forms of health care access became ill at the same time, as is often the case with colds and other common childhood infections, mothers like Veronica spent the greater part of a day or more first visiting a pediatrician, followed by long waits at a charity clinic or community health center hoping to have an undocumented child seen for the same condition. This results in time off from work and loss of income. As Veronica pointed out, this can be logistically difficult if no transportation is available, and no buses or taxis serve the semi-rural *colonia* in which she lives.

A few days later, I spoke with Javier, Veronica's eighteen-year-old son. He was brought to the United States at the age of ten alongside his younger sister, while his three younger brothers were all born in Texas. Growing up, he and his sister were undocumented like their parents. Javier considered his brothers to be "lucky" by virtue of their place of birth, which affords them access to treatment in times of acute illness, regular checkups, and dental care. The rest of the family must go without. Like many other undocumented children in mixed-status families, he recalled that his parents often told him to "not get sick." He says, "I remember if we would get sick, and it was like, 'Suck it up. We don't have money to take you to a doctor.' There wasn't much we could do."

This chapter examines the unequal health experiences in mixed-status families, including the hierarchies that different forms of access to medical care create between individual members. Immigration and health care policies intersect at numerous junctures, and health challenges associated with im/migration are often the result of the pathogenic role of social inequality. Health policies have multiple direct and indirect impacts specifically on these families, including their hesitancy to enroll citizen children in programs due to fear of deportation or to avoid jeopardizing chances of future regularization. There is little doubt that the rise in anti-immigrant policymaking since the mid-1990s has fostered an unhealthy environment for mixed-status families. They report worse health compared to their citizen counterparts, and hostile immigration policies further exacerbate these disparities.

A number of strategies are employed by these families, including seeking health care in multiple sites, as well as drawing upon social networks for alternative forms of care. In this context, parents experience constraints to access by not being able to take their children to the physician when they would like to. They must rely on "leftover," salvaged, and potentially ineffective medicines. As formal systems fail to meet the needs of a large segment of the population, alternative and informal channels of care proliferate, including illicit medications, unlicensed providers, and home treatments. Heavy border enforcement also impacts mixed-status families when specialty care is required outside the region, and exacerbates stress and anxiety for mixed-status family members. Without adequate access to care, chronic illnesses are aggravated, while specialty treatment is out of reach. Mobility associated with health care access and delivery is both fostered and hindered in communities along the

U.S.–Mexico border. In the cases described here, immobilities in this dynamic region are associated with barriers accessing health services in all directions. Some families have avoided enrolling eligible members in programs such as Medicaid and Women, Infants and Children (WIC); this chapter examines how notions of "deservingness" have become internalized and result in a chilling effect that extends to U.S. citizens, in what Laura Enriquez has called "multigenerational punishment."[1] While many of the issues and strategies overlap with the uninsured more broadly, the socio-spatial context of the Rio Grande Valley provides a unique backdrop for mixed-status families, highlighting cross-border opportunities and limitations produced by life so close to the border. As in other areas of everyday life, the construction of illegality for parents and siblings in mixed-status families also influences opportunities for U.S. citizens, impacting their health and social mobility.[2]

The Intersection of Immigration and Health

Members of mixed-status families report worse physical health compared to their U.S.-citizen counterparts.[3] Their children are more likely to have poor health, be uninsured, and lack a usual source of care compared to children from non-immigrant households. Parental immigration status is also associated with lower health care utilization in children,[4] especially the legal status of the mother due to women's role as primary care provider.[5] Hostile policy environments result in intense feelings of anxiety, fear, and depression,[6] which exacerbate pre-existing health conditions such as high blood pressure and diabetes.[7] Experiences of racism and discrimination are in turn linked to risk factors that pattern health outcomes.[8] Undocumented immigrants and their family members experience a pervasive fear of deportation that negatively impacts their psychological, emotional, and physical health.[9] The association between worry about the deportation of others (i.e., of family members) and cardiovascular risk factors has been quantitatively confirmed using reference points such as body mass index (BMI), waist circumference, and continuous measures of systolic and pulse pressure.[10] This shows that the physical and mental health consequences associated with heightened anti-immigrant policy environments reach beyond undocumented persons themselves, impacting others in their family and community.[11]

An examination of the origins of these disparities requires a careful consideration of legal status as a structural constraint impacting health.[12]

Immigration policies and health care intersect at numerous junctures, and the range of health challenges associated with immigration is wide and often the result of the pathogenic role of social inequality.[13] As populations are increasingly interconnected, large-scale social forces impact the health of unequally positioned groups of people. Immigration status affects health through mechanisms including fear, stress, differential access to resources, experiences of prejudice and violence, family separation, and differential access to safe work and housing.[14]

Eligibility for health care coverage is also significantly determined by legal status. While U.S. citizens under the age of eighteen are able to access Medicaid and the Children's Health Insurance Program (CHIP), undocumented children and parents are ineligible for all publicly funded services besides perinatal and emergency medical care. Even if they were eligible, these programs would not provide comprehensive access. Given the low income levels of mixed-status families in general, but particularly in this region, most such families are unable to pay privately for medical services. Deferred Action for Childhood Arrivals (DACA) recipients faced the same restrictions as undocumented immigrants, even though they are considered lawfully present. Nonetheless, DACA recipients (and, much less commonly, undocumented persons) were sometimes able to obtain insurance through their employers, or have access to student health coverage if they are enrolled in a college or university.

A focus on just individuals, however, would miss the cumulative effect on families, and especially the ways in which the health of citizen children is directly and indirectly impacted by the illegality of family members. Although U.S.-citizen children are eligible for benefits such as Medicaid and CHIP, studies have shown that such children in mixed-status families access these programs at lower rates than those with citizen parents.[15] Complex eligibility rules can produce a chilling effect on participation by mixed-status families.[16] Fear of deportation leads some families to limit or delay services for children, or withdraw from programs altogether.[17] Risk of deportation has been shown to negatively affect uptake of Medicaid as well as WIC among mixed-status families.[18] In Texas, a decline in enrollment in CHIP appears to also be linked with aggressive immigration enforcement under the Trump administration, as well as with the passage of Senate Bill 4, which allows local law enforcement officers to investigate the legal status of those they detain. Moreover, some undocumented parents fear that enrolling their children in public programs will affect their own future chances at regularization. Applicants for permanent residency status must prove they will not be dependent on the government—that is, they cannot be deemed a public charge—and this has led some families to avoid health services and programs for their children.[19] When immigration and health-care access policies are combined, an environment is created in which families may become discouraged or frightened from enrolling in public health insurance coverage or utilizing health care services.[20]

The structure of public health insurance in the United States allows for variable eligibility to occur within families, which is associated with lower access to care for all.[21] This creates dilemmas for parents, who may worry about favoritism and thus may choose not to enroll any children in publicly funded programs, resulting in reduced overall household resources.[22] Although this could offset costs and increase the family's budget for other medical needs, parents sometimes felt that performing equality in the household was more important. On the other hand, stratified access to care can lead to preferential treatment of some children based on legal status, as well as to resentment, inequalities, and hierarchal relations within the family.[23]

In the case of mixed-status families, these exclusionary effects can be read as unintended consequences of policy or as a deliberate effect of state power. Leisy Abrego and Cecilia Menjívar describe the "legal violence" that occurs when laws protect the rights of some while simultaneously marginalizing others, ultimately increasing their vulnerability to inequality.[24] Such violence is especially devastating when it restricts practices at the core of family dynamics via ideas of "good parenting," such as the ability to access resources for children in times of illness. Policies that restrict or mystify access have broad spillover effects on others living in the same household, leading to "multigenerational punishment." This is a distinct form of legal violence, wherein "the sanctions intended for a specific population spill over to negatively affect individuals who are not targeted by laws."[25] Legal violence and marginality often go hand in hand with notions of "deservingness"—which Sarah Willen defines as the ways in which some groups but not others are considered worthy of health-related attention, investment, and care, and thus linked to larger questions of inequality and the interconnectedness of multiple systems of entitlement.[26]

Border communities account for the largest percentage of the uninsured population in the United States and continue to be classified as medically underserved areas. There are stark cultural, political, and public health implications associated with continued exclusion of these communities; achieving health equity in the United States will be impossible without addressing their needs. The cumulative effects of social disadvantage are well established and suggest that "the costliest consequences of unauthorized status will emerge later in the life course, as current generations of unauthorized parents, children, and youth move into midlife and older age."[27] Many—if not most—of these effects cannot be reversed even if individuals transition out of their undocumented status. These costs will be shouldered by U.S. society as a whole. The sheer numbers—an estimated 11 million undocumented persons, including 4.5 million citizen children—is cause for large-scale concern because they deter the integration of communities and socialize citizens to a second-class status.[28]

Unequal Access to Medical Care

Children who grow up in mixed-status families often have an acute awareness of the different opportunities and resources available to some siblings and not others. Many spoke of simply being told to "not get sick," since cost was the greatest barrier to visiting a doctor for these mostly low-income families. Erin, thirty, an uninsured DACA recipient with undocumented parents, noted that the cost of one medical visit could equal a week's wages for her family. Growing up, she said the calculus was always "either we take care of our health or we buy food." Jonathan, a twenty-two-year-old undocumented college student who grew up with two U.S.-citizen brothers, discussed his parents' unwillingness to call an ambulance in urgent situations: "The medical bills were always so high, you had to avoid going. I remember in eighth grade I got a concussion playing football at school, and my mom drove me over an hour to the hospital herself, because she didn't want to end up with a $600 bill for the ambulance. What if I would have damaged my brain?" In these situations, parents must make a difficult calculation, weighing cost with the severity of injury to their child.

On the other side of this issue, many parents shared their regret at being unable to take their children to the doctor for an illness or accident for which they would have immediately taken a child that had insurance coverage. Instead, treatment often consisted of home remedies, over-the-counter products, or leftover medications—a combination of concessions and strategies to deal with the lack of access. Thirty-four-year-old Janice confided that it is a difficult decision for undocumented parents, particularly for mothers, who are often in charge of negotiating health issues. She said,

I struggle a lot when they get sick, because sometimes you don't have money. It's very difficult, because those children who were born here have Medicaid and more privileges. With them, you immediately go to the doctor if they get sick or have an accident. It's not the same for those without. Like, one time my little girl, who doesn't have Medicaid, fell. She was playing, running, and she banged into a chair and ended up with a bump that swelled up and almost burst open. For a heavy blow like that, you really have to get X-rays. You know it's something that is worth going to the doctor for, but then you don't have money for it. All you can do is try to get the swelling to go away. So you put Vicks [VapoRub ointment] or something like that on it to bring down the swelling. If that happened to someone with Medicaid, you would immediately go to the doctor, because your insurance would cover it.

Such disparities in treatment were keenly felt by siblings, but they were also felt beyond individual households. When I asked seventeen-year-old U.S. citizen Michael about how legal status affected health care access, he pointed to the living room where his little brother was playing a video game with a friend. Michael explained that the friend, who was undocumented, lived next door and was in the same second grade class as his brother:

He's like eight years old and he has *dientes picados*. Cavities, little black spots on all of his teeth. They're actually like cracked and open. It's really serious. And he doesn't have Medicaid, because he's not a citizen, so it's difficult for him. Right now his parents are happy, because his [baby] teeth are falling out and he's getting new ones. But you know, the new ones will get that way too. He doesn't get the advantages that we do. I feel really sorry for him.

Dental issues are distinct from those associated with medical coverage and remain one of the most significant health concerns of uninsured people across the United States.[29] Tooth decay resulting from severe early childhood caries can leave lasting effects on children's physical development, including malformations and crooked permanent teeth. But equally important, it creates "stigmatized biologies," which can have lifelong social effects.[30] Children with dental pain, for instance, are less able to concentrate in school, and resulting disadvantages are not easily reversed by legalization. These are embodied differences expressed through "bad teeth" that, in turn, reproduce systems of social inequality. As children with poor oral health grow up to become adults, their teeth reveal the cumulative effects of their disadvantage, heightening their self-consciousness and impeding their social mobility. As a result, unequal access to dental care has lasting effects on children's well-being and success in life.

Collective Strategies: Sharing Medicines and Feigning Symptoms

While other studies have suggested that stratified access to resources within a family may lead to preferential treatment toward some children, and to resentment,[31] this study also detected more positive and supportive attitudes. This may be in part because it included relationships among siblings, in addition to those across generations. As one person stated, "In a mixed-status family, you stay closer together. You help each other out in one way or another."

This mutual assistance was especially evident in the sharing of prescription medications. Medicines prescribed to a citizen child were frequently used to treat undocumented siblings (and often, parents). Jonathan is nineteen years old and undocumented, and arrived in the United States at age eight. His father is a legal resident, and his mother is undocumented. He has three brothers; the eldest is now a naturalized U.S. citizen by marriage, while the two youngest are U.S. citizens by birth. He described sharing medications in the following way: "When I would get sick, I would take medicine from my little brothers. My parents would say, 'Oh, he is sick with a sore throat, too,' so, whatever they give them, they'd give the leftovers to me."

Jennifer, a twenty-two-year-old U.S. citizen, also described the use of "leftover" medication not only within the family, but also in the wider community: "There's always leftovers. Even the neighbors would call us and be like, 'Oh, my son is coughing,' or, 'We have a cough, do you have anything?' 'Oh, yeah, I took her to the doctor and *aquí está la medicina que me sobró* [here's the medicine that was left over].' So it's always counting out medicines to see who needs it." Michael, a citizen, similarly emphasized that the privilege is spread around: "We can buy a little pill here or there if we need it. I'm really thankful for that, because we have friends and neighbors that are undocumented and don't have that opportunity. If they come asking, we gladly give it to them, for coughs, antibiotics, rashes. I know it's wrong, because with medicine it has to be the measurement that you are prescribed, but it helps, so we're alright with that."

Medications are socially embedded phenomena, and saving, sharing, and reusing medicines is broadly practiced. This not only serves the immediate need of treating illness but also creates the obligation of reciprocity between individuals (within a family) and households (within a community), serving as an asset in conditions of scarce resources. However, it can become problematic—for instance, when a course of antibiotics is cut in half, rendering it less effective for both individuals. The socially valued and pragmatic act of sharing may in fact lead to twice the negative outcomes; half of an antibiotic regimen may be worse than none at all. In this way, the well-being of individuals—including those, like U.S. citizens, who have sufficient access to care—is directly affected by a family's mixed status. But in situations where social bonds are important to the survival to the family, it is impossible not to share.

Recognizing the need for mutual assistance, citizen children often advocated for their siblings. Cecilia, an undocumented thirty-three-year-old mother of four children with different statuses, commented, "Our middle daughter always notices. When her older sister gets sick, she's the first one to say, 'Mom, give her the medicine you gave me.' Or she says, 'Well, mom, talk to the doctor and see if he will see my sister too.'" Indeed, participants reported that many physicians took pity on their uninsured siblings and would prescribe "a little extra." Lisa is a twenty-two-year-old U.S. citizen with one undocumented and two citizen siblings. Her parents are undocumented. She reflected on this, noting:

> If I went to the doctor, like if I had an earache, if they saw that my [undocumented] brother was sick too, they knew the situation. They would prescribe a little bit more. They would be like, 'Okay, well, it's the same thing.' They would give him free exams, in a sense. That was only with certain doctors that understood the situation and understood the norm here in the Valley.

The "norm" is that a high percentage of U.S. citizens in the region have undocumented family members, and that many low-income families are uninsured. In some cases—perhaps when a doctor was less sympathetic—children feigned symptoms for their sick siblings or parents. Jennifer stated,

> If my parents got sick, I would go to the doctor and tell him my dad's symptoms and get medicine for him. "It hurts right here, and this is what happened." [laughing] There were a few times where I wasn't sick. It would be just a regular checkup, and I'd be like, "I feel this, this, and this" for my mom or my dad or my brother.

Cross-Border Care and Unregulated Medicines

The unique sociogeographic context of the Rio Grande Valley offers additional strategies for those without access to health care. As formal systems fail to meet the needs of a large segment of the population, alternative and informal channels proliferate. These include traveling to Mexico for health services or to purchase medications. Elvia, a fifty-five-year-old legal permanent resident who has lived in the United States for over two decades, still travels to Mexico regularly to see her family physician in Reynosa, just on the other side of the river. She says,

> I go whenever I need to. Like recently, I was undergoing menopause [*tuve el cambio de la vida*] and having heavy bleeding. I went to my doctor in Mexico because the doctors here wouldn't give me anything, no pill, nothing. The one time they did give me something, it was too expensive. It is so much cheaper to buy it over there. So I went to my doctor over there, and she gave me a shot that made it stop, and medications that I could afford.

In addition to affordability, many people described Mexican medicines as "better" because they are "stronger" or "the full dose," as opposed to what is prescribed in the United States. Medical returns to Mexico are common even among those who do have health insurance—like Elvia—because they may prefer the culture of medicine practiced in these border clinics. The perceived contrast to medicine in the United States derives from the difference in organization of health care services in Mexico, and those with access to cross-border services often express higher patient satisfaction.[32] Even citizens benefit from these cross-border opportunities, traveling to small Mexican border towns like Nuevo Progreso. Within its five-block tourist district there are more than seventy dental clinics, sixty pharmacies, and ten doctors' offices, all of which advertise cheap prices and English-speaking staff.[33]

People drew on their intimate ties to people with greater ability to cross the border, whether Mexican or American. This is a direct result of increased enforcement and an inability to travel themselves for care. Elvia often brings back medicines for her two undocumented teenage grandsons. "Like with the flu," she said. "Well, I just bring them medicines over from Mexico. I go to the doctor we always consult with over there, and tell him, 'They have this, this, and that,' and he will write me a prescription. The medicines are much cheaper over there." Similarly, Lisa said, "If we ever have something, one of my dad's cousins is a doctor in Mexico. We call him up, and we tell him the symptoms. 'This is what we have, this is what we feel. What do we take?' Then they'll send us the medicine, or my grandma would cross over [from Mexico to the United States] and bring the injections that we would need."

Notably, Lisa had full access to care growing up as a U.S. citizen with Medicaid until she turned eighteen. However, in her childhood narratives of mixed-status family life, she consistently employs the inclusive first-person plural ("we"): "If we ever have something . . . we call him up"; "Grandma would bring the injections that we would need." Her illness experiences are not separated from those of her siblings and parents. This illustrates how the effects of illegality of some family members extend to the entire social unit, even for those who are lawfully present.

Lisa's parents relied on relatives in Mexico to bring or send medications, rather than crossing the border themselves. Traveling to Mexico for medical and dental services was an otherwise common strategy over the past several decades; however, increased border militarization and amplified scrutiny of papers has decreased the ability to do so. Thirty-nine-year-old Anabel—who has three citizen children and an older daughter born in Mexico—discussed the difficulties locating health care for her family, saying, "We can't even go to Mexico, to Reynosa, for treatment. You can't leave here." Even as Mexican citizens, they are no longer able to obtain medical care there because they would be unable to return to their home in the United States.

There has been an increase in strategies such as purchasing prescription medications offered—unlawfully and in an unregulated manner—by vendors at local flea markets. Based on observations at booths and discussions with vendors, these include antibiotics of various classes, steroids to treat inflammation, insulin, weight-loss medicines, and birth control pills. As women's health services have been increasingly defunded in Texas over the past several years—not only by restricting access to abortion services but also by closing locations where uninsured women could access any form of health care—emergency contraception has been in high demand, particularly a small, white, hexagonal pill called misoprostol. Also known as miso or Cytotec (*cytoteca* in Spanish), when taken in combination with mifepristone the drug induces a miscarriage-like abortion during the early stages of a pregnancy. Punitive new regulations in the state of Texas (the subject of a 2016 U.S. Supreme Court case) have forced the closure or reorganization of women's health clinics, leaving many women without any options.[34]

Unlicensed Providers

Informal practices, including the use of unlicensed providers, are another direct result of stricter border policing and the inability to travel for transnational care. While in the past, people were able to travel to Mexico for medical and dental services, increased surveillance and stricter inspection of identification documents (often with biometric features) now precludes this. Today, providers also travel more frequently in the other direction, crossing into the United States from Mexico using a Border Crossing Card (a B1/B2 visitor's visa, often referred to as a "laser visa") that allows frequent, short-term transnational opportunities. In this way, they become "doctors without borders," treating patients who have been trapped within these border buffer zones. In direct response to the lack of access to care and inability to travel for services, unlicensed practitioners (generally dentists) operate out of homes in the *colonias* or at flea markets. Rebecca, a twenty-seven-year-old undocumented mother of two U.S.-citizen children, said,

> There is a dentist at the flea market. Seriously, we are in such an extreme circumstance, we are resorting to this type of care. In the back there is a chair, and you are directed to enter the doctor's "office." Well, it is outdoors. You don't want to think about it, full of dirt and everything, open air. All they have there is a chair and they do it [dental work].

Marina, a forty-two-year-old undocumented woman, explained: "There are no dentists for us here. Some come from Mexico and work in homes, but it is risky for them because they could get caught, could get in trouble. It's not the same, like being in a clinic where you know exactly how everything was cleaned, and that they have everything they need. But we need them." In addition to working out of people's homes, some dentists have their own residences in the United States out of which they practice illicitly. Michael described this in the following way:

> My crown came off, and we eventually found a doctor who lives here, but has his office in Mexico. He had all his stuff in his house and he did the dental work there at a good price, like $100. Other dentists charge like $200 just for the X-ray and then $200 for this and then for that. Just too expensive. So, he always has a line outside of his house, and you go in through the back.

Remedios Caseros and DIY Health Care

Many participants relied on home remedies. Like other uninsured persons, they turned to over-the-counter medicines, such as Vicks VapoRub, plant products like aloe vera, and teas made from chamomile, mint, and other herbs. Some simply preferred naturopathic care over conventional medicines, concerned about side effects or unnecessary chemicals. Jesse, a master's student at a local university, regularly consulted over the telephone with his aunt's naturopathic doctor in Mexico. Diagnosed with anxiety at the university's student health center, he said, "I think the stress kind of weakened my immune system and made me sick." For his panic attacks, he preferred to take herbal treatments suggested by the Mexican doctor over the phone, rather than the medications prescribed by the student clinic, since he wanted to avoid side effects.

For injuries and accidents, some participants engaged in "do-it-yourself (DIY)" care. As with some other strategies, this is not unique to living in a mixed-status family, but rather linked to being uninsured. For example, Darius was a twenty-two-year-old DACA recipient who grew up without adequate access to health care. He told the following story about his father—who runs an upholstery business—assisting him with a gash on his leg:

> For a cut, my dad would sew us up. Like this one time, I fell down. He cut me here [points], this chunk of meat [flesh] because it wouldn't close. So, he just cut me with the scissors. I guess it's handy that he does upholstery [laughs]. He's not afraid, and he knows how to do the stitching. Yeah, with all those kinds of bloody things, my dad would be the doctor.

A particularly risk-loving nineteen-year-old, Andy, described avoiding the emergency room for a number of serious injuries. This included multiple car accidents when he and his friends raced in some of the open country roads that ran in-between the citrus groves. He was just as afraid of his parents' wrath, he said, as being reported to immigration authorities: "If I end up in the emergency room for doing something stupid, then my parents are going to be like, 'What is wrong with you? Don't you know Immigration will come if you go to the hospital? How can you put yourself at risk like that?'" He described how, after getting into a fight after school, he and his cousin "YouTubed how to fix a broken nose," looking for advice on the internet. I gasped and cringed, and finally asked, "So, did it work?" "Oh, yeah, he just popped it back into the right position."

Trapped by the Checkpoints: Lack of Access to Specialty Care

While families develop strategies for common health issues, greater challenges arise when there are unexpected, severe, or life-altering medical problems. Those who are unauthorized or have unclear legal status are not able to travel to other parts of the state without facing inspection at one of the permanent Border Patrol checkpoints, yet many still needed to do so for specialized medical care. This situation worsened under the Trump administration, which clamped down on approving temporary authorization for travel for humanitarian reasons. In the past, agents were more likely to exercise discretion in deciding not to detain or deport parents with sick children or other extenuating circumstances.[35]

Ivete is a twenty-three-year-old undocumented woman diagnosed with chronic kidney disease related to high blood pressure at the age of fourteen. She was living in Mexico at the time she was diagnosed, but she and her family moved to the United States shortly thereafter. After becoming pregnant and giving birth to a baby girl, her blood pressure became dangerously high, and she had a seizure. This led her to develop kidney failure at the age of twenty. When I spoke with her, she had been on thrice-weekly dialysis for three years already. While she was eligible for DACA, she had not yet applied, because her life was a whirlwind of dialysis appointments every other day and then an exhausted recovery on the days she stayed home. She had recently become eligible for a kidney transplant; however, without DACA, she could not proceed. She explained,

> I'm stuck here. I applied for a kidney transplant and received a letter saying that they need for me to come to San Antonio to do labwork and to bring my Social Security number. But I can't cross the checkpoint. I can't do much of the process from here. There are a lot of steps to get a kidney, it usually takes three or four years, and I am getting close to my eligibility date.

After the 2017 announcement by the Trump administration to rescind DACA, this opportunity—and the kidney transplant—disappeared for Ivete. While her specific experience is the result of a preexisting and incurable disease, it nonetheless encapsulates the life-and-death realities that many undocumented people face on a daily basis.

Undocumented parents faced an excruciating choice between risking deportation or forgoing treatment for their child. While rare, access to specialty

or tertiary care often required travel, for instance to Houston for cancer treatments or to San Antonio for severe burn wounds. Participants had difficulties
accompanying family members—including their own minor children—if specialists were located in cities beyond the checkpoints. A community health
center physician relayed the story of an eight-year-old girl he diagnosed with
leukemia the year prior. The only treatment available for her complex pediat-
ric case was at MD Anderson Cancer Center in Houston, which lies on the
other side of the border patrol checkpoints on U.S. Highway 281 (or alternatively, U.S. 77). Although the girl was a U.S. citizen and her care was covered
through Medicaid, her mother was undocumented. Even a copy of her medical records with the diagnosis and a letter from the physician addressed to U.S.
Customs and Border Protection did not suffice to permit the mother to cross
into the interior of the state. There was simply no guarantee that the mother
wouldn't be deported if she approached the checkpoint with her child. In an-
guish, he said, "She had to put her daughter on a Greyhound bus, with her
fourteen-year-old brother as the guardian," accompanying her on the trip to
Houston, according to the physician. "It's just immoral," he added, "for us as
a society to expect a mother to stay behind while her eight-year-old daughter
has to travel 400 miles away for cancer treatment. To tell her, 'No, you're not
allowed to go.' In what world is that alright?"

Other families reported an inability to travel to specialized schools for
children with disabilities.[36] One undocumented single mother, forty-four-year-
old Sarah, has a U.S.-citizen son, Hector, who is deaf and blind. The closest
specialized school for the deaf and blind was located in Austin, three hundred
miles north of the Rio Grande Valley. Sarah was unable to take him there herself because she could not cross the checkpoint, so every school year she had
to find a way to transport Hector to his residential schooling program. At first,
she relied on friends to drive him; as he got older, she sent him by plane as an
unaccompanied minor. However, Sarah was afraid to take him into the airport
herself because of the heavy Border Patrol presence at airports in the region.
"I would have someone else go inside with him, but it broke my heart that I
couldn't say goodbye each time, or to be there when he landed to come home,"
she said. Moreover, parents were expected to be heavily involved with the
educational experiences at the residential school, especially by learning sign
language themselves to effectively communicate with their children. "One of
the first things that the teachers at the school told me was that I need to engage more with him over there, but I couldn't," Sarah said. "They asked me,

'When are you going to come?' Well, I can't go. I see that he's losing more and more communication skills. Instead of knowing three hundred signs, he just knows a few."[37] Hector's communication abilities were extremely underdeveloped, leading to frustration and inhibiting the boy from expressing his full academic and social potential. Over the course of this study, Hector graduated from the school in Austin and returned home to live permanently with his mother. Despite the school's strong emphasis on successful transition to adult life through the development of communication and independent living skills, Hector now spends most of his days in his room, alone. His mother coaxes him out as often as she can, taking him out for ice cream and clothes shopping—his favorite activity—but he remains largely isolated and despondent.

Immigration Enforcement, Stress, and Anxiety

Undocumented immigration status can negatively impact mental health and psychological well-being.[38] The intensifying anti-immigrant policy environment has disrupted neighborhood cohesion, community trust, and family ties—all of which takes a toll on the health of mixed-status families.[39] Life in illegality and the constant threat of deportation—either one's own deportability or that of family members—unsettles people's sense of security. Even the threat of deportation can provoke poor health, and this is not limited to one's own deportability but includes concern about the threat of deportation to others. Research has documented significant associations between worry about deportation and depression and anxiety,[40] as well as lower rates of health care utilization.[41] These worries are marked on the body and can be measured as cardiovascular risk factors.[42]

Even though medical facilities—similar to schools and places of worship—are considered "sensitive locations" where immigration raids are not to occur, fear of deportation can still keep some undocumented immigrants away, leading to delayed or deferred care, which has potentially significant public health implications for all. A hallmark of the condition of deportability, people's hesitation is in equal due in part due to unsubstantiated rumors about deportations and actual enforcement events that have occurred in their community. For instance, there were frequent anecdotes about Border Patrol agents or vehicles waiting outside of hospitals. (Agents I spoke with claimed they were parked there because they were bringing someone they had apprehended into the emergency room for medical attention.) One person recalled the community outrage when the region's largest hospital decided to clothe their security guards in the same green color as Border Patrol agents, which was read as an attempt to scare off undocumented persons from utilizing their emergency room. This practice had since been discontinued. However, as there are no county hospitals that can be charged with serving uninsured patients in this region, for-profit hospitals like this one face significant financial burdens when they take them in. High-profile stories about people being deported from hospitals and other medical faculties only underscored their hesitation. How often the fear of deportation translates into people actually forgoing care remains unclear and difficult to measure.

Uncertainty, fear, and stress often have serious effects on mental health, ranging from depression to anxiety. Some turn to self-medicating with alcohol and other drugs. Others simply suffer, as there are few mental health services available to them. Because mental health issues are seen as stigmatizing or embarrassing, participants were rarely forthcoming about them and often only opened up when trust had been established over time through follow-up interviews. Herminia is one of the participants who talked openly about her and her husband's mental states. She said, "I feel like we are emotionally sick, my husband and I. We are depressed and ill because of all the stress. Stress provokes depression." She also talked about how the couple increasingly avoided social events, losing all interest and withdrawing into their home. "I'm not used to socializing with anyone anymore, or having friends. When there's a get-together or family gathering, I no longer want to go." Her children, both U.S. citizens, had been urging her to get out and socialize more. Clearly concerned about their parents' mental health, they coaxed them into attending events as often as possible. Still, the parents no longer maintained friendships, so they were isolated in their home except for visits by their adult children.

Deportability also exerts influence over the sense of security of entire neighborhoods. Sitting around the kitchen table with an elderly couple, Saul and his wife, Olga, we discussed how the fear of immigration authorities impacted mixed-status families. Suddenly, Saul turned to his wife and said, "You remember the time the neighbor came over and asked for our help? There was nothing wrong with her, just anxiety, a panic attack, but she was afraid to go to the hospital because she thought immigration would come and take her away." Nodding in agreement, Olga added, "So she came here and we had to drive her there. She wouldn't call the ambulance, because she was afraid, and didn't want them to have her phone number or address. She was scared and asked us to call and give them our address. But then we decided to just drive her." This example—of being afraid to call an ambulance out of fear of alerting immigration authorities—illustrates the direct and indirect effects of immigration law enforcement on the health of mixed-status families and the communities in which they live.[43] Perhaps unsurprisingly, the shift from being undocumented to being lawfully present has been associated with positive health outcomes.[44]

Internalizing Notions of Deservingness: Avoiding Becoming a "Public Charge"

In addition to wanting to avoid deportation, undocumented parents often want to avoid damaging their chances for legalization.[45] Parents, social workers, and eligibility specialists described families' hesitancy to enroll citizen children in programs such as Medicaid, CHIP, or WIC—for which they are eligible—due to fear of deportation or to avoid jeopardizing chances of future regularization. Juliana is thirty-three years old and has lived in the United States for eleven years. She has four children, all U.S. citizens. She said, "Well, at first I was hesitant to enroll them in Medicaid because they told me that if I ask for assistance, it would affect me later when there is immigration reform." Similarly, to retain the hope of qualifying for legal status one day, thirty-eight-year-old Luz stated that she was initially afraid to take part in the WIC program while pregnant. She remained unwilling to accept benefits from the state-run Supplemental Nutrition Assistance Program (SNAP) for her four U.S.-born children, stating:

> At first I didn't want to ask for WIC or anything, because they say that this could affect you if you want to fix your status. And many people say, "Don't ask for food stamps," because if you ask, you're done, even if they aren't for me. The woman [at the WIC office] told me, "They're not for you; they're for your son." But, yes, I am afraid and don't want to have them.

At the same time, many families were willing to exchange these potential repercussions for the greater health of their children. Lisa describes how her family weighed potential future opportunities against immediate health needs:

> When my parents came here, they really weren't looking for anything, being supported by the government, feed off the government. They were just looking for a better life. I went to a doctor when I was six, and a social worker came up

to my mom and told her that she could get Medicaid [for us]. But we have talked in my family that we're going to have to pay back all that money that the government provided to us to go to the doctor, or that there was going to be a penalty for having Medicaid for us who were born here in the United States. But I think, in times of need, for our parents our health is more important than having to pay a fee afterwards.

The broader implication was that some participants refused to accept any services, because they wanted to avoid the perception of being a public charge. Eligibility specialists at two different clinics even recalled instances where families attempted to actually *pay back* services received during a pregnancy. One hospital worker recalled a woman and her husband who came into the emergency room with $2,000 in cash, which they had saved up and attempted to use to pay back the Emergency Medicaid service that had covered their child's birth. Or, as Lisa noted, families made plans to "pay a fee afterwards" in order to clear their "debt" with the U.S. government.

However, it is neither necessary nor possible to pay back these services. The U.S. Citizenship and Immigration Services (USCIS) has had a policy clearly stating that the use of noncash public benefits—including Medicaid, WIC, and SNAP—should not be used to determine if someone is a public charge when they apply for residency or citizenship.[46] Enrolling eligible family members in these programs is not intended to put other members at risk of being determined a public charge, and parents should not have to fear repercussions for accessing them on behalf of their children. Benefits specialists were well aware of these policies and encouraged parents to enroll children, but still faced skepticism. This may be because some other programs *do* fall under the public charge assessment—namely cash assistance programs such as Supplemental Security Income and Temporary Assistance for Needy Families. Various information—not entirely incorrect—circulates within the community and is weighed alongside enrollment specialists' attempts to persuade parents.

However, this hesitation is also founded in the reality that changes can be made to policies about public charges. In 2018, the Department of Homeland Security proposed new rules that would allow immigration officers greater discretion to scrutinize the use of certain taxpayer-funded public benefits, including ones that were previously off-limits, such as CHIP, WIC, and Head Start.[47] These proposed changes were clearly meant to target mixed-status families. Thus the constant possibility of immigration reform—always promising legalization but never quite delivering it—ends up being a major disciplinary practice that keeps people in their place.[48] To prepare themselves for a potential yet still unavailable form of legal relief, some parents refused to draw on public resources, even if they and their children were entitled to them.

Finally, many people simply felt that health care access was superseded by the need for status regularization, commenting that they "could not expect to have it all," or that it was "asking too much." These ideas and feelings of undeservingness were frequently internalized in this way. Aaron, a twenty-six-year-old college student and DACA recipient, said, "If undocumented persons were to be able to go to work out of the shadows and get better jobs, they can take care of themselves . . . You just can't have it all." He echoed the sentiments of many others by suggesting that people simply want the ability to work legally, which would then allow them to better deal with their families' health needs.

Unequal Access for Mixed-Status Families

Using the lens of health, we can see that the illegality of just one person in a family can influence resources and well-being for all, including legal residents and U.S. citizens. This is most clearly evident in the variety of strategies that families must cultivate for different members, including seeking care at multiple sites, finding ways to acquire and stretch medications, and engaging in informal care practices. This can be burdensome for parents, especially mothers, illustrating the gendered nature of this logistical work. Meanwhile, undocumented siblings must watch as their citizen brothers and sisters get better health care than they do. Parents experience regret at not being able to treat all their children equally. In some cases, parents were reluctant to sign up their citizen children for public programs to which they were entitled, like CHIP and Medicaid, leading to a chilling effect by discouraging the legitimate exercise of legal rights by the threat of sanction. This impacts children's health as well as overall household resources. Being in a mixed-status family can impede access to specialty care, as well as parents' ability to accompany children of theirs who require complex medical treatments or specialized education because of a disability.

In response to these limitations to health care, families develop a set of strategies. Sharing medication within the family and larger community is common. Other tactics to help out uninsured family members include U.S. citizens feigning symptoms to get medicine for siblings or parents, and relying on the goodwill of doctors to prescribe "a little extra." Some individuals used their ability to cross the border to Mexico to obtain care or medicines to bring back to family members. Meanwhile, several participants described unlicensed providers—usually dentists—operating in the community and willing to treat people at lower cost. Finally, some dealt with a lack of access to adequate care by using home remedies or by treating medical problems on their own.

The uniqueness of the Rio Grande Valley shapes these experiences in myriad ways. First, the proximity to Mexico allows for cross-border medical travel and access to significantly lower cost services and medications. On the other hand, the checkpoints limit mobility in the other direction and impact people's ability to access necessary treatments and services in the interior of the country. Finally, the everyday surveillance in the region fostered fear and rumors of Border Patrol waiting outside hospitals, causing hesitation to seek out medical treatment in emergency rooms. Fear of accessing medical services increases in times of more exclusionary anti-immigrant rhetoric and practices.

Health care access is simply one lens through which to view the exclusionary effects on entire families. The following chapter examines the deliberate violence of family separation through detention, deportation, and removal. It highlights the consequences for families, including the mental health impacts and economic instability created for the household when someone is deported. It also illustrates their agency in developing strategies in anticipation of this possibility, such as advance planning as families prepare for the worst, as well as methods for reunification.

CHAPTER 7

FAMILY SEPARATION

DEPORTATION, REMOVAL, AND RETURN

THE SUN WAS starting to set on a warm, gusty October evening. After greeting his mother and four tiny kittens on the front porch of their weary and weathered trailer, I sat down on the couch to speak with Jason. The fourteen-year-old had just arrived from the neighbor's house, where he had been playing video games. His mother headed into the kitchen to prepare dinner, and within minutes the aroma of sautéed onions wafted down the hallway.

Jason and his younger sister were born in Texas and are both U.S. citizens, unlike their parents. Their father was detained and deported to Mexico six months ago, following a random traffic stop. Their mother is unable to work; she suffers from chronic kidney failure and must go for dialysis three times a week. She often drives herself to and from the exhausting four-hour appointments—much to the dismay of the nurses—because there's usually no one else to drive her. Their economic situation had quickly worsened, with no wage earners in the household and their father only able to send small amounts of cash to his family in the United States. Their income, his mother tells me, is about $250, sometimes $300 a month. They hadn't paid rent for over three months and feared being evicted.

Jason told me he had started selling snacks at his high school—small bags of chips and candy for 50 cents—to help pay the bills. "Whatever I get," he said, "I use it for what we need. Any money left after that, I buy more snacks to sell at school." I asked him, "Have you ever told anybody that your dad was deported? Like your friends?" Nodding, Jason replied, "Mm-hmm. They help me with it. They feel sorry for me. Yeah, because right now I'm the man of the house and I take care of everything. It's my responsibility." "That's a hard responsibility when you're in ninth grade," I said. After a long and heavy pause, I continued, "What do you do when you feel like it's too much?" Staring into the distance, Jason responded, "I just sit around and think about it." The pressure clearly weighs on him.

Deportation is a fact of life for mixed-status families in the borderlands. In contrast to the interior of the United States, it is a constant threat and frequent occurrence, experienced by the majority of families in this book. And it is swift. Special processes can be invoked for anyone apprehended within 100 miles of the border, resulting in individuals being deported to the other side of the Rio Grande on the very same day. But because they have familial and social ties to the United States—the inevitable outcome of policies and programs restricting cross-national flows—they are motivated to return, and often do. Meanwhile, deportation disrupts family life, producing economic and psychosocial stressors, and altering relationships between parents and children.[1] Family members of the deported—including minor children—have to step up to support the household financially; even when they do, rents are late, food insecurity rises, and the emotional toll of a missing family member weighs heavily.

Detention and deportation have an enormously detrimental impact on individuals, families, and communities. Some 5.3 million children in the United States live with undocumented parents, and 85 percent of them are U.S.-born citizens. Because of the increasing efforts and resources being devoted to apprehending undocumented immigrants, children like Jason are at constant risk of separation from their parents. Laura Enriquez describes this as "multigenerational" punishment, whereby U.S.-citizen children and their parents share in the risks and penalties associated with undocumented immigration status.[2] Immigration enforcement, especially deportation of parents, has significant spillover effects on citizens in mixed-status families—sometimes referred to as "forgotten citizens"[3]—as well as lawful permanent residents. Experiences of deportation also impact the larger community beyond individual families, negatively affecting social networks, influencing trust, and making people reluctant to rely on others. In addition, they erode relationships between immigrant communities and law enforcement, impacting public safety when undocumented persons underreport crimes in their neighborhood because of their own or their family members' precarious status.[4]

This chapter examines family separation through deportation, illustrating how the detention and deportation of relatives shapes children's sense of security and well-being and increases economic uncertainty in the household. The families described in this book are well acquainted with the fear and costs associated with deportation; they are more affected than in other regions because geographic context alters the landscape of deportability. Not only is the density of mixed-status families high, but interior checkpoints and traffic stops along major roads and highways increase the likelihood of apprehension.

Following several families whose members have experienced deportation, this chapter details the consequences and elaborates on participants' "emergency planning" measures, to be enacted in the case of family separation. These measures include crafting plans for a relative to take care of children, creating legal documents to transfer custody, saving money for legal battles, and arranging to keep property intact by transferring titles. Preparing these emergency plans is not a new phenomenon; they have increased in recent years in response to evolving enforcement priorities. Citizens in the family are designated as caretakers or legal intermediaries, and often carry the burden as de jure owners of family land, businesses, and property. This shifts household power dynamics, empowering citizen children in a complex micropolitical economy of deportability. However, such advance planning, especially by legally transferring property or custody of children, also reveals that the event is akin to social death for the deported. The chapter ends by exploring how deported family members are brought back, relying on ties in Mexico, connections to smugglers who can aid their return, and their ability to pay. In the Rio Grande Valley, many families are touched by the specter of deportation. I argue that geographic context alters the landscape of deportability, making everyday security much more precarious in the borderlands than in other parts of the United States. This reality affords us the opportunity to better understand the stakes of increased immigration enforcement as it expands nationally.

Deportation, Removal, and Return in the Borderlands

Deportation regimes are profoundly effective and efficient in provoking fear. They do so through a combination of highly visible deportations of a few people and the enduring everyday deportability of countless others.[5] They are also highly dependent on a given political moment, and each administration can have significant influence over immigration enforcement priorities and policies. The president, through U.S. Immigration and Customs Enforcement (ICE), has broad authority and discretion over enforcement efforts through the issuance of memos and guidelines.

Under the Obama administration, new measures appeared to recognize that mixed-status families now constitute a primary feature of the contemporary immigration experience. Under the slogan "Deporting Felons, Not Families," there was a pronounced shift in focus from removing ordinary status violators apprehended in the interior of the United States to removing criminals and recent border crossers. While there were much higher rates of removals than in the preceding administrations, there was also a deliberate commitment to placing in much lower priority those who had established roots in U.S. communities and had no criminal record.[6] But this also created divisions within communities: the focus on "felons, not families" helped to dichotomize immigrant groups through discourses of deservingness, ultimately marginalizing many.

Under the Trump administration, anti-immigrant rhetoric soared and was accompanied by a reversal of the previous treatment of low-priority cases. This carried with it a rejection of the idea that deportation would inflict more harm than good on communities, and immigration enforcement activities leading to the separation of families became more visible. Rather than the result of changing laws, these shifts emerged through memos and guidelines issued by the administration, which drastically expanded the category of people classified as "priorities for removal." This has been paired with an increased willingness on the part of ICE agents to pursue individuals without criminal records and wherever they can be found.

The families in this book know well the fear and costs associated with deportation. The percentage affected by deportation here is notably higher than estimates provided by other scholars.[7] The difference is geographic context, which alters the landscape of deportability. At least 81 of the 100 families had been affected by deportation at some point. Overall, 75.4 percent of the 167 individuals interviewed disclosed that a family member had been deported. While this was often someone in their immediate household, it also included extended family members (e.g., cousins or aunts/uncles). Perhaps unsurprisingly, people rarely shared this information during the initial interview; rather, it emerged in follow-up conversations over the course of the five years. Their experiences spanned multiple decades, changes in the law, and different enforcement priorities. Since the average time living in the United States for the families in this book was almost two decades, it should not be assumed that the apprehensions were linked to criminal activity. Indeed, most of the deportations they reported were prior to the Obama administration's shift in focus to those with criminal records.

There are several processes unique to the border region that set the experience of deportation apart from other parts of the United States. "Voluntary return" is an informal process whereby an individual who has been detained agrees to be expelled immediately from the United States, without formal removal proceedings before an immigration judge. However, officers do not always provide people with information about the consequences of accepting voluntary return, which can impact future claims for legal status or may cause them to become barred from lawfully reentering the United States for up to ten years. In addition, there is an "expedited removal" process that can be invoked for anyone apprehended within 100 miles of the border, which removes procedural protections and allows immigration officers to operate as both prosecutor and judge, and often deport individuals on the same day. People are asked to sign papers indicating their agreement to "voluntary" removal and are prohibited from seeing a judge or contesting the order—in other words, it eliminates procedural protections so that individuals are essentially denied due process. These two procedures—voluntary return and expedited removal—have different immigration consequences if and when a person decides to apply for a visa or residency status (discussed in the next chapter). Both processes are invoked commonly in the border region, making the circumstances different than in other parts of the country. In some of the more isolated communities, people live in media and immigration attorney "deserts"—that is, where there is little oversight by the public—and thus may be at greater risk of being rounded up. This is especially of concern following reports of immigration enforcement agents in South Texas contriving some facts—for instance, about the use and location of surveillance cameras—and hiding others.[8]

Michelle's Fifth Grade Deportation

Michelle, twenty years of age, grew up in a mixed-status family. A younger brother of Michelle's is a U.S. citizen, but everyone else in her family is undocumented. Now a mother herself, Michelle's own, newly founded family is also mixed-status, since her partner and her daughters are U.S. citizens. (Michelle is the person described in the introductory chapter, who was unable to obtain a birth certificate until her child was four years old.) Although she remains undocumented, she emphasized, "I've been here since I was practically a baby. And before that, my parents and my sister, they would come and go across from Mexico. But me, I started school here." Michelle's mother died when she was seven years old, the result of complications during childbirth. Ever since then, she says, "I've been real attached to my dad, so wherever he goes, I go."

Michelle and her sister had to go with their father when he was targeted for deportation because of a disgruntled neighbor's phone call. As she told the story:

> We were living in this pretty house. We really liked it because it had a mandarin tree. But we had a neighbor, who didn't want us to use this little side yard that was part of the space we were renting. Before we got there, she used it to park her car, but it wasn't her space. So she would see us outside and she would be snooping around, always arguing with my dad. He would water and cut the grass there, and she would tell my dad to stay off that spot. My dad was like, "Well, I'm paying rent for it." The lady was real rude. We always had trouble with her. So she's the one that called the people [the immigration authorities] on my dad.

I interjected, "So they came to your house?" Michelle continued:

> Mm-hm. We were getting ready for school. I think I was ten or eleven years old. And it was the weirdest thing. It's kind of personal, because I had just started my [menstrual] period that day, for the first time. I was in fifth grade. It was going to be our first day of school, too. They knocked on the door while I was changing. My dad told us, "Well, we have to go. Get your stuff." My sister was in the shower and she had to get out and get dressed. And then they took us.
>
> They put us in a van around five or six in the morning. When we got to the immigration office, we were separated from my dad. I remember the officer asked me to sign a paper. My sister's now like, "Because you were small, they couldn't do that to you, that was wrong." On that same day, they made us walk across this little bridge [across the border to Mexico]. I remember it was just a little pathway, not like the big bridges with cars. And then we were standing there for three hours, waiting for my aunt to pick us up.

The family stayed with the aunt in Mexico for the next year. "To me," she says, "it felt like forever, but my sister says it wasn't that long. I remember going to just one school year over there. And then we came back. We went through the river. They [smugglers] had a boat, and we had to be on our knees, and from there we had to walk. It wasn't that far."

Michelle's story highlights several important points. An angry neighbor reported them out of spite. As described in Chapter 3, denunciation is always a possibility when people know or suspect one's undocumented status, and people must always be guarded, lest it be used against them. This can and does lead to conflicts within communities, and can be used to pressure or extort undocumented persons. The process by which Michelle and her family were returned is common in the border region. Michelle and her family experienced a "voluntary departure," which typically entails a short detention period, usually less than six hours; during this process, fingerprints and pictures are taken, and paperwork is signed. The person is then released to their home country; this is a common procedure at the border for Mexican nationals. Lastly, the family returned to the United States after a year. In cases where deported individuals have family remaining in the United States, they are motivated to return, and the duration of their stay in Mexico depends on many factors: kin ties, financial resources, and connections to smugglers. Michelle's is a melancholic coming-of-age story, where the life transition of menarche, which by itself can already be a trying event in a young girl's life, is paired with fear and loss.

The event left an indelible impact on Michelle, shaping her perspective as a young woman. Some of the rippling effects of the deportation on Michelle today include her inability to drive ("I get so scared, so I'm not driving right now") and a persistent fear that authorities will revoke her four-year-old daughter's U.S. citizenship: "I'm afraid they're going to take it away from her," she says, "because I'm from over there."

Where Do U.S.-Citizen Children Go When Their Parents Are Deported?

Michelle was deported alongside her father and sister because they were all undocumented. But what happens to U.S.-citizen children in the wake of parental deportation? Michelle's little brother, who is a citizen, was sent to stay with another aunt, who lived nearby. Across the United States, the bulk of citizen children stay in the country, often in the care of relatives or friends. This trend was very evident in the study that informs this book and is likely even more robust in the borderlands than elsewhere because of historically deep cross-border ties.

Staying in the United States with relatives as caretakers is not the only possible outcome if parents are deported. In a worst-case scenario, children may be placed into the foster care system. This, however, is rare. Very few deportation cases include involvement with the child welfare system, and often those children were already in the foster care system at the time their parents were apprehended.[9] Nonetheless, there have been cases in which the family reunification process has stalled or parental rights have been terminated due to parents' inability to attend child custody hearings or comply with court requirements because they were not physically in the United States.

Some deported parents will take their children with them when they return to their home county; an estimated half a million U.S.-born children live in Mexico.[10] The transition to Mexican culture and schools can be difficult. Often unregistered and undocumented in Mexico—in an ironic twist—these children may be shut out of public services, lack support systems, and often do not finish their education.[11] In other cases, there are bureaucratic difficulties with transferring school records from the United States. Often described as "invisible," they can end up in an educational limbo, since most do not read or write Spanish. As a result, they may be held back a grade, become easily discouraged, and stop attending school. Their growing presence has prompted concern for governments of both countries, prompting campaigns in Mexico to document and better integrate these binational children.

For the families in the study, and in the border region more broadly, there is no such trend of taking U.S.-citizen children to Mexico when parents are deported. This is largely due to geography: many families have relatives on both sides of the border, so can rely on a temporary caretaker. Smuggling opportunities are common, and as a result, most parents tend to return to the United States to reunify with their families. Since the mid-2000s, narco-violence has increased in the border states of Tamaulipas, Nuevo Leon, and Coahuila—often the places of origin for migrants living in the Rio Grande Valley—so parents feel uncomfortable relocating their families there. As Michelle told me, "If anything ever happens, my daughter won't go with us. I'll leave her with my sister while we get all that fixed. In Mexico, kids are getting shot—that's scary. No."

A major theme that emerged in discussions with mixed-status families was concern about siblings. Undocumented young adults worried especially about the fate of their younger, U.S.-born brothers and sisters. Robert and Ricardo, two brothers who were both Deferred Action for Childhood Arrivals (DACA) recipients, stated, "If we get deported, our brothers would be the only ones who get to stay here. But they don't have anyone else, so it's going to be hard for them. They're going to suffer." Similarly, Olivia told me, "If we get deported, my little sister is the only one that can stay. What is she going to do? She's four-teen. I mean, her only choice would be to go with us to Mexico, and she has no future over there. No future at all. This is her homeland. This is where she was born. This is where she needs to be. This is what her future is."

Childhood Trauma and the Health Impacts of Family Separation

Scholars have begun to systematically measure the health impacts of deporta-tion, including the psychosocial and health consequences for the children of immigrants.[12] Children in mixed-status families frequently worry about family separation and can exhibit high levels of stress, which may lead to poor mental health.[13] Those studying the health implications of immigration raids have found that the presence of such activities in a community led to higher levels of stress and lower self-rated health scores.[14] Separating children from their parents, or even the threat thereof, represents an adverse childhood event. This can cause irreparable harm through "toxic stress," or prolonged exposure to highly stressful situations, and affect children's short- and long-term health. Children whose parents have been deported or detained are more likely to experience a host of social concerns and mental health problems, including de-creased school performance, depression and other internalizing problems such as anxiety, and externalizing problems such as aggression and conduct issues.[15] Watching relatives be detained or deported disrupts children's sense of onto-logical security, or the confidence in the constancy of one's surrounding social and material environments of action.[16]

Fifty-one-year-old Rosa told me that hearing about deportations in her neighborhood always saddens her. "It separates the parents from their children, who have to stay here. And it causes psychological damage, trauma, to be sep-arated from their parents. If it were me, I would take my children with me, even if they are from here. Give me my children. If they are going to throw me out, then let my children go with me. This government is evil, separating children from their parents." Elvia is a grandmother who was caring for her four-year-old granddaughter after her son was deported. "We told her he had gone away to work. She would see his pictures around the house and would talk to them: '¿Papá?' But no, we didn't tell her anything, just that he was away working."

Beyond manifestations of ill health, the emotional scars of missing a family member are evident when families are torn apart. Fifteen-year-old Jaime, a U.S. citizen, spoke of the emotional impact of his father's deportation: "I love my dad. We've always been close. Ever since I was little I was always working with him in the [auto repair] shop and we always had time together. So when he was deported, it was hard for everybody, but it was definitely hardest for me because, oh my god, I love my dad." Especially for adolescents, a parent's deportation takes an enormous emotional toll, and even the threat of deportation has been shown to affect mental health, school performance, and likelihood of experiencing poverty.[17]

Parental Deportation and Economic Hardship

Economic hardship is one of the most significant impacts on the family of the deported. When the primary family wage earner is deported, the entire mixed-status household suffers economic hardships.[18] In one study focused on the aftermath of six immigration raids, family income dropped an average of 70 percent in the six months after the arrest of a parent, often the father.[19] Nationally, more than 90 percent of those deported and detained are men.[20] While men are at higher risk of detention and deportation, it is frequently women who have to hold the family together after the event. Thus deportations are both gendered and gendering.[21]

Jaime, who spoke in the last section about missing his father, relayed the following story about the economic impacts on the family:

> My dad got stopped while driving, and sent to Mexico. Well, we brought him back. But during those six months, I realized a lot of things. My dad is the head of the household. So, when dad's gone, we just don't know what to do; we're in a panic, like, were we going to still be able to live in our trailer? He pays the rent. He pays the bills. You never really appreciate it until he's gone. It was really hard. We only had a sofa to sleep on. We had no heater. The floors on trailers are freakily cold, and the landlord didn't want to fix the water heater. I'm not saying this for people to feel sorry for me. Just that, during those six months, it was really hard and it just made me want to get a job, but I was still only fifteen and I couldn't.

Twenty-three-year-old Daniela remembers the time her father was stopped for a traffic violation: "They didn't even give him a ticket or anything; they just automatically called immigration." With the primary wage earner temporarily gone, the rest of the family turned to the informal economy for extra income: "I remember my mom had to sell plates because we didn't have any money. We would all wake up at 5:00 A.M. to help make plates to sell." "Selling plates" is a popular way to fundraise in Mexican American communities and is often used to procure money for medical expenses, funerals, and other unforeseen costs, or to benefit churches or community sports teams. Sold for between $5 and $10, they usually consist of Styrofoam takeout containers with barbequed chicken, potato salad, rice, and beans, or occasionally chile relleno, brisket, fajitas, mole, or enchiladas as a main dish. Selling plates can help to supplement missing household income, but rarely replaces it.

Children in mixed-status families grow up with the knowledge that they will have to pitch in to support the family in the case of deportation. One U.S. citizen participant said, "My mom told me that if they ever get detained, that I would have to start working with my uncles as a carpenter on the ranch." For children in mixed-status families, including citizens, there is an ever-present possibility that they will have to alter their own life plans and career aspirations to support the family in the case of a parental deportation.

Advance Planning for Parental Deportation

One evening I was sitting at the kitchen table in the Hernandez family home and talking with three sisters—Cristina, Amy, and Kayla, all in high school—as their mother busied herself in the kitchen behind us, heating up tortillas on the open stove flame and putting away dishes. She presented us with plates of delicious chicken in mole sauce, and as we ate, she pushed, "Have some more! Eat!" Her husband sat on the couch, talking with research assistant Milena, as they ate and waited for the mother to sit down. Several times he called for us to join them in the living room to watch the movie *McFarland, USA*, which was running on TV. "It's a good movie, *mijas*!" he called from the next room. The girls laughed and rolled their eyes, "Dad! We're being *interviewed* right now!"

The possibility of family separation seemed so antithetical to this scene of family life and the small joys of home on a Thursday night. And yet, it was one of the questions I was asking the girls in what had become a group interview. Eighteen-year-old Cristina told me, "Being in a mixed-status family makes us a lot closer. So if you were to take one person away, it would be more devastating.

I don't think people realize that. In a mixed-status family, every time you get stopped by a cop, you're just wondering, like, 'Is this when they're going to take away my family?'" Amy, the second oldest, added, "Or you're thinking, 'Is this the end?'"

Many families have strategies already in place in case the parents are deported, much like any other emergency plan for fire, hurricanes, or other disasters. Most commonly, this involved prearranging for a relative to take care of minor children. In several cases, aunts or grandmothers agreed to come across from Mexico to care for the children, if they had a Border Crossing Card or dual citizenship. This would ensure that the children could continue going to school in the United States, so experience as little disruption in their environment as possible. Of course, having a relative cross over from Mexico while the parents were deported in the other direction is a paradoxical twist of mobility patterns.

Some families formalized this arrangement with the aid of legal documents, completing power-of-attorney paperwork or even transferring custody of their children to a family member—an aunt, grandmother, or, quite often, an adult sibling of the child. This practice picked up among immigrants with U.S.-born children across the nation after 2010, when Arizona passed an anti-immigration "show me your papers" law that became a template for other state legislative efforts.[22] For citizen siblings, this created extra responsibilities, with one adult sister noting, "My role is to be responsible if our parents are deported. I would take care of my brother and sister. We did talk about that. We've got to be prepared for any situation."

Marisol and her mother had the following exchange about the scenario she and her siblings faced while growing up. It was a weekday morning, and Marisol was making everyone breakfast tacos with egg and potato. As Marisol flitted about the kitchen, her mother sitting nearby and fussing over her newborn grandson, we talked about the recent rise in deportations. Marisol said, "They often don't consider the fact that families have both undocumented persons and legal citizens. So people like me were always afraid immigration would come and take my parents and my brothers, and leave me all alone. *Pues* but now I'm already twenty-one, so I'm OK." Her mother interjected, "But you were very scared." "Yes, when I was little, I was afraid they would come at any moment and turn me into a foster child because my parents didn't have papers. That was what I was always scared of. That you all would be sent to Mexico and I would have to stay with someone else." Nodding, her mother told me, "That was the fear that she always had, that because she was a citizen she would be treated that way." Marisol's parents had signed power-of-attorney documents naming her oldest brother the guardian when he turned eighteen years old. This clued her in, at an early age, that her family was not like others, and gave her a lasting sense of insecurity. She began plating up the food and after a short silence told me:

> When I was nine or ten, that's when I started processing everything. My mom would panic so much, and be like, "If we're gone, you have your brother and sister." So we grew up knowing that if my parents got deported, we were going to be taken away to foster care or something *if* it was before my brother turned eighteen. I would always think to myself, "As long as he turns eighteen, it's okay. They're not going to send us anywhere."

Being prepared for any situation included many other small details of daily life besides assigning a guardian and substitute caretaker. This included learning to fend for oneself ("My mom tells my little brother, 'You need to learn to cook, because what if one day I'm gone?'") and learning to drive at a young age, even before they were eligible to apply for a license. One young teen told me, "Just in case Border Patrol came, I know how to drive. If they took my sister, my mom, and if my dad was at work, I would be able to drive my other sister."

Other families were maximally prepared for a legal battle. In a few cases—particularly among those that had been active with local community organizations—families had assembled a packet and even saved cash in case someone was detained. As Jennifer, a twenty-four-year-old U.S.-citizen daughter of undocumented parents, explained:

> We have all the papers gathered for me to take to an attorney and say, "Hey, my parents got detained. Here's our money." You have to prove that you've been living in the United States, that you've been a good citizen, that the kids need you. I spoke to attorney friends, "What do I do? What happens if someone gets detained, what is the first step?" So the plan is to grab those files, and I would be in charge of getting an attorney and starting the process to get them out of detention. Fortunately, we have that file all ready to go.

I asked about such plans in case of parental deportation during a conversation with the three Hernandez sisters, all U.S. citizens. The oldest at eighteen, Cristina, told me, "My dad always says that if one of them would be deported, they know exactly what to do. Not signing anything, not to speak, and then try to get lawyers. Us three, we can't really do much, but now that I'm an adult probably I can get my dad out." Her sister, Amy, the second oldest, chimed in, "So, yeah. We have somewhat of a plan." Meanwhile, I noticed that the youngest, Kayla—known for her energy and clownish antics—sat wide-eyed and uncharacteristically quiet. Laughing, Cristina poked her, saying, "I don't know if Kayla knows anything about this [laughs]. She's silent because she's like, 'When did this happen?'" Kayla, fourteen, smiled sheepishly but was clearly just coming to understand her parents' limitations and deportability, and hadn't yet been clued into the family's arrangements.

Some families reconsidered or strengthened their emergency plans after the 2016 election. A number of community-based organizations and churches in the Rio Grande Valley began offering workshops and legal aid clinics to assist in filling out power-of-attorney documents. Others had started saving extra money, which Olivia jokingly called her "Trump GoFundMe account."[23] One participant stated that her neighbors had bought a house in Mexico "as soon as Trump won." For many others, the election motivated them to begin the process of filing their residency paperwork, if they had the opportunity to petition for adjustment of status. Five participants with DACA who were married to U.S. citizens decided—shortly after the election—to begin the paperwork process to obtain residency via their spouses. As noted in Chapter 3, many of them had previously said they did not want to rely on their spouses for a status, but this resolve had changed for them with the election.

Perhaps unsurprisingly, social media has served as an important tool for people seeking information about immigrant enforcement activity or details about what to expect when loved ones are being deported. However, sites like Facebook are also insecure and may be monitored by authorities. An app called Notifica was launched that allows users to send out secure messages to their support networks.[24] Similar to a panic button, users can preload personalized messages (e.g., one tailored to a lawyer and different ones to be sent to a child or spouse); these are sent out automatically to recipients in the case of an apprehension.

Finally, several families arranged to keep their property intact in case the parents were deported. Homeownership among undocumented persons is very high in the Rio Grande Valley; an estimated 57 percent of undocumented persons own their homes.[25] The Garcia family owns a tidy, four-bedroom house they built after coming to the United States eighteen years ago. After the 2016 presidential election, the parents transferred the title to their home, land, and cars to their U.S.-citizen children, both of whom are now in college. As Evelyn, the forty-eight-year-old mother, explained, "I told my husband, 'Let's put the house in our sons' names, since they are from here.' And I told my kids, 'Here are the papers to the house, and here are all the papers to the land that it is on.' Because you never know, for any reason, we might leave and not be able to return."

The Garcia family, like others in this book, engaged in the type of planning that usually happens in preparing for death. But here, it was in case a deportation occurred. Similar to preparing a last will and testament, families legally transferred property and assigned guardians for their children, often completely but temporarily reorganizing their family structure. This highlights how deportation is indeed a form of social death, or the systematic process by which people are prevented from engaging in social relations and denied their humanity.[26] The devaluation and lack of "deservingness" associated with undocumented persons, like other criminalized populations of color, challenges the very understanding of personhood in the United States. Deportation as an everyday practice normalizes social death.

"Deportation Doesn't Just Affect a Person; It Affects a Whole Community"

The effects of deportation reach beyond individual families. Deportation negatively impacts immigrants' social capital through fear and makes people hesitant to confide in or rely on their neighbors. It also produces distrust of law enforcement, eroding relationships between immigrant communities and police officers. Olivia stressed, "Deportation doesn't just affect a person, it affects a whole community. If my neighbors, who are also undocumented, were to get deported, it's not something just affecting their family. I've known them for a decade now. I have seen their kids grow up. If their parents would get deported, it would be something that would actually hurt me, hit me very hard." Similarly, twenty-three-year-old Eric, a U.S. citizen with undocumented parents, said, "There are these kids down the street whose parents were deported, for no reason. They left them with no mother, no father. Those kids, they don't deserve that. Sometimes when my little sister plays with the girl, to try to make her forget about her parents, she'll see her cry. My little sister plays with her to keep her distracted about those things."

People's lives are interconnected beyond their own family, and deportation has multiple meanings and implications for the people in one's circle. David, a thirty-three-year-old schoolteacher who is a U.S. citizen, recalled a story from his childhood in which his babysitter shielded the family, resulting in her own deportation:

> When I was growing up I had a nanny, a friend of my parents from Mexico. She was undocumented, and I remember one day I opened the door to the Border Patrol. They asked, "Is so-and-so here?" She saw them and said, "Oh no, she's not here," and slammed the door on them. But because I was small, he tricked me. He knocked again, and when I opened, he says, "Do you know where she [the nanny] is at?" "Oh yeah, she's over there." And then, "Can you get her to come?" She tried to close the door, but he put his hand in and caught her. Then I realized, oh, I wasn't supposed to say that. They took her right there in front of me. I mean, he was courteous about it. He said, "Listen, I'm not going to handcuff you in front of the child. Is the child by himself?" and she says, "No, he's not." She lied for me. They would have taken me, too, and then they would have called my parents, and we would have all been deported. She lied to protect us.

As a result of this experience, David was acutely aware of his privilege as a citizen, and he simultaneously felt he could better empathize with undocumented people in his community. This included the parents of his students, many of whom lacked papers. This story illustrates the toll of deportability on the larger community, where many citizens are aware that their neighbors are in precarious circumstances and have witnessed the devastating consequences of detention and deportation firsthand.

"I Have No Idea How Pesos Work": Imagining Deportation and Return

In addition to asking about deportation experiences and emergency planning, participants were asked, "What would you do if you were deported?" This was to probe specifically about the possibility of return to Mexico. The overwhelming majority—especially young adults—said they would find a way to come back to the United States, citing family ties and the violence on the other side of the border. Even those who had very strong family ties in Mexico expected to return. As one person noted, "The plan is if you're deported, [you] go back to Monterrey. We have a house there. I mean, at least visit the family while we get money to bring you back. It's just, relax. If we need to call somebody from Monterrey to take you in, then we can do that." The only ones who said they might remain in Mexico were older individuals, whose children were grown and out of school, and who had become nostalgic to be with aging family and friends on the other side.

DACA recipients, in particular, had a lot to say about this hypothetical scenario, since they had transitioned from an undocumented to a liminal status and seemed to have given it a lot of thought. Olivia used to see deportation as a one-way ticket to Mexico, noting, "When I was younger, I thought if I ever get deported, I'll go to my grandpa. That's where it ends; there is no other way." But as an adult, she had reconsidered the possibilities of this scenario, especially now that she had strong ties to the United States after many years of living there and was also married to a citizen:

> Now that I'm a DREAMer, I find this is not set in stone. Now that I'm older, now that I'm married, now that I'm thinking about starting a family, it's very scary. If I ever get deported, I can't stay over there. I would have to come back, one way or another. This is where my family is. This is where my husband is. This is where home is.

Like Michelle, whose own childhood deportation story was shared earlier in this chapter, Olivia has transitioned from being an undocumented child to becoming an undocumented parent of a mixed-status family, as part of the social reproduction in these communities. The cycle of deportability continues, and in each of these cases parents will need to have difficult conversations with their own children and consider another round of family plans in case of deportation.

Twenty-five-year-old Daniel, a DACA recipient since 2012, grew up in the United States with no memory of Mexico, like many other DREAMers. The idea of being forced to relocate to a country he doesn't know was inconceivable to him:

> It would be extremely difficult. Like, I speak Spanish, but not very well. I think in English. It would be difficult for me to assimilate. I'm not exactly sure how the economy works; it's a completely different type of culture, different type of people. It's like, even though you're Mexican, you don't know the customs. I might as well be moving to Europe. It would put me out of my element. It's just

so different. I've never handled the currency. I have no idea how pesos work. No idea.

Bringing Them Back: Family Members Return to the United States

Those who are deported but have developed strong ties to the United States demonstrate a greater resolve to return. Recent border- and immigration-enforcement programs have contributed to a "caging effect" since the mid-1990s, which has disrupted seasonal migration flows and increased familial and social ties to the United States.[27] Rather than risk returning to Mexico, more people have stayed and started families in the United States. In addition to these strong family ties, many undocumented immigrants in Texas own property and businesses, and they are not willing to abandon them.

In many deportation cases, family members are able to return a short time later. The duration of their stay in Mexico depends on many factors: whether they have family members in Mexico they can stay with, whether they have connections to smugglers who can aid them in their return, and whether they have the money to pay. Edgar told the story of organizing his father's return to the United States following deportation:

> We arranged for my father to be brought back. It was horrible, because there was a period of three or four days where we didn't know where he was. So one only assumes the worst, right? We were able to find some *coyotes*, who cross people over from Mexico. We paid $500 first and the rest, $2000, once he was brought to our house. I paid for that out of pocket, $2,500 in total. I had just gotten my income tax return, so I was able to pay. We met a really nice guy, whose family did that [smuggling] from their own land, and so there really wasn't any violence around them. They were Christian people, so they brought him over safely and everything. He wasn't exposed to the cartel, like the first time he crossed. Back then, he had to go with them and pay a quota. He said that they were all drugged up with guns, so you can imagine how that was.

While this amount is pretty high for a straightforward crossing, Edgar's family was most concerned about the father's safety, not cost.[28] However, as Wendy Vogt points out, the "security" offered by smugglers in an environment where extortion and kidnapping is common works to "coproduce new forms of violence and profit within the economy of the journey."[29] This is the case even if smugglers are perceived to be "a really nice guy" or as "Christian people."

In some cases, people's return was hastened by good connections. Elizabeth's father went across the border to Reynosa one morning to get his wisdom teeth removed. He was unable to obtain the procedure in the United States because the cost was too prohibitive; still, he was in extreme pain, so knew he needed to get them extracted as soon as possible. Using someone else's documents, he crossed into Mexico but was stopped on his return to the United States:

> When he was coming back, my dad got detained. They saw the American num-
> bers on his phone, like the 956 area code, and he had a U.S. cell phone carrier.
> So they knew that he had been living over here; that's how they got him. They
> detained him and sent him to Mexico, but that same day he came back [to the
> United States]. The people that bring you over here are not cheap, but that same
> day he was back and working again. He's like, "I've got to go to work tomor-
> row." [laughs] He crossed through the river and he worked the next day. Yep.
> That's my dad. [laughs] With his teeth all fixed.

Nonchalance aside, for children, their parents' crossing was viewed as an act of love. As one high school–aged participant said, "My mom was deported, but she crossed once again all so we could be united. She took the risk for us."

Family Separation in Mixed-Status Families

No other process has a more violent and immediate impact on mixed-status families than deportation. Deportation breaks up families when people's primary social and kin ties are in the United States. Mixed-status families have been disproportionately affected by recent policy reversals and new deportation priorities, which have disregarded family and community ties. Faced with the removal of a family member, children must step up to help allay the economic impacts. They are also deeply affected emotionally. If they are U.S. citizens, children may be left behind with family or friends when their parents are deported; alternatively, they must join them in Mexico, a land they do not know, resulting in a difficult transition. Sadly, foster care is also a possibility for citizen children whose parents are deported. As a result of the ever-present possibility of family separation, older siblings worry about their little brothers and sisters who might be left behind. Deportation also separates people from their rightfully owned property, including homes, cars, land, and businesses.

Families have developed a set of strategies—what I refer to as advance planning—to deal with the challenges associated with family separation, should it occur. They prearrange care for their children with relatives or friends living in the United States. Alternatively, a family member may come over from Mexico to care for the children. These arrangements may be formalized with power-of-attorney paperwork, or by transferring custody of their children to others, including adult siblings. They also plan in advance for legal battles in case of detention, preparing folders of paperwork, with an attorney on standby, and setting aside dedicated funds for this purpose. Others take pains to keep their property intact by transferring deeds to a home or property to their U.S.-citizen children. But deportation is a form of social death, and planning for the event resembles the preparation of a will, as family structures are completely reorganized for legal purposes. A number of options can be employed if someone is deported: most likely, they will return—especially if the United States is their primary country of orientation—by hiring smugglers, or they may rely on family members in Mexico to provide housing, jobs, and other forms of support.

The uniqueness of the border region shapes the experiences of mixed-status families. First, the intense levels of everyday surveillance and entrapment mean that encounters with Border Patrol and law enforcement are frequent. Deportation is swifter here than in other parts of the United States, particularly because procedures like voluntary departure and expedited removal are accompanied by lack of due process. In addition, in this region, people are more likely to live in immigration attorney "deserts" than elsewhere. For these reasons, a high percentage of families interviewed had experienced deportation, and entire neighborhoods felt the effects of harsh immigration enforcement.

The next chapter further examines mixed-status families' intimate relationship with the law, exploring the family dynamics associated with regularization. This process may shift power relations between parents and children, for example, or provide children with a sense of agency in an otherwise insecure environment. However, it also demonstrates that the path to lawful status is neither short nor easy.

CHAPTER 8

FIXING PAPERS

STATUS ADJUSTMENT IN MIXED-STATUS FAMILIES

WHEN BRITTANY WAS eight years old, she learned about her parents' legal status. "I figured out they were undocumented when my dad started working in the fields." She said, "I was like, 'Why don't you work at a store? It's way easier, and you don't have to be in the hot sun.' Working in the fields is really hard work, and they pay you really low. But that's all there is for him." Her father explained to her that he didn't have the necessary Social Security number to get another job:

> He told me, "When you're an adult, hopefully you can fix my papers, since you're a U.S. citizen," and that's when I saw it: I'm going to fix my mom and my dad's papers. I couldn't *wait* to be an adult from that moment on. As a little kid, that was a big deal for me. I felt powerful, you know, like I could actually *do* something for my parents, give back for all they've done for me.

When I met Brittany, she was twenty-one years old and could finally start the process of petitioning for legal status. "We're still saving up the money, since it's about $6,000," she told me. The family had laid out a plan for the next few years: Brittany would petition for her mother first, and then her younger sister Erica, who is two years younger, would petition for their father when she turned twenty-one. "It's my mom that gets me more worried," she said. "I see her nervous all the time. My dad's a little more relaxed about it." Brittany had started taking on as many shifts as possible at her restaurant job in order to save up the money.

A year later, I caught up with Erica, Brittany's sister, who updated me: "Right now my sister and my mom going through the process, but it's slow. I know some people take ten or fifteen years to finally get their papers. Let's hope for the best. Maybe she'll be different and it will process faster." Erica noted that her grandparents were also waiting, as a next step in this protracted family odyssey. "I just wish it could have been sooner. I want her to get her papers so that she can petition for my grandparents. It's a lot of wishing, you know. I just need to have patience. Maybe one day I'll check the mail and it's going to be in there. That day, I will feel at peace finally."

Mixed-status families have an intimate relationship with the law. This chapter explores how the regularization process plays out in families and the dynamics it produces. Most people refer to this process as "fixing papers"[1]—in Spanish, "*arreglando papeles*"—a phrase which suggests that something is broken and simply needs to be (and can be) repaired, as opposed to interpreting people's situations as illegal or criminal. When undergoing regularization, the family's relationship with immigration authorities changes, as Ruth Gomberg-Muñoz notes, from "one largely characterized by mutual avoidance to one of intimate, regular, and prolonged surveillance."[2] Roberto Gonzales has argued that illegality is a master status, and that "its only undoing is legal citizenship."[3] Deportability only ends when one becomes a U.S. citizen; even permanent residency status can always be taken away and remains vulnerable to the effects of criminalization. Yet fixing papers is a long and complicated process, full of expense, contradictions, and unknown consequences. During this process, law impacts family bonds in distinct ways, often shifting or reversing power relations between parents and children. It also empowers children, who, like Brittany, finally feel they have agency and some sense of control over their family's destiny. U.S. citizens frequently also help with regularizing their siblings, another practice that is common in mixed-status families but that has received little scholarly attention to date. However, as this chapter shows, the path to lawful status is neither short nor easy for families, and it creates many inequalities along the way.

Not all intimate ties are recognized by the state as "family," so as meriting rights, protection, and opportunities.[4] Through law, regularization and citizenship opportunities are premised on the "right type" of family, with assumptions about age, gender, sexuality, biological relatedness, and location at the time the request is submitted. One critical aspect of regularization is mode of entry; this chapter illustrates the distinction between those who entered unlawfully (without inspection) versus those who overstayed a visa (with inspection) using specific family cases. It follows those who have engaged with the legalization process—both successfully and unsuccessfully—petitioning through a spouse or a family member, especially U.S.-born citizen children or siblings. The promise of future regularization carries over into everyday lives as "hypercitizenship," a form of discipline in which people modify behaviors in the face of constant criminalization and deportability.

This chapter also offers stories of the trajectory of Deferred Action for Childhood Arrivals (DACA) recipients in their transition from undocumented to "DACAmented," which was experienced as precarious status. Taking stock of the five years of DACA, it highlights the positive impact the program had on mixed-status families. At the same time, it is part of a disturbing pattern of granting provisional and temporary legal statuses in lieu of lawful permanent residency, leaving entire populations in a constant state of marginalization, limbo, and revocability.[5] Policies like DACA are part of a disquieting trend of policies of precarity, in which populations remain both documented and deportable.[6] Regularization creates hierarchies based on discourses of deservingness and solidifies prior and produces new forms of inequality. Also explored in this chapter are the "dead ends" faced by some, who are blocked by eligibility criteria, financial constraints, and prior visa-related or deportation offenses. Lastly, for those who are successful in obtaining legal relief or status, other perils loom: jealousy, stratification, and hierarchies created within families and communities when others are left behind. The flip side of this phenomenon is survivor's guilt; once people regularize their status, they must be cautious to avoid seeming boastful or provoking feelings of bitterness or resentment.

Biases in U.S. Immigration Law

Law has the power to demarcate boundaries and define inclusion, and in doing so establishes the very contours of the family. While U.S. immigration laws privilege family membership in the reunification process, they can also undermine family structures by defining what counts as kinship—that is, who is included—as well as by designating and marginalizing some members as "illegal." The family reunification system actually treats people not as a family unit but as individuals in a complex hierarchy in which some statuses and relationships are considered more important than others.[7] A family member's undocumented status affects people indirectly in many more ways, as prior chapters have demonstrated. This, along with inconsistent rules and discretionary practices of state bureaucrats, highlights the precarity of legal protection even for citizens in mixed-status families.

U.S. immigration law is constantly changing, but it is always embedded in larger sociopolitical contexts. Through the 1980s, the experience of illegality was much shorter in duration and impacted fewer people in mixed-status families.[8] In the 1990s, many people were able to legalize their undocumented status through marriage to a citizen without long wait times or innumerable barriers. However, policy changes in the 1990s and 2000s made it much more difficult for people to legalize through family ties, regardless of the length of their residence in the United States. These changes, combined with stricter border enforcement, which keeps people trapped in the United States, has led to the large numbers of mixed-status families we see today.

The current legal system is simply not designed to provide relief for mixed-status families. Not only are pathways to legalization more limited than ever before, but even these pathways are reserved for people who are either already legally present or have never entered the United States.[9] In 1964, the quota system was replaced with per-country limits and a preference system for family reunification. The irony is that at the same time other factors encouraged the rise of mixed-status families—the very group now more likely to be broken up through deportation—despite this stated preference for family reunification. Today, family-based immigration visas account for roughly two-thirds of all visas (ahead of employment-sponsored, diversity lottery, and refugee visas). These can be divided into one of two broad categories: immediate relatives of U.S. citizens and those classified under a family-preference system.

Since all countries are allotted the same number of visas, wait times are particularly long for countries with large numbers of applicants (specifically, Mexico, India, China, and the Philippines). At the time of writing, an adult unmarried person from Mexico with a family sponsor can expect to wait twenty-one years to legally enter the country on an F1 visa, based on U.S. Customs and Immigration Services (USCIS) processing times.[10] After considering this situation, it is perhaps no wonder even those who are eligible may forfeit the wait and attempt entry without a visa or by overstaying a non-immigrant visa.

The current configuration of laws produces a social hierarchy that excludes specific groups from attaining or exercising citizenship. Immigration law and citizenship categories are experienced differently by different groups of people. These laws and policies are imbued with racial, class, and gendered biases, and are premised on the "right type" of family. Intimacies, especially in the form of families, comprise material sites through which states have historically sought to create and sustain deeply unequal relationships at global, national, and local scales.[11] In the United States, nation-building has long relied on the white, heterosexual, nuclear family as its point of reference, ignoring other forms. When racial categories were removed from immigration law in 1965, the family became the primary route for admission. As migrants from Latin America and Asia began to dominate family-based immigration opportunities, the inherent biases of white supremacy and heteropatriarchy have been increasingly challenged. This has led to ever-louder calls to reduce or restructure family-based admissions, sometimes disparagingly framed as "chain migration." This rhetoric misrepresents legal realities, however, since the ability to sponsor green cards for family members is very limited; U.S. citizens can only sponsor spouses, children, parents and siblings—with caveats based on age and marital status—while green card holders can only sponsor spouses and unmarried children. It is not possible to bring in more distant relatives, one of the many inherent biases in the law's definition of family.

Gender bias also has a long history in immigration law. It was not until June 2017, in the case of *Sessions v. Morales-Santana*, that the U.S. Supreme Court reversed portions of the Immigration and Naturalization Act, written in the 1940s, that made it easier for the children of American mothers than the children of American fathers to obtain citizenship. According to the policy, a child born abroad to a U.S.-citizen father only automatically became a citizen if the father had lived in the United States for ten years (at least five of which were after he turned fourteen years of age). However, a child born abroad to a U.S.-citizen mother automatically became a citizen at birth if the mother had spent only at least one year in the United States. Justice Ruth Bader Ginsburg wrote in the decision that the outdated ideas about gender in the application of citizenship were "stunningly anachronistic" and "date[d] from an era when the lawbooks of our Nation were rife with overbroad generalizations about the way men and women are." The assumption in the law was that an "unwed mother is the natural and sole guardian of a non-marital child." The Court thus revised the laws in favor of the stricter rules that applied to fathers, meaning that it made this policy more equal but also more restrictive.

Heteronormative ideas about marriage and family continue to undergird the system, despite the 2015 U.S. Supreme Court confirming that same-sex couples have a constitutional right to marriage. Although it is now possible to regularize status through a same-sex spouse using the same marriage-based immigration benefits under federal law that "traditional" marriages have received, there are still biases in the practices the USCIS uses to evaluate their legitimacy.[12] Evidence to prove that a relationship is bona fide often assumes couples conform to a traditional American family archetype. However, prejudice and institutional barriers may hinder same-sex couples from proving a bona fide marriage. For instance, if they lived in states that prohibited same-sex marriage prior to the 2013 Supreme Court ruling that the Defense of Marriage Act (DOMA) was unconstitutional, they may not have been able to file taxes jointly or may have avoided comingling assets because of the potential for discrimination. As a result, they may lack evidence of joint assets and liabilities. Some immigrants avoid labeling their relationship as such in conversations with family and friends, or on social media, if their home country has discriminatory attitudes and persecutory laws toward same-sex couples. This may lead to difficulty finding third parties to corroborate and legitimize the relationship. While the 2013 Supreme Court decision was a victory for same-sex couples, in practice, immigration law can still disadvantage these petitioners. Furthermore, marriage equality laws fundamentally exclude those in other kinds of intimate relationships, privileging and preserving a specific type of institution and leaving unaddressed the assumption that governments should be regulating benefits for sexual relationships at all.

U.S. law is also full of de facto status crimes, or "specific activities that are only transparently recognized as 'criminal' when they are attached to statuses that invoke race (gang member), ethnicity ('illegal alien'), and/or national origin (suspected terrorist)."[13] In other words, there is an ongoing and permanent criminalization of certain groups, who are rendered ineligible for full citizenship as a result. This criminalization is evident in regularization as applicants must prove "good moral character." While clean criminal records are an important piece of evidence for this, assimilation into U.S. society and involvement in their community are also considered. However, undocumented persons' ability to have good moral character is already in doubt from the start because they have violated immigration rules. This concept is itself inextricably classed and raced.[14]

This emphasis on good moral character produces a form of discipline in which immigrants learn to police themselves and restrict their own actions to avoid trouble.[15] For instance, Darius, a twenty-two-year-old DACA recipient told me, "My parents would always say, 'This is not your country for you to be doing whatever you want.' You pay your taxes and stuff like that, just be invisible to people." This included avoiding trouble and being careful to follow all laws and rules. This was echoed by Ricardo, another DACA recipient, who said, "That's one reason I've never worked in a business or a store, because I don't want to have a bad image. In those cases, almost everyone works under a different name, using someone else's documents. That's not for me. I want to have a clean record and not use false names or some papers that I borrowed." Beyond staying "invisible" and avoiding identity loans, other participants emphasized behaviors such as dutifully following all traffic signs (full stops!), making sure they had liability insurance on their automobiles, paying utility bills on time, returning library books by their due date, and generally following civic procedures and expectations to the fullest extent. Attempting to prove their moral worthiness, respectability, and orderliness—often explicitly in contrast to what they have seen ordinary "Americans" doing—results in a disciplined form of hypercitizenship.

A "Family Affair": Mixed-Status Families Navigate Immigration Law

Immigration processing is a "family affair," as various members must become actively involved, and the outcomes profoundly affect everyone, including extended relatives.[16] Many discover obstacles early in the process: they may not have the right kind of family; the applicant may have an immigration or criminal record, making them ineligible; or the costs may be too steep. Those who are lucky enough to proceed find the process burdensome, full of uncertainty and vulnerability, expensive, and a strain on relationships. Gomberg-Muñoz concludes that the regularization process is "a comprehensive system of inequality that benefits some while wreaking havoc on the lives of mixed-status families and the undocumented population at large."[17]

Two parts of the U.S. immigration system collide when people attempt to regularize their status, and highlight that this process was not designed for mixed-status families. On the one hand, individuals are eligible for permanent residency status through a family member. On the other hand, the law requires them to leave the United States and petition for residency from abroad; but by leaving, they are immediately barred from reentering the country for a certain time. The Illegal Immigration Reform and Immigrant Responsibility Act of 1996 (IIRAIRA) established three-year, ten-year, and permanent bars to reentry if an immigrant has accrued "unlawful presence" in the United States, leaves the country, and then wishes to reenter lawfully. Generally, someone who enters the United States without inspection, or who overstays a period of authorized admission on a visa, will be deemed to have accrued unlawful presence. Individuals who accrue more than 180 days, but less than one year, of unlawful presence are barred from reentering for three years; those who accrue more than one year of unlawful presence are barred for ten years.

It is here that mode of entry matters so much: Did the petitioner arrive in the United States the "hard way" or the "easy way?" IIRAIRA established the legal distinction between people who enter unlawfully (that is, the "hard way," without inspection and in a clandestine manner, often via the desert or river) versus those who overstay a visa. The important difference is that visa overstayers have been lawfully admitted to the United States in the past—that is, a state official recorded their entry in some fashion—while unlawful entrants have not. Although visa overstayers represent the majority, unlawful entrants are more likely than visa overstayers to come from particular countries, like Mexico, and from particular class backgrounds.[18] Thus one of the ironies is that people often become ineligible for a visa if they are undocumented (because they entered unlawfully), whereas if they had petitioned via a family member while living outside the United States, they would be successful. As Gonzales has noted, "This Catch-22 produced a population of settled and now highly vulnerable migrant families—one consisting mainly of Mexicans—with few rights and no practical way to legalize their immigration status."[19]

A waiver of the three- and ten-year restrictions is possible if the applicant for permanent residency status is the immediate relative (spouse, child, or parent) of a U.S. citizen. Since 2013, applicants can apply for a "provisional unlawful presence waiver" before leaving the United States for the consular interview in their home country, which allows them to return shortly afterward. In 2016, this was expanded to include all individuals statutorily eligible for an immigrant visa. This new process was specifically developed to shorten the time that U.S. citizens and lawful permanent residents had to be separated from their relatives. Today, families are usually separated for less than a week. Nonetheless, the process still retains the punitive implication promoted by the international separation of family members.[20]

The legalization process also affects the subjectivity of U.S. citizens. Gomberg-Muñoz found that when their spouse is excluded from the opportunity or their application is not approved, it may feel like an affront to their own status as citizens. This contradiction arises because policy emphasizes family unity but simultaneously rejects this possibility in some cases. In addition, "when U.S. citizens strategically identify themselves as citizen wives and mothers, they uphold distinctions between statuses and reinforce the idea that citizenship is a legitimate basis on which to distribute rights;"[21] this legitimizes the very policies that excluded their loved ones in the first place. Citizens who go through the petitioning process often learn that they actually have no "right" to family, at all, under immigration law. This can estrange citizens from their own sense of national belonging, making them feel that the process is a degradation of the value of their citizenship, rather than a celebration of it.[22] This was evident in some of the stories families shared with me. As U.S. citizen and former Marine Miguel noted following the unsuccessful attempts to regularize his sister's status, "That's the sad thing. No matter how much you do as a citizen, for example, you can be in the military, you can be a senator, you can be Mr. Perfect and she can be Ms. Perfect. But the government has the final say, and you feel crippled because of it."

Fixing Papers Through U.S.-Citizen Children and Siblings

Despite widespread misconceptions, U.S.-born children do not "anchor" families by providing automatic pathways to citizenship, nor do they provide protection from deportation. Instead, as this book has underscored, the entire family remains entrapped in a labyrinth of precarity.[23] When they turn twenty-one, U.S. citizens can indeed petition for their parents to gain permanent residency status (not citizenship), but depending on a number of factors—like the parent's mode of entry to the United States or their ability to afford a lawyer—it can take anywhere from half a year to five or six years for the process. If someone were to enter the country with the intent of gaining access to services and legal status by giving birth to a child in the United States, they would be waiting a minimum of twenty-two years to benefit from the opportunity. This is not a very effective pull factor, despite the political rhetoric that surrounds "anchor babies" and proposals to limit birthright citizenship.

As noted in Chapter 2, citizen children in mixed-status families often grow up knowing that their role might include petitioning for their parents. Cristina, the oldest of three sisters, recalled, "My parents always reminded me that I would be the one to turn twenty-one first. So I just remember my mom saying, 'When you're older you'll be able to help your dad.'" While many, like Brittany and Erica in the introduction to this chapter, were excited and ready to help their parents, for others this created enormous emotional stress. Norma, a twenty-two-year-old U.S. citizen, told me that her relatives frequently hounded her about it:

> They say, "Norma, you've already turned twenty-one; why haven't you fixed your mom's and your brother's papers yet?" But it wasn't because I was lazy. I had this image in my head that I would have to go to court with a lawyer, stand up and talk in front of a judge. And what if I said something wrong and ruined it all? They did put a lot of pressure on me. I felt the pressure, and it stressed me out.

More typically, families were on the same page when it came to moving forward with the process. Because the study that informs this book was longitudinal, the legal status of some family members changed over the course of the five years. During our third visit to the Rodriguez family's home, mother Evelyn proudly stated, "So, my husband is a resident now!" After I had congratulated them both, she continued, "He received it through our son Eric. I have yet to apply. The lawyer recommended my husband go first." How long did it take? "The application process took three months, and then another five months for the residency to be approved. Five months, that was quick. My mother is a resident. She got it through one of her brothers. It took a long time, like fifteen or twenty years." Notably, his mother had gone through the process before it was possible to apply for the provisional unlawful presence waiver, which partially explained the difference in their timelines.

I was curious how their son Eric felt about the process. Evelyn said, "He knew he was going to fix our papers someday, when he turned twenty-one. And then we told him, 'It's almost time, you have a week until you turn twenty-one.'" Her husband interjected, "He knew because his brother was always talking with him about it." Evelyn continued, "And then when the time came, Eric was like, 'Let's go! Where do I sign?' So we got a lawyer, we had to save up $4,000—that's $8,000 for both of us." Her husband chimed in: "My brother lent us the money. We've already paid it back." In a separate conversation later, I asked Eric what was going through his mind at the time. He told me his reaction was indeed, "*Que chido* [How cool]! I get to fix their papers, now we get to go do it." He was excited to finally help out his parents after all these years.

John is a U.S. citizen with undocumented parents and two older sisters who were recipients of DACA. In Chapter 5, he described having joined the Marines to satisfy his wanderlust and see the world beyond the Rio Grande Valley. However, he also confided that he had decided to serve in the military because it would help him in regularizing his mother's status. He told me, "I knew a few people in the military who joined to gain citizenship and to help their families out. You join, and then you apply. So you get a clearance, and then as they're processing your paperwork it goes a little bit faster than for someone who is not in the military." There is a special opportunity, called "parole in place," that applies to undocumented persons who are the spouse, child, or parent of an active duty member of the U.S. Armed Forces, an individual in the Selected Reserve of the Ready Reserve, or an individual who previously served.[24] Under the usual policy, individuals—like John's mother—who enter the United States without inspection must return to their home country for a time and undergo a consular interview. However, the "parole in place" opportunity grants special permission to the petitioner to remain in the United States without having to leave, thus speeding up the process.

Some families were unable to go through the regularization process altogether, often facing a dead end of one sort or another. And, in some cases, the process simply didn't make sense. Claudia, a U.S. citizen, told me that she had been excited to petition for her undocumented mother but that another route had become more prudent: "Once I turned twenty-one, I found out the petition takes such a long time. It kind of discouraged me. But by that point, my mom had also married my stepdad, so the lawyers told her, 'It's a lot easier and quicker route if you go through the marriage route versus your kid petitioning you.'"

Fixing Papers Through Marriage to a Citizen

For many undocumented persons, petitioning for legal permanent residency status through a spouse may be a better option, especially if they have no children or have very young children. This section illustrates how this process works, using the stories of four young adults: Michelle, Olivia, Brian, and Justin.

Michelle was hesitant to apply for DACA despite being eligible. She worried that if she applied, the government would have all her information, so could come for her at any time. Michelle did have a U.S.-citizen boyfriend, who was also the father of her child. As noted in Chapter 3, however, many people desired marriages "for the right reasons," not out of desperation for legal status.[25] They rejected advice to use marriage as a way to regularize their status, and it was important to them that their partners knew their love was sincere. Michelle emphasized this by recounting a conversation with her boyfriend:

> He really wants to get married because he wants to help me get my papers fixed. I was like, "No, I don't want people to think that I'm getting married to you just because I want my papers." When we first started dating, one of his aunts was like, "She got pregnant because she wants you to fix her papers." I was like, "What, no!" They had fights because of that and would tell him that I was going to just use him. So I said, "Now I don't want to get married, because what are they going to say? 'Oh, she's just marrying you for papers.'" We haven't gotten married yet because of that. I was like, "We're getting married because we want to get married. If you want to help me with that, okay, later, but don't say that that's the reason." It makes me feel bad thinking that other people are going to say, "Oh, she's just looking for the papers."

Michelle reluctantly agreed to look into the process of regularizing through marriage, but only because she had been convinced her boyfriend truly wanted to be with her. The last time I spoke with the couple, however, little had changed. Michelle was so overwhelmed by the thought that people judged her in this manner that she had little motivation to engage seriously with the opportunity.

Olivia, on the other hand, had similar feelings the first few years I knew her, but ultimately decided to go through with the process. Olivia had DACA and was married to a U.S. citizen, but refused to get papers through him because of his family's suspicion about her motives even years later. As described in Chapter 3, she told her husband the day they got married, "I'm not marrying you because I want a legal status, I married you because you are the love of my life, because I want a family." She was adamant that, even though she could easily just get a lawyer and file the paperwork, it didn't feel like the right way for her. This all changed, however, following the 2016 election and the rapid increase in anti-immigration policies and rhetoric:

> Over time I feel more pressured that it's something that I have to do, regardless if I'm okay with it or not. I am being pressured by what's going on with politics. I feel more cornered to proceed that way, more than I did a year ago, with everything that's going on in politics and the fact that my mom's getting older. God forbid, if she were to get sick, the first thing she's going to do is want

to see her parents in Mexico, and who would she go with? Nobody. The fact is, with a permanent resident status I will be able to travel out of the United States. And now that I am making more money, and we bought some land and want to start a family, I need to think about the future.

In a quite different scenario, Brian and his girlfriend, Norma, had planned on getting married for some time; they had been together since starting college and had set a date more than a year in advance so that all their extended family and friends could attend the wedding. Brian had DACA, so was able to take advantage of a process known as "advance parole" to speed along the approval process. Advance parole allows a person to leave the country and receive advance authorization to reenter the United States (to be "paroled") on their return. The USCIS only granted advance parole to DACA recipients if the travel abroad is in furtherance of: (1) humanitarian purposes (e.g., to obtain medical treatment, attend a relative's funeral services, or visit an ailing family member); (2) educational purposes (e.g., study-abroad programs and academic research); or (3) employment purposes (e.g., foreign assignments, conferences, or trainings). Like several other DACA recipients I met, Brian was approved for advance parole to visit his elderly and ailing grandparents in Mexico. Since travel for "vacation" purposes was not a valid basis for advance parole, he had to provide statements by his grandparents' physicians attesting to their deteriorating health status. Within three weeks of applying and paying the $575 administrative fee, he traveled to Mexico for a week and was reunited with his grandparents for the first time in fifteen years.

Advance parole offers a unique advantage during regularization: For those who first entered the country without inspection (that is, the "hard way"), obtaining legal status can be difficult because of the three- and ten-year bars. However, because of the authorization to reenter legally, advance parole essentially provides them with a fresh stamp in their passport and a fresh start. This now-lawful entry allows them to proceed much more easily with the adjustment of status needed to become a permanent resident, without being subject to the bars and with a much quicker timeframe for approval.

A year later, after getting married to Norma, Brian began the adjustment of status process. He told me,

> Right now it's $1,070, just for the appointment to get a hearing. And then it's like $2,000, plus the lawyer's fees, which are like $750. I can do the paperwork by myself. I did the advance parole application myself, but then I saw a lot of

people with packages that were like really thick, and I'm like I don't want to mess up, you know? You have to be careful and fill out everything right, because if you miss something, *te van a rechazar*, they will reject it. You're going to have to pay again and you're going to lose your money. So, we don't want to risk it.

Justin was the first person I met who was able to petition for adjustment of status through a same-sex marriage. This was a new possibility following the 2013 U.S. Supreme Court decision in *United States v. Windsor*, holding that Section 3 of the Defense of Marriage Act (DOMA) is unconstitutional, paired with the 2015 ruling in *Obergefell v. Hodges*, which upheld same-sex couples' fundamental right to marry and requiring all fifty states to perform and recognize marriages of same-sex couples. "With the possibility of DACA getting taken away" after the 2016 election, he told me, "my partner started talking about marriage." He continued,

> We always talk about our future. He always says, "Oh, we should travel, we should go to Europe. Once we get married." We've been together for over three years now, so we have talked about those things. After the Supreme Court decision, now that it is a possibility. We talked with an immigration lawyer about same-sex marriage, and she said it is the exact same process; nothing is special or unique about it. It's the same thing. Our relationship is not different from any other relationship. It's filled with love.

When I saw Justin again the following year, he already had received his permanent residency status and had just bought a new house together with his partner. While they still hadn't traveled to Europe, they were planning a belated honeymoon there the following year.

From Undocumented to DACAmented: Precarious Status

The most common status transition for the families in this book was the opportunity that arrived with DACA. This allowed youth and young adults to move from an undocumented status to one that offered temporary protection from deportation and a two-year, renewable work permit. Twenty-six-year-old Adrian remembered well the day he received his approval letter. He had forgotten to go to the mailbox one day, but rushed out early the next morning:

> I actually got it on Christmas. So my mom was like, "Aw, it's your Christmas present!" I remember I opened it, and I was like wow, you know, this is it!

[laughs] I couldn't believe that such a small thing makes such a big difference. I was real excited. It was a huge relief. Especially for my mom. I could see that it was a huge relief for her because she knew that I didn't have any limitations anymore when it came to education.

The 2012 executive order by President Barack Obama that created DACA swiftly and dramatically changed the lives of the many undocumented immigrants who had come to the United States as children. Nearly 790,000 people were approved by the program, with 124,300 in Texas alone, the second highest number in the country behind California.[26] Some 28,000 DACA recipients resided in the Rio Grande Valley.[27] In fact, the Rio Grande Valley contained one of the largest concentrations of DACA-eligible individuals per capita.[28]

How can we take stock of the five years of DACA? By pure coincidence, the data collected for this book covered the full term of the program. When I began these series of studies in late 2012, my intention was to examine mixed-status families. I was very aware of the DACA program, but it was not the focus of my research. However, I soon discovered that the positive impact of DACA on mixed-status families was so enormous that it needed to be accounted for; the increased benefits for entire families were very similar to when U.S. citizens were part of the family. As noted in earlier chapters, DACA recipients assumed important roles and responsibilities in their families—driving those who were not permitted to get a license; supporting their families through internal remittances from their new jobs; using their names and Social Security numbers to secure loans, mortgages, and other services; and even traveling abroad to Mexico as representatives for their parents. In addition, since the study's research assistant was a DACA recipient, we had ongoing conversations with each other and with participants about the program, its processes, pitfalls, and benefits. In some cases, our interviews also became sites of intervention and education, as young adults struggled to understand the opportunities and limitations that came with their new status. Milena often played the dual role of researcher and concerned advocate, sharing resources and advice as needed.

Some have referred to DACA as a "natural experiment," because it provided an opportunity to assess a policy in which people are subjected to different interventions (in this case, arbitrary cut-off dates) when a formal randomization design was not feasible.[29] A number of existing studies have taken stock of DACA in its first years. The National UnDACAmented Research Project

(NURP), a multisited, longitudinal national study, surveyed 2,684 DACA-eligible young adults, followed by 481 in-depth interviews. Their findings shed light on how DACA improved individual lives and boosted local economies.[30] They especially noted the benefits for recipients' psychological well-being, including how it gave them renewed hope and motivation for their futures and a greater sense of belonging in the United States, and how it lessened their fear of authorities and the constant threat of deportation.[31] Other studies have confirmed that DACA had positive effects by increasing labor force participation and income levels.[32] Key findings in a 2016 nationwide survey by United We Dream, the Center for American Progress, and the National Immigration Law Center showed that 95 percent of DACA recipients were working or in school; 48 percent got a job with better working conditions; 63 percent got a better-paying job; 90 percent got a driver's license or state ID; 54 percent bought their first car; and 12 percent bought their first home.[33]

There is simply no doubt as to the success of this program. Participants reported similar social and economic progress, as well as increased well-being. They experienced a profound increase in economic opportunities, such as getting a new job, obtaining a driver's license, opening their first bank account, and obtaining a credit card, but they were also excited specifically about being able to cross the checkpoint and travel to other parts of the United States for the first time.[34] As nineteen-year-old Alan told me, "Everything I've wanted to do, I've accomplished once I got my DACA. All I wanted was a job and to be able to walk across the street without being scared. I don't have to be afraid of being arrested or anything. I can cross the checkpoint and visit family. I just wanted freedom from the cage, you know?"

For many, it offered new hope for the future at a time when their lives seemed to be heading to a dead end. Erin, who was thirty years old and worked as an elementary school teacher, told me,

> I was like, "Why am I going to college when I'm not going to be able to work?" I was going to become a teacher, but I'm not going to be able to teach. I was giving up. Then there was my mom, pushing me, telling me, "No, you keep going. You never know when it's going to happen. Something's going to happen." I was asleep when the announcement about DACA came on. My mom came in and turned the TV on, and there were all these DREAMers holding signs and celebrating. I was crying. I couldn't believe it. I was like, "Wow, here's my opportunity!"

Many, like Erin, transitioned from a situation of hopelessness to thriving in the careers they had always dreamed about. Studies that have examined DACA recipients show that changes to legal status positively impacted mental health and psychological well-being.[35] DACA eligibility was associated with clinically meaningful reductions in symptoms of psychological distress.[36] There are positive emotional consequences of transitioning out of undocumented status for immigrant young adults, and the change from undocumented to lawfully present is associated with better overall health outcomes.

There were several unique regional problems affecting youth in the Rio Grande Valley who applied for the program. One issue related to entries on a Border Crossing Card. This visa became a liability for those who overstayed because they sometimes became ineligible for DACA due to frequent and multiple entries and a lack of clear last entry date. Also, in the Rio Grande Valley there appeared to be more problems with obtaining birth certificates compared to the rest of the country; for example, I met one person who was born in Mexico, but the birth was never registered there because her mother was in transit to the United States at the time. In other cases, people had had home births that were not registered properly. Finally, in this predominantly low-income area, many youth do not move out on their own once they begin college or full-time jobs. As they continued to live with their parents, they often didn't have utility bills or other forms of evidence in their name to show continued residence in the United States. For many, applying for the program was often financially prohibitive, especially if more than one family member was eligible. Families often had to decide which sibling would "go first," based on age, college ambitions, or other factors.

To apply for DACA, one had to be at least fifteen years of age. This coincided with an important rite of passage in Mexican and Mexican American culture: the *quinceañera*. Many families explicitly associated the program with this life transition, so used this money to help finance the application. "When my sister had her *quinceañera* last year, she used the money she got as gifts to apply for DACA," Daniela told me. "We couldn't have done it otherwise. But to her, it was a gift as well, right?" At least one family decided to forgo the party for their daughter and instead pay for applications. As her brother Andres told me, "We had all this money saved up for my sister's fifteenth. Then when DACA came, my dad used the money for both of our applications. So my sister wasn't too upset that they used that money for that. She's like, 'It'll come back.'"

Although the ability to work legally was uniformly mentioned as a major benefit of the program (and income often linked to the ability to do other things, like being able to afford college or medical care), many DACA recipients lacked a strong resume. Daniel, who had earned money for college by selling books at a flea market, said, "It was intimidating, because I knew I was a little bit older than other people applying for their first job, and yet I had no professional work experience. A lot of people would say, 'You're twenty-three and this is your first job?' so it was a little difficult to overcome that stigma. I would just tell them, 'I owned my own business.'" In this way, Daniel attempted to cover his lack of job history and primary participation in the informal market.

Working legally afforded DACA recipients the ability to do something they never had: pay income taxes. Olivia explained why this usually despised activity was something she welcomed: "I was so proud when I did my taxes, because I felt like I was paying my share. That's something that I was excited about." To her, it was a form of participating in U.S. society, a marker that she belonged and could contribute. Olivia and her citizen husband also now had the opportunity to purchase property. As she said,

> My husband and I got half an acre that is now under our name. We already paid it off and have the title. I was able to have it because of DACA. That's another thing I'm very proud of because, eventually, I'll be able to build my own house. It's close to the water. It's really nice. Part of the American Dream is the stability of a home. Because of my future plans, as far as having a family, I myself think that having a home is very important insurance. Having a house is very important to me. It might not be much, I guess, but to me owning a home is a triumph that I'm very proud of.

Activities that, to most people, would seem fairly mundane—such as traveling to another city, getting a first job, paying taxes, building a house, and starting a family—took on enormous significance for DACA recipients. It allowed them "freedom from the cage," as expressed by Alan above, and permitted them to think about long-term plans for the first time in their lives. Even parents reflected on the program's importance in this way. Herminia, mother of two DACA recipients, told me:

> Now that they have DACA, they are more open. They had been hiding in a hole, in the dark, and now they are coming out into the light because they are not afraid if people know they are undocumented. They see that they are like

everyone else. Their personalities are changing, and they are more themselves. They see that other people are in the same situation. And through this, I have become more knowledgeable about the situation in this country. Before, I also thought there were few people in the situation we are in.

However, even before the program was rescinded, it had a dark side. It was only a temporary program, not a legal status, and recipients were subjected to scrutiny, surveillance, and additional costs when they submitted their renewal applications every two years. As Gonzales and Chavez have noted, the constant vacillation between hope and fear engendered by the possibility of immigration reform and the DREAM Act is a major disciplinary practice that informs the subject status of undocumented youth, adding to their levels of stress as it seems to always promise the possibility of change.[37] The unpredictability of the DACA program added to this sense of underlying insecurity, especially as a transition in the U.S. presidency loomed.

In many ways, DACA represented another form of confinement, this time a temporal one. There has been a policy shift in U.S. immigration law from the amnesty of the Reagan period to a proliferation of provisional and precarious statuses.[38] These temporary statuses create "new and pernicious forms of inequality."[39] The renewal process associated with DACA underscores this, as it represents a shift from random encounters with the state and institutions of immigration enforcement to routine surveillance and regulation that lasts indefinitely. As a result, people become documented but are still deportable. This produces a persistent vulnerability and insecurity. Cecilia Menjívar has noted that these forms of "liminal" or temporary legality, now increasingly common in other receiving countries as well, represent a form of internal immigration control that presumably prevents long-term settlement with no opportunities for permanency.[40]

This very precarious status was emphasized by Ricardo, who told me, "To be honest, it still feels the same as before DACA. We're restricted at so many levels, but we get these documents and, alright, we can do all these things now? Yeah, right. They can strip it away whenever they want. That's one of the reasons why I still feel that way, because it can be taken away." This was echoed by Adrian, who in the meantime had become a father (his wife was also a DACA recipient). He told me,

When you're undocumented, you feel hostile. You're never at peace. And having in the back of my mind that they can take away DACA, now it doesn't only affect us, it affects our family. I can't imagine not being able to work again, now that I have a degree and a good job, and I need to support our baby. So you're still in that fear of losing everything you've worked for. And now you've got more to lose.

Since September 2017, the uncertain official duration of the DACA program has ended, but the precariousness associated with it is not over. When the end of the program was announced, it was put in the hands of Congress, but a resolution has been elusive. There were protests, walkouts, petitions, and general outrage, since most Americans supported the program. For DACA recipients, the decision was devastating. During the year prior, we asked recipients to imagine what it would be like if the program were to end. I also spoke with many participants in the days and weeks following the decision to talk about what it meant for them. Twenty-two-year-old Edgar told me,

> I don't know what my life will be like if I had to go back to being undocumented. It's a very dark place. For me, it was. I hated it. When I think about that time, I see I am a different person now. Don't want to be back there ever again. Never ever. Yes, because I been there before and I know exactly what it's going to be like. I don't want to be there, I really, really don't. Once you've tasted being documented, I don't know if you can go back.

Robert, who was working in his dream job as a firefighter because of his DACA work permit, was slightly more optimistic: "I always remember what it was like to be undocumented. Yeah, as soon as I step outside and its burning hot, I'm like I remember being in the fields and hating to be outside. You never forget it. But have I gotten comfortable? Yes. It would be hard to go back, but we'll make it work. We'll find a way."

Dead Ends in the Regularization Process

While I spoke with many who were able to go through the regularization process and become lawful permanent residents, or who qualified for DACA as a temporary path to start realizing their dreams, I also met many people who did not qualify for any kind of relief, who were simply not able to fix their papers. This occurred for a diverse set of reasons.

For many, money was a major barrier. Many families experience "sticker shock" at the massive expense that immigration processing incurs.[41] At the cost of $4,000–7,000, many people had to save for a very long time, while others took out loans. As Evelyn explained, "The problem is money. The lawyer charges you to do the paperwork, and it goes on for a long time and costs more and more. Some people get loans, but most people without papers have no credit, so either you don't qualify or they give you a very high interest rate." Indeed, the costs for legalizing status are often out of reach for many mixed-status families.

Others had simply "timed out" of their opportunities. This was most often the case because they had reached an age ceiling that terminated eligibility or because they had gotten married. In these cases, sponsorship via a family member became impossible, even with creative attempts. Camila and her sister were adopted by their grandmother, who is a U.S. citizen. "But we couldn't qualify to get our residency through her after all," she told me, "because we had turned eighteen by the time the whole adoption process was over. We just fell out of the category again." The two were also not eligible for DACA because of the timing of their entry to the United States: "We have gone in and out of categories like three times. We have tried a lot of things and nothing works. We're always missing one little thing and don't qualify." Similarly, Miguel tried to legalize his sister, Selena, but found out that he had missed an important deadline to list her as a dependent while she was still young enough: "I tried to fix her papers while I was in the military, in Afghanistan, and I couldn't because my sister was already eighteen. If she would have been younger, I would have been able to put her as my dependent and fix her papers. But since she was over eighteen, I couldn't."

Vanessa, at age forty, was too old to apply for DACA, which stipulated a maximum age of thirty years. She had another channel for legalization, but that also did not work out. She explained, "My mom is a U.S. citizen by derivation. Her grandmother spoke English and was from San Antonio. Her father was born in Mexico, but the law that said if you were a citizen and had a child abroad, they are automatically a citizen. So she and all of her siblings became American citizens by derivation." Derivation is the process by which a person can receive U.S. citizenship even if they are born abroad, under certain circumstances. This is the same process that was described earlier in the chapter, recently heard by the U.S. Supreme Court due to its differential treatment of unmarried men and women. Vanessa continued, "I didn't qualify, because I was already an adult and married." In the case of gaining citizenship through her mother, who in turn had received it later in life after discovering the derivation process,

Vanessa had timed out both because of her age and because of her marital status, so she could not be included on her mother's application.

In other cases, individuals faced a three- or ten-year bar and were unwilling to go to Mexico, thus opting to end the process altogether. Jennifer, a U.S. citizen who wanted to petition for her parents, told me, "We've already talked to an attorney. My parents have a ten-year ban since they didn't cross with a visa. But ten years is a long time. And if my parents go to Mexico, my little siblings would have to go with them. My little brother wouldn't fit in, and we're really paranoid that something might happen to him. We've heard a lot of cases where kids are being kidnapped." Jennifer's mother, Juana, weighed in and affirmed, "It's just not reasonable for us to go to Mexico for ten years. It's better that we wait for some kind of immigration reform."

On the other hand, those who entered the "easy way" on a visa (most commonly the Border Crossing Card) and overstayed it often had to seek out what, if any, official record of their exits and entries to the United States existed. If there were any, they too faced the three- or ten-year bar. This sleuthing was made possible using a request under the Freedom of Information Act (FOIA) and usually involved sending simultaneous requests to multiple government offices, including the USCIS, the Department of Homeland Security, and Immigration and Customs Enforcement. As Gerardo told me,

> It was our error. We still had our valid laser visa. We could still go back and forth to Reynosa. It was my mistake, and it is still affects me to this day. The lawyer told us, "There are ways that they can prove that. You committed an offense, an infringement of the law, if you left and reentered the country after being here for more than six months. It is like trying to deceive the government." Right now we are using a FOIA request to see if there were any exits registered at the bridge [border]. If exits were registered later than the six months we were given on the visa, it ends up being the same as if you had signed a voluntary departure order. There is no pardon, and we would face the bar, which could be ten years.

Even when FOIA requests come back "clean," sometimes other records are left undiscovered that can offer unpleasant surprises for applicants and their lawyers. For example, as Gerardo noted, "Since our children used Medicaid, they can see exactly what dates we were here." It is unclear whether or not this information is actually used when parents try to regularize their status, but the underlying fear remained.

Others were stuck in a Catch-22 if they had made certain administrative mistakes. For example, one person had checked the "U.S. citizen" line in her college application ten years earlier because she did not fit into one of the other two categories provided (permanent resident or international applicant with a student visa). Her lawyer explained to her that would now be evaluated as "impersonating a U.S. citizen" if she tried to file paperwork to change her immigration status. As a form of identity fraud, which is a federal offense, it would immediately put her into deportation proceedings. As noted in Chapter 2, there are cases of "identity loan," where parents, for instance, borrow their U.S.-citizen children's name or Social Security number for a utility bill or driver's license. Since the law has no mechanism to account for this kind of social exchange within a family, the consequences can be devastating—it can terminate people's ability to gain lawful status.

Several lawyers explained to me that their clients' petitions for U.S. citizenship had been denied because they had been registered to vote at some point, a privilege afforded only to full citizens (not to legal permanent residents). In almost all cases, they had been registered without their knowledge, either by employees at the Department of Motor Vehicles when they obtained their driver's license—the lawyers speculated that, rather than being ignorant, these employees might have known full well the consequences—or by overzealous community organizers conducting door-to-door voter registration campaigns. Regardless of their knowledge or permission, this counted as impersonating a U.S. citizen and could lead to a denial of their case and even a deportation order.

Lastly, deportation spelled the end of any opportunities to legalize status. Twenty-five-year-old Manuel had been deported, so despite being married to a U.S. citizen he could not regularize via his spouse. As noted earlier in the chapter, his brother Eric was able to legalize his parents. This meant that, out of the entire family, only Miguel was left out of the opportunity, due to his prior deportation. Similarly, Michelle's younger sister was going to fix her father's papers, but after the entire family's deportation following a jealous neighbor's denunciation (discussed in Chapter 7), that all changed: "My dad lost the opportunity when they deported him. And we're like, why? We've been living here our whole lives, he has an honest job, he's raising three girls by himself."

Deportation and convictions of deportable offenses trigger an "irreversible chain of events that ends in permanent banishment from the United States."[42] This underscores the growing linkage between U.S. immigration and criminal justice systems—often termed "crimmigration"—that reproduces racial and class inequalities but conceals them with putatively race-neutral standards.[43] Furthermore, signing an order of voluntary departure to avoid deportation—common in this region because of the opportunity of expedited removal near the U.S.–Mexico border—also has severe consequences that prohibit future legalization. This disproportionate targeting of undocumented Mexicans for criminal immigration violations jeopardizes their ability to regularize their status in the future.

"Ya te crees mucho": Social Hierarchies Created Through Status Differences

For those who succeed in obtaining some form of relief, other perils loom: jealousy, stratification, and hierarchies that are created through changes in legal status. While this book has traced stratification in mixed-status families, here I specifically refer to situations in which an individual's lot improves because they were able to become a citizen or a permanent resident, or obtain DACA. Vanessa, a forty-year-old mother of four U.S. citizens, describes her extended family in the following way: "Half of my family has papers, and the other half doesn't. But unfortunately the half that is already legal sometimes discriminates, because they think they are better than us." She continued,

> I have a friend, a neighbor, who just fixed her papers. Before that, she was a modest person, but I have seen how having papers changed her. She's the same person, of course, but now she calls the police on everybody for every little thing, like if your dog walks on her property. She calls the police when she didn't before, because now she has papers, you know what I mean?

Twenty-three-year-old Carmen, who had received DACA, talked about some of the impacts of her new status: "Now I'm not scared anymore. I feel comfortable. I feel 'white' in some ways. We joke about it, my friends say, '*Ah, ya te crees mucho porque tienes papeles*' [Now you think you're all that because you have papers]," she laughed. In fact, several participants used that exact phrase, *ya te crees mucho*—which translates as "you think very highly of yourself," or perhaps "you think you're all that"—to describe people's reaction to their improvement in status. While this phrase is usually said jokingly, it also hides envy and to some degree social disapproval as one person sets themselves apart from the group.[44] Carmen also associates both "being comfortable" and being seen as "better" than others with being "white." This, too, reflects the perpetual racialization of immigration laws and practices and hierarchy of perceived social acceptance, with undocumented immigrants the least accepted, followed by those with DACA, and then lawful permanent residents and U.S. citizens, the latter category frequently conflated with whiteness.[45] (In a similar demonstration of the conflation with whiteness, in Chapter 2, twenty-three-year-old Adrian recalled how when he received DACA, his parents and siblings jokingly called him "gringo.")

By drawing lines between the "deserving" and "undeserving," immigration and citizenship laws produce insidious social hierarchies. This deservingness distinction has especially entered popular and political discourse since DACA was announced. Advocacy for this program, and for the larger DREAM Act project, has built popular support because it posits that undocumented children and young adults of the 1.5 generation are not responsible for their plight. Politicians and the larger American public have supported these efforts because it is a convincing and poignant argument: it is not their fault, they did not ask to be brought to the United States, they are innocent. However, this line of reasoning depends on another set of complementary actors: their parents, who by default become culpable, even criminal, by their very participation in the migration event.

This inequality is further entrenched when socially valued behaviors are added, such as attending college or not having a criminal record. College-goers, in particular, have been able to galvanize merit-based deservingness by highlighting the tension between their achievements and the legal barriers in their paths to success.[46] A focus on these high achievers leaves many others out, who become viewed as undeserving of protection, so have less political support. High achievers, only a fraction of the population of undocumented youth, do not reflect the many complications and complexities of immigrants' lives. As Gonzales has noted, this strategy is vulnerable to "slippage," as the same people who gain public sympathy because they are viewed as "innocent" children and youth eventually grow up.[47] On the other hand, in some scenarios DREAMers have been able to flip the script on this and craft a new message. Rather than framing parents as guilty, they can be framed as responsible and courageous for their decision to seek out a better life for their children.[48] As many said to me, "My parents are the *true* dreamers."

The flip side of this phenomenon is survivor's guilt. It is not uncommon for people who are able to regularize their status to avoid seeming boastful or creating feelings of bitterness or resentment.[49] This was especially common with DACA, as youth frequently pointed out that they still worried about their undocumented parents and siblings. For instance, twenty-two-year-old Edgar told me, "With DACA I would say we had some fresh air in our lives. But my parents are still in that undocumented place. They're still there." As noted earlier in the book, this often meant that people who could now do new things, like travel, held back for fear of creating resentment or "showing off" in front of their undocumented family members.

This "survivor's guilt" even led some to consider leaving the United States altogether. If not everyone in the family could benefit from these opportunities, they reckoned, it might be better just to return. Melanie was one of the U.S. citizens who grew up knowing her role in the family as a future petitioner for regularization of status. During the course of this study, she had successfully gone through the process with her father. But she told me that, after her father became a permanent resident, he was conflicted about his new status because his wife was still undocumented and had no chance for fixing her papers:

> A lot has changed for him since becoming a resident. But he doesn't feel comfortable until my mom can do the same. I told him, "Let's go to Mexico to visit your brothers," and he was like, "I'm not going without your mom. I can't leave her here." I guess he feels guilty. He was telling me the other day, "I was talking to your mom about moving back to Mexico. Soon we will be in our sixties, and there's no point in us living here. We can't travel, we can't do anything." Whereas if they were to go back, they could come visit us, travel anywhere in the world with their Mexican passport. My dad also said, "We're super poor here. It's no different from living over there." Isn't that ironic? He just got his residency, and now, because of my mom's situation, he really feels like it's all not worth it.

Fixing Papers in Mixed-Status Families

"Fixing papers," or undergoing status regularization, is a major preoccupation in mixed-status families. It represents simultaneously the possibility of release from the grip of illegality as well as a shift from avoiding immigration authorities to exposing oneself fully and submitting to prolonged, willful surveillance. In fixing their papers, mixed-status families' intimate relationship with the law becomes most apparent, and the construction of illegality for some members continues to influence others as they become involved with legal procedures. Immigration processing is truly a family affair. U.S. citizen children grow up with the knowledge that they will be called upon to fix a parent's or sibling's papers. This impacts their own subjectivity and the dynamics of the family, sometimes leading to unusual power configurations—with the future fate of individuals often in the hands of the youngest members—and even role reversals between parents and children. In the course of petitioning for a family member, however, U.S. citizens may also discover that their own rights to family are not absolute, and the process can leave them feeling powerless and as if their own citizenship has been delegitimized. Even when someone is able to fix their papers, they may face teasing, discrimination, or guilt as hierarchies are created within families when one person can legalize but others cannot.

Mixed-status families actively strategize in ways that can mitigate the exhausting process of fixing papers. When U.S. citizens are able to petition for their parents' or siblings' legal status, they are empowered through the process that allows them to actively assist. It provides feelings of relief and the ability to be at peace. Marriage to a citizen can also function as a way for individuals to obtain legal status, but this is often contested, as people are reluctant to do so if it means others will believe the marriage is a sham. They may resist the opportunity to make life easier by gaining legal status, all to show commitment to the relationship first. Another strategy to hasten the legalization process for family members is for U.S. citizens to join the military, since the "parole in place" program allows them to apply for family members' permanent residency without having first to leave the country. Additionally, the legalization process may be sped up for those with DACA if they are able to leave and then reenter the United States after having been approved for advance parole. This lawful entry allowed some individuals to become permanent residents much easier, without being subject to the bars, and with a much quicker timeframe for approval.

The uniqueness of the region shapes the experiences of mixed-status families when tackling the legalization process. In the Rio Grande Valley, the mode of entry (the "hard way" or the "easy way") is highly variable compared to many other parts of the United States, with both options impacted by geography and availability of the Border Crossing Card. Mode of entry greatly impacts possibilities for legalization. Region also impacted possibilities for temporary relief under the DACA program, with unique issues impacting the application process, such as multiple entries with the Border Crossing Card, use of midwives who may not have formally registered the birth, and general lack of funds and evidence because of endemic poverty.

CONCLUSION

Know that we are people like you, families like yours, just with limitations. Our voices are silenced, so you have to listen harder. But when you do hear us, as you see people's pain, what are you going to do with that information? Make it public. Sitting in the classroom, you can't understand the lives of the people who are sweating and suffering outside. People have to hear it firsthand. Otherwise it's like they're watching a different movie than the one we live in, and there's no direct relationship to their own lives.

THESE WERE THE WORDS of fifty-nine-year-old Martín Mendoza, who has lived in the United States since the early 1990s with his wife and three children. For most of this time, he lived "in the shadows," like many of the other estimated eleven million undocumented persons. Martín recently received permanent residency status after one of his citizen children petitioned for him, but his wife remains undocumented. His eldest son had Deferred Action for Childhood Arrivals (DACA) status, but lost it when the program ended. His middle and youngest children are U.S. citizens. Martín has always held a steady, modest job, and paid off the land he and his wife purchased many years ago. He and his family have been active participants in their community, involved with schools, churches, gyms, environmental organizations, and art clubs, and engaging in ample volunteer work. His three children graduated with degrees from the local university and have since moved on to professional employment outside the Rio Grande Valley. Martín's story is not uncommon, but it exemplifies the ways in which mixed-status families are incorporated into life in the United States. Like other families in this book, the Mendoza family has experienced ups and downs: changes in legal status, including returns to illegality; sending children off to college and watching them graduate after a few struggles along the way; purchases of land, vehicles, and other property, all riddled with uncertainty; protection through deferred action but also deportation that threatened the very foundation of their family; and ongoing anxiety about shifts in federal immigration policies.

This book has complicated the idea of living "in the shadows" as it is used in scholarly and popular discourse. It portrays mixed-status families as resilient, socially engaged, and living as active members of their communities, while at the same time recognizing their profound marginalization. Families like Martín's are complexly and deeply integrated into the social fabric of the United States, but they are also decisively rejected from it. The daily lives of some 16.7 million people in mixed-status families are marked by precarity and exclusion. Some might ask: If people are suffering so much, why not return to their country of origin? As this book has illustrated, people have planted deep roots in the United States. Their children, siblings, spouses, grandparents, grandchildren, cousins, aunts, uncles, nieces, nephews, in-laws, godchildren, and/or godparents may be U.S. citizens or lawful permanent residents. They have become integral parts of local communities, investing time, energy, and money in the futures of those communities. Conditions in their home country continue to be challenging and marked by instability, and for many, their connections to Mexico are fragile after living in the United States for decades. Human social relations are infinitely more complex than artificially delineated borders and constructions of citizenship.

When I began the research that forms the basis of this book, things were beginning to look up for the families I got to know. The DACA program had come into effect, revitalizing young DREAMers' outlook on life and opening new doors for education, employment, and well-being. Their families had reason to be optimistic. A few years later, in 2014, President Obama announced a similar program, Deferred Action for Parents of Americans and Lawful Permanent Residents (DAPA), which would have benefited parents in mixed-status families. The same executive order expanded the number of people eligible for DACA to include those who arrived later or were previously excluded by the age ceiling. Together, these programs would have allowed an additional four million people to remain in the country with a work permit and protection from deportation.

But the programs were never implemented. A federal district court in Brownsville, Texas, issued a preliminary injunction, blocking DAPA and the expanded DACA program in response to a legal challenge brought by Republican lawmakers. The actual focus of the case was quite mundane: the state of Texas argued that it would suffer significant financial damages if required to subsidize the cost of driver's licenses to the large numbers of people qualifying under the new programs. The larger political context, however, was an unwillingness to allow the president to enact policy change via executive orders, despite years of blocked and failed efforts at immigration reform in the halls of Congress.

Following the injunction—issued, astonishingly, by a court located in the Rio Grande Valley, giving this research an unforeseen and bittersweet turn—people took to the streets. Alongside many of the people in this book, Milena and I joined protests in front of the United States Courthouse in Brownsville, where we held signs proclaiming, "Keep families together," "DON'T DEPORT MY MOM," "Our Families Deserve Justice! #Fight4DAPA" "FAMILIES BELONG TOGETHER," and "#HereToStay." Once back at my desk, I frenetically wrote policy briefs and op-eds, arguing for the benefits of these programs on mixed-status families, including the 4.5 million U.S.-citizen children. But the blocked initiatives, I argued, would have offered only temporary relief in an immigration system long overdue for major reforms. They signaled an urgent need to provide a solution for immigrant families, which would allow people to go to school and work, thereby boosting their contributions to society.[1]

Following an appeal of the case, the U.S. Supreme Court heard *United States v. Texas* in June 2016 but was unable to reach a decision. It deadlocked in a 4–4 tie. This unusual but not unexpected outcome was the result of the vacancy left following the death of Justice Antonin Scalia and reflected the politically divisive nature of the case. Since the deadlock affirmed the lower court's judgment "by an equally divided Court," the two initiatives remained blocked until the Trump administration formally and quietly rescinded them in 2017.[2] This disappointing and anticlimactic outcome was overshadowed by other even more drastic efforts by a president whose formal entry into politics was marked by xenophobia, racism, and anti-immigrant rhetoric—as well as an eagerness to physically separate children from their parents newly arrived at the border.

The remaining pages summarize the scholarly and policy implications of the issues presented in this book. While they reveal the uniqueness of this "buffer zone" along the border, they also have significance for an increasingly bordered U.S. interior. From the outset, this engaged anthropological research was committed to social justice and to informing public policymaking through robust, theoretically grounded findings. This work represents both a form of social critique—that is, by uncovering the structures of injustice and inequality—as well as a form of advocacy, supporting the struggles of the families whose lives are laid bare here.[3]

The Construction of Illegality Impacts Everyone in a Family

The stories presented here speak to critical concerns in the study of law and migration by highlighting legal status as a major axis of stratification. Historically in law and policy, immigrants were treated as "Americans in waiting" and were assumed to be on a trajectory toward, or in transition to, full citizenship.[4] However, as the construction of the "illegal alien" became central to U.S. immigration policy, new ideologies and practices related to race, citizenship, and state authority have emerged. Over time, undocumented persons became "impossible subjects," persons whose presence is a social reality paired with a perpetually unattainable legal existence.[5] The book's primary argument is that the construction of illegality for some members in a family influences opportunities and resources for everyone, with spillover effects even for legal residents and U.S. citizens. These occur at multiple levels, including through institutions, relationships with authorities, social interactions, and the formation of individuals' subjectivities.

Within larger institutions, the concept of bureaucratic disentitlement helps explain the effects of illegality on members of a mixed-status family. This refers to insidious practices by which administrative agencies deprive individuals of their statutory rights or entitlements by complicating processes, withholding information, providing misinformation, or isolating them. Several examples in the book have illustrated these practices, beginning with the denial of a birth certificate for Michelle's U.S.-citizen baby in the introductory chapter. Schools are an important site of bureaucratic incorporation, often very tolerant of irregularities that children and parents from mixed-status families bring with them and enacting inclusive practices to lessen their impacts. However, other experiences in schools may be explicitly hostile, such as bullying or demeaning comments, like those of a teacher who called Rosa's daughter a *mojada*. Undocumented students may be excluded through institutional practices such as assignments that require travel, or when they are left out of college application workshops in contrast to their citizen siblings. Parents may experience discrimination when enrolling citizen children for services to which they are entitled, as Juana discovered in applying for the Children's Health Insurance Program (CHIP). In this case, the social worker threatened to report the family to immigration authorities if they didn't withdraw their application. Through bureaucratic disentitlement, a variety of institutions—ranging from vital statistics offices, public schools, and sites of application assistance for state and federal programs—actively block the incorporation of mixed-status families.

Incorporation is also impacted by aggressive immigration enforcement practices. Deportation critically affects the economic and emotional base of the family unit. The condition of deportability is insidious not because deportations are a common occurrence but because there is always the potential for them to occur. Deportation regimes are profoundly efficient in provoking fear through a combination of targeting a few people while fostering an enduring sense of danger and fragile existence for many. As a result of this everyday threat, children in mixed-status families grow up worrying about the apprehension of parents or siblings, which fosters chronic stress. The fear of denunciation, that someone will report their parents or siblings to authorities, is ever-present and impacts their willingness to trust others. They may wonder: What will happen to me if my parents are deported? Living with uncertainty shapes their confidence in the constancy of their surroundings. Distrust in law enforcement further impacts public safety and the secure foundations of entire neighborhoods, as people may be afraid to call the police to report crimes.

Social relationships are also affected by the illegality of family members. There may be resentment toward parents or jealousy toward siblings as individuals are faced with different life opportunities. People may feel like they live a double life and improvise with "little lies" in order to hide the family's legal status. As a result of these forms of concealment, friendships may be threatened, and differences in legal status can create tensions between romantic partners. Feelings of embarrassment, shame, or fear affect people's ability to form strong and trusting social bonds.

As these stories have shown, a person's subjectivity—their everyday sense of being in the world—is acutely affected when they are part of a mixed-status family. Several U.S. citizens relayed in their stories that they "felt undocumented too" by virtue of their family members' status. Some, like Jennifer, were even shocked when they found out they were *not* undocumented. Children in the family may develop a lasting fear of law enforcement, become afraid of driving, or live with a heightened sense of existential precarity. Undocumented siblings may grow up feeling like they are valued less than their citizen siblings. Role reversals and peculiar power dynamics emerge as citizen children (often the youngest in the family) have disproportionate influence and access to more resources. They become the family representatives by putting important documents in their names or by traveling abroad to maintain kin ties in Mexico. At the same time, they may harbor guilt or limit their own activities—such as recreational travel or attending college out of state—because they don't want to accentuate divisions within the family.

These stories illuminate the lived experiences of inequality that are produced by legal regimes, contributing to scholarship on the practices of citizenship and the penetration of the contemporary state into institutions of kinship. These concerns are set within a larger body of work on the processes of intergenerational transmission of legal status.[6] U.S. citizens in mixed-status families have frequently been derided as "anchor babies" and treated as a threat to the nation; because their parents are assumed to have broken the law to arrive, their very birth is unacceptable and castigated as a "pull factor" for additional immigration. As a result, they become "suspect citizens," often construed as undeserving of full citizenship, and may not develop feelings of belonging to the nation of their birth.[7] However, these processes are not new. The children of immigrants have long held a tenuous place in U.S. society and been characterized as perpetual foreigners.[8] Thus, such constructions must be understood within broader histories of power and patterns of marginalization. They are a logical outcome of racial and ethnic exclusions that are fundamental to the U.S. nation-state project.[9]

A related set of processes can be seen in the growing public support for undocumented youth raised in the United States. Despite being legally excluded, DREAMers have successfully obtained recognition for their humanity by demonstrating identification with the values and norms of the nation.[10] Because they have framed their experience as that of de facto Americans, the broader public has increasingly supported the notion that an injustice has been committed against youth with certain positive attributes (that is, well-integrated, educated, and law-abiding). Because of their ability to fit into this national community, they have assumed the most prominent position among undocumented immigrants. However, this simultaneously accentuates stigma toward other groups, magnifying any negative attributes. Ultimately, DREAMers' collective political power is constrained precisely by the reproduction of certain ideals of citizenship.[11]

The stories in these pages do not intend to valorize citizenship. As I have shown, U.S.-born citizens can be disenfranchised by a family member's illegality; however, these experiences occur in relation to and alongside their undocumented parents and siblings. We must continue to trouble the taken-for-granted construct of citizenship, since it is precisely these legal constructions that produce and advance the inequalities presented here.

Contesting Illegality

While illegality impacts everyone in the family, people are not simply passive recipients of this fate. Through their resilience and creative responses, people in mixed-status families actively contest and resist juridical categories and amend the circulating hegemonic structures of meanings concerning the law.[12] As Nando Sigona argues, our attentiveness to the condition of illegality should not result in constructing people as "passive and agency-less subjects overdetermined by structural conditions, or undocumentedness as a homogeneous and undifferentiated experience."[13] It would be an injustice to the families in this book if I did not also show the ways they adapt routines and mundane social interactions to the circumstances of their precarious lives.

This book highlights agency in particular through its focus on family unity. The overwhelmingly common response by families living with status uncertainties is to stick together and solve problems cooperatively. These include mundane strategies to share financial resources, such as splitting bills or allocating particular responsibilities based on legal status. Enormous effort is put into fostering the education of the next generation, which families viewed as the ticket out of poverty and out of the lingering effects of illegality. Responding to the lack of access to medical care, people share medications within the family and with others in their community, seek out cross-border care, use home remedies, or engage with alternative providers. In response to the threat of family separation through deportation, mixed-status families plan in advance, arranging for family members to be smuggled back and organizing childcare with relatives or friends. They may formalize fostering arrangements through power-of-attorney paperwork or even transfer custody of children. They also advance plan for legal battles in case of detention, with cash, folders of paperwork, and an attorney on hand. They strategize to keep family property intact in the case of deportation, by transferring mortgages to U.S.-citizen children. Preparation for deportation resembles the preparation of a last will and testament—and indeed deportation represents a form of social death—as families transfer property and assign guardians for their children, often completely reorganizing their family structure for legal purposes.

Resilience also fosters political resistance and the pursuit of legal remedies. Undocumented parents successfully sued the state of Texas when it refused to issue birth certificates to them. Activism and community organizing in South Texas *colonias* has resulted in safer, healthier neighborhoods and has answered anti-immigrant policies and proposals with large-scale protests and media attention. To counter stigma, empower themselves, and educate others, undocumented youth tell their stories in public or disclose status in order to humanize discussions. U.S. citizens like Jennifer advocate for immigrant rights and seek employment in fields such as immigration law, where they use their own experiences to help others. Citizen children like Sarah's son stick up to bullies, while undocumented parents like Rosa meet with school counselors and principals to demand respect for their families. People turn to social media to create community and to share information in response to bureaucratic disentitlement or in response to enforcement tactics, informing others of the location of roadblock checkpoints. In public protests, parents and children draw upon intimate ties to challenge deportability and demand an end to family separation. Youth mobilization helped galvanize support for DACA, and they continue to fight for more permanent and just policy solutions.

As the writing for this book comes to a close, several people in its pages are in Washington, DC, occupying congressional offices to demand a permanent solution for DREAMers. They drove twenty-six hours from the Rio Grande Valley without stopping, only to switch drivers. On social media, they pose proudly and defiantly in front of the Washington Monument and take group selfies in the Rotunda of the Russell Senate Office Building, wearing bright orange coordinated T-shirts to show their unity. Their cause enjoys broader public support than ever, despite an otherwise deeply politically divided country and immigration debates in the media that have brought their border homeland into a largely unfavorable national spotlight.[14]

Place Matters

Finally, configurations of illegality and their effect on incorporation are geographically specific and historically contingent.[15] This book has argued for the analytical significance of place by focusing on the U.S.–Mexico borderlands, specifically the geopolitical "buffer zone" created in the Rio Grande Valley of South Texas. The stories presented here have been attentive to a unique regional context and its impact on the everyday incorporation experiences of mixed-status families. The border remains an analytically powerful construct for examining patterns of inclusion and exclusion and is an important reminder of the enduring territorial authority of the state. Borders are not just static lines of spatial demarcation, full of walls and fences and checkpoints. They are also dynamic and inhabited places full of people.

The border region is a place where immigration policies can be put under a microscope, because their effects are experienced more discordantly than in the interior of the country. The 100-mile buffer zone produces a geographic boundedness of daily life, with people describing being "trapped in a cage," "stuck on an island," "*encerrados*," or living "in a jail with a beach." Mixed-status families in this region experience stuckness and immobility, unable to travel outside the region together, which hampers shared experience and the maintenance of social ties with kin in other part of the United States. Wasted potential results as students are unable to attend colleges past the checkpoint (for undocumented youth) or because they are unwilling to leave family members behind (in the case of U.S. citizens). Bordering processes create extreme barriers to receiving specialized medical care, resulting in stratified opportunities for well-being and life expectancy. Daily life is filled with surveillance, exemplified by routinized Border Patrol presence and its accompanying technologies—sensors, drones, aerostat radar systems, and coordination of information with local law enforcement departments. Immigration enforcement agents are also deeply embedded in local communities, with many people counting them among their family, friends, neighbors, and teachers. At the same time, deportation is swifter than elsewhere and lacks due process. Physical and social movement is constrained through larger bordering processes that may be violent and racialized. While racial profiling is complex when the majority population consists of Latinos, the checkpoints construct all residents, including U.S. citizens, as suspect. These practices thus contribute to the reformulation of citizenship and social membership more broadly.[16]

However, this binationally oriented zone also opens up unique possibilities for inclusion. Many people have families on both sides of the Rio Grande, and proximity to the international boundary facilitates frequent travel and exchange through the Border Crossing Card. Mixed-status families in South Texas find that their legal status challenges are shared in common with others in their community. Being undocumented is frequently an open secret. As a result, people's identities are complex: undocumented Mexicans may feel like citizens because of their high levels of incorporation in the United States, while U.S. citizens may more readily identify as Mexican because of feelings of racialized exclusion from the nation. And then there are a range of deeply significant compound or blended identities (e.g., American Mexican, Mexican American, or Latinx) as well as regional ones (e.g., Tejana).

As a case study, this region can offer lessons to the rest of the United States on two issues: (1) the incorporation experiences of a growing demographic—namely, people living in mixed-status families; and (2) the impacts of increased interior immigrant enforcement on communities. Sets of policy recommendations emerge as a result, with implications beyond the border region.

Policy Implications

At the beginning of this chapter, Martín stated, "Our voices are silenced, so you have to listen harder." This is the very foundation of meaningful ethnographic work, which seeks to witness everyday experience, and is crucial in the project of "humanizing" migration. By uncovering the deep, layered consequences of immigration laws for families, we can work toward policies that lift people up rather than exacerbate inequalities and inhumanity.

Engaged scholarship must be valuable for the public sphere. Ethnographic work can highlight the complex and diverse social realities in order to inform policy debates. This book illustrates the effects of illegality on families with the goal of redirecting contemporary political discussions with the understanding that anti-immigrant policies do not only affect the undocumented. In doing so, it extends prior analyses to focus on the impacts on the social unit of the family rather than on individuals. This shift in the analytical unit is valuable in other areas beyond immigration. For instance, it can help policymakers understand the true social impacts of mass incarceration in a criminal justice system that is clearly in need of reform. The United States has the highest rate of incarceration in the world, and more than half of those incarcerated are parents of minor children. In an era of social exclusion and limited economic prospects of those convicted, our current laws and practices remove individuals from their social networks rather than building upon or restoring them. As more people become ensnared in a cycle of criminalization through policing practices in low-income neighborhoods and targeting people of color, the life-long effects of incarceration are felt not only by the convicted but also by their families and communities.[17] This issue links back directly with immigration policies. Reentry after deportation is now the leading charge in sending people to federal prison. As a result, these practices of criminalization disproportionately impact precisely those individuals who have existing ties to the United States and who are compelled to reunite with family members by attempting re-entry.

The stories from the border presented here in some ways offer an exceptional case study of incorporation of immigrant families. However, this region also represents a harbinger, a potential "canary in the coal mine" that can offer lessons to the rest of the United States. Around the country, communities are seeing increased immigration enforcement that relies on interior controls such as traffic stops and coordination with local agencies. As illustrated here, the result is racial profiling, fear, and distrust in law enforcement, in addition to the diversion of resources from local authorities' primary duty of keeping communities safe. In addition, because immigration enforcement widely profiles the population during daily activities (for example, driving to work or school), it treats all residents—citizens and lawful permanent residents included—as potentially suspect. As initiatives like 287(g) continue, more communities and more residents will be affected. Policymakers must strongly consider the civil rights implications of these arrangements, especially given the history of high cost to localities, patterns of racial profiling, and trail of pretextual arrests. It is also time for the "100-mile" rule utilized by U.S. Customs and Border Protection (USCBP)—which allows agents to stop and search automobiles, busses, trains, aircraft, or other vehicles—to be seriously scrutinized by federal lawmakers. It has been generally been invoked to defend practices along the U.S.–Mexico border, highlighting its arbitrary and potentially discriminatory implementation. This practice has been on the rise elsewhere and is part of a larger pattern of increased surveillance of all residents as USCBP claims sweeping authority to operate in in the interior of the United States.

One compelling question remains: Do the long-term effects of illegality persist even after that illegality is reversed? Some researchers have argued that the negative effects of illegal status are not as permanent and wide-ranging as those of race, for instance, and that with legalization significant intergenerational gains can be made in areas like educational attainment.[18] However, in other areas, especially health, there is greater potential for long-term and enduring effects of early trauma, anxiety, and impacts on well-being. Further, as this book has argued, the effects of illegality are not limited to those who are undocumented; disadvantages for U.S. citizens have been a constant cautionary message throughout. Part of the reason why this question can be better explored now is a demographic one: never before have so many citizen children affected by parental illegality come of age as in our current historical moment. More research following the outcomes of the members of mixed-status families is needed to better understand the reproduction of inequalities across generations and its implications for education and health policy.

Despite its temporary nature, DACA equalized many relationships, responsibilities, and roles within families, making recipients more like their U.S.-citizen siblings by offering them the opportunity to work, become geographically mobile, and liberating them from the constant fear of deportation. It augmented the economic security of their families, increased their sense of belonging to the United States, and, for the first time, offered real hope for the future. The status shift out of illegality for these young adults was so impactful that any expectation that they return to that state is especially cruel. While additional comprehensive accountings of DACA are still needed, future studies should also examine the effects of its rescindment on entire families. During the study that informs this book, participants were asked to imagine what their lives would be like if DACA were taken away; their responses indicate that it would be qualitatively different than if they had simply been undocumented the entire time. As Edgar said, "Once you've tasted being documented, I don't know if you can go back." A return to illegality is devastating as it cuts off people's livelihoods, life chances, and dreams, not only at the individual level, but for their families as well.

The recent trend toward granting temporary and precarious statuses has only underscored immigrants' inequalities and impossibilities. The production of categories of liminal legality and semi-membership, as well as the persistent hope for immigration reform, adds significantly to the insecurity experienced by the families in this book. Any legal remedy simply cannot be a temporary or provisional one. While this book has focused on the spatial confinement of life in the border region, there is also a temporal confinement that occurs through programs like DACA or Temporary Protected Status (TPS), which put people in legal limbo or liminal legality for periods of uncertain duration.[19] These forms of temporary reprieve and ongoing surveillance presumably seek to discourage long-term settlement and attachment to the United States. However, the experiences of recipients prove that their commitment and contributions to society greatly outweigh any negative implications, and thus granting permanent legal status would be a more beneficial policy solution.

The most equitable solutions for improving the well-being of all members of mixed-status families involve some pathway to legal, permanent residency status. Citizenship, as a legal construct, is not a scarce resource; the limits of this category are equally invented. However, appealing to citizenship as the only solution also perpetuates inequalities. Any measure must steer clear of invoking existing hierarchies of deservingness, or producing new ones, by focusing on citizenship as the goal. By drawing lines between the "deserving" and "undeserving," citizenship laws can produce insidious social hierarchies. Scholars, advocates, and policymakers must avoid doing the same. As long as there is a category of people deemed "undeserving," changes in the political tide can shift the discourse to cast all immigrants as such.[20] We must resist framing only U.S. citizens in mixed-status families as a priority for interventions, because doing so privileges the very idea of citizenship that produces violence on their families. We must resist framing undocumented youth brought to this country as children as innocent, because this line of reasoning depends on the vilification of their parents, who by default become culpable and even criminal. We must resist valorizing only those individuals who have been able to adhere to traditional norms of success and exhibit socially valued behaviors, such as attending college or not having a criminal record. And we must resist narrow definitions of the family that are not inclusive of all types.

Family unity is the very foundation of immigration law in the United States. That it is widely accepted as such became quickly apparent in the widespread challenges to a new policy decision to separate children from their parents upon arrival at the U.S.–Mexico border. This directive to prosecute them criminally for illegal entry into the United States was a shift from prior enforcement practices, and a clear attack on the principle of family unity. Americans from across the political spectrum viewed these separations as acts of cruelty rather than justice and support a fundamental and moral right to family unity. Proposals to cut the number of family-based visas (in an effort to "end chain migration," for example) further undermine family unity as the basis of a values-driven immigration system. Reuniting with family members, or petitioning for legal status for the ones already here, is a complex and lengthy process that should not create additional barriers to stabilizing generations of American families.

We must all listen harder in order to craft a compassionate, humane immigration system that proactively keeps families together.

NOTES

Introduction

1. The Head Start program is a federally funded, comprehensive child development program available for children from low-income families between zero and five years old.

2. Pew Research Center 2016.

3. Preston 2016.

4. Grimes 2016.

5. Danz 2000: 1006. See also Joseph and Marrow 2017; López 2005; Marrow 2011a, 2012.

6. Chavez 2017.

7. Suárez-Orozco et al. 2011.

8. See Chavez 2007, 2014; De Genova 2002; Willen 2007. I use the term in quotation marks in this first usage to indicate it is a construct; for readability, I have dropped them afterwards, but they remain implied. Further, I have opted to utilize the term "undocumented" in the book, as it is likely to be the most familiar to readers (as opposed to irregular, extralegal, unauthorized, or clandestine migrants, all of which are precise in their own ways and in particular contexts). While I agree with De Genova that the term "migrant" should generally supplant "immigrant" in order to "problematize the implicitly unilinear teleology of these categories" (2002: 420–421), particularly from the standpoint of the migrant-receiving nation-state, I utilize "immigrant" in various places in the book when referring to participants' own accounts and trajectories or in reference to specific laws and policies.

9. Gomberg-Muñoz 2016: 150. See also Inda and Dowling 2013.

10. Abrego and Menjívar 2011.

11. Luibhéid, Andrade, and Stevens 2017.

12. Sigona 2012; Silbey 2005.

13. An estimated 100,000 persons in a county of 849,843, or 11.7 percent of the population (Migration Policy Institute 2016).

14. Dorsey and Díaz-Barriga 2015.

15. Mathema 2016, based on an analysis of the 2010–2014 American Community Survey.

16. See Passel 2011; Warren and Kerwin 2017; Wasem 2012. Estimates range from 2.3 to 4.6 million, depending on source and definition of family/household, and these numbers have grown since some estimates were calculated.

17. Capps, Fix, and Zong 2016; Warren and Kerwin 2017.

18. Passel 2011.

19. Boehm and Terrio 2018.

20. Zayas 2015.

21. Passel 2011.

22. De Leon 2015; Nevins 2008.

23. That is, unmarried son and daughters (Travel.State.Gov 2018).

24. Gonzales 2015: 36.

25. Suárez-Orozco et al. 2011.

26. Mangual Figueroa 2012; Menjívar and Abrego 2009; O'Leary and Sanchez 2011.

27. De Genova 2002; Willen 2007.

28. Boehm 2008; Romero 2008.

29. See also Boehm 2012; Coutin 2003, 2007; Heidbrink 2014; Heyman 2002.

30. Luibhéid, Andrade, and Stevens 2017: 17. See also Hordge-Freeman 2015.

31. Ibid.: 21.

32. Boehm 2012.

33. On studies of immigrant families, see, e.g., Boehm 2008; Coe 2011; Hondagneu-Sotelo and Avila 1997; Parreñas 2005. On the incorporation experiences of the second generation, see, e.g., Foner 2009; Kasinitz et al. 2008; Portes and Rumbaut 2001.

34. Heidbrink 2014.

35. Chavez 1988.

36. PewHispanic.org 2010.

37. Gomberg-Muñoz 2016.

38. Tsing 2015: 2.

39. Foner 2009.

40. Alber, Coe, and Thelen 2013.

41. O'Leary and Sanchez 2011.

42. Heidbrink 2014.

43. Migration Policy Institute 2016.

44. This was used as method explicitly during an NSF-funded portion of the research project that focused on forty families; however, during the first two data collection periods (2013–2015), multiple family members were interviewed as well.

45. Melo 2017a, 2017b.

46. See explanation above; not all phases of the project included two to five people per family.

47. Gonzales 2015: 28.

48. Participant confidentiality is of utmost importance. The privacy of the families in this book is protected by the use of pseudonyms; I have changed all names and personally identifying details. Additionally, in a few cases, details of their stories were omitted or changed to make them less recognizable.

Chapter 1. Belonging in the Borderlands

1. Throughout, I use the conventional grammatical use of Latino/Latina. However, Spanish, like other Romance, Germanic, Greek, Celtic, and Slavic languages, contains an implicit gendered bias, particularly in the use of the masculine noun and pronoun when referring to groups of people. To achieve gender neutrality and greater inclusivity, many have advocated for terms like "Latinx."

2. Migration Policy Institute n.d.

3. Ibid.

4. Center for Public Policy Priorities 2017.

5. Migration Policy Institute n.d.

6. Gonzales and Ruiz 2014.

7. Ibid.; Marrow 2011a; Schmalzbauer 2014.

8. Dauvergne 2008; Heyman 2008, 2010; Hollifield 2004; Sassen 2000; Stuesse and Coleman 2014.

9. Garcia 2006; Heyman 1991; Vélez-Ibáñez 1996.

10. O'Leary and Sanchez 2011.

11. Valerio-Jiménez 2013.

12. Heyman and Symons 2012.

13. Vilanova 2002.

14. Ibid.

15. Coleman and Stuesse 2013.

16. Government Accountability Office 2017.

17. Cresswell 2006: 735.

18. Sheller and Urry 2006.

19. Blunt 2007: 2; Winton 2015.

20. Massey, Durand, and Malone 2003; Ngai 2014.

21. Ngai 1999.

22. Gonzales 2015: 19.

23. De León 2015; Nevins 2008.

24. Golash-Boza 2015.

25. Macías-Rojas 2016.

26. Gomberg-Muñoz 2016. See also Armenta 2017a; Provine et al. 2016.

27. Heyman 1999.

28. Heyman, Núñez, and Talavera 2009.

29. Nuñez and Heyman 2007.

30. Dorsey and Díaz-Barriga 2015.

31. Passel and Cohn 2017.

32. Gonzales 2015; Warren and Kerwin 2017.

33. Warren and Kerwin 2017.

34. Passel and Cohn 2017.

35. Ibid.

36. The U.S. Department of State (2018) has ranked Tamaulipas as Level-4 risk ("Do Not Travel"), the same as countries such as Afghanistan, Iraq, Libya, and Syria, warning that "violent crime, such as murder, armed robbery, carjacking, kidnapping, extortion, and sexual assault, is common. Gang activity, including gun battles, is widespread. Armed criminal groups target public and private passenger buses traveling through Tamaulipas, often taking passengers hostage and demanding ransom payments. Local law enforcement has limited capability to respond to violence."

37. Luna 2018.

38. Her good friend/children's godmother.

39. Yarris 2017.

40. Warren and Kerwin 2017.

41. Garip 2017.

42. Richardson 1999: 1.

43. Arispe y Acevedo 2009.

44. Garcia 2006.

45. Hendricks 2010.

46. Núñez and Heyman 2007.

47. Nájera 2015.

48. Ibid.: 17.

49. Richardson 1999; Richardson and Resendiz 2006.

50. Harvey 2010.

51. A 2017 report by the Institute on Taxation and Economic Policy indicates that undocumented immigrants contribute an estimated $11.74 billion to state and local coffers each year via a combination of sales and excise, personal income, and property taxes. See Gee et al. 2017.

52. Ura 2016.

53. Richardson 1999.

54. Harvey 2010.

55. Bastida 2001.

56. Heyman and Symons 2012; Richardson and Pisani 2012; Richardson and Resendiz 2006.

57. Díaz-Barriga and Dorsey 2011; Dorsey and Díaz-Barriga 2010.

58. Fleuriet and Castañeda 2017.

59. Dreby 2015; Gonzales 2015.

60. Migration Policy Institute n.d.

61. Aranda, Vaquera, and Sousa-Rodriguez 2015.

62. Ibid.

63. Junior Reserve Officer Training Corps (JROTC) is a federal program sponsored by the U.S. Armed Forces in high schools and also in some middle schools.

64. Díaz-Barriga and Dorsey 2011; Dorsey and Díaz-Barriga 2010.

65. "Tejano/Tejana" refers to someone who is a native of Texas, but also references "America's largest ethnic subregion, Mexican South Texas." Arreloa 2002: 2.

66. Schmalzbauer, in her study of Mexican immigrant families in Montana, also notes that U.S. citizen children of the second generation predominantly consider themselves to be Montanans, not Americans. Their deep social rooting in the local environment means they are best described as "Mexican-Montanans" rather than "Mexican-Americans" (2014: 165).

67. Chavez 2017.

68. Ibid.

69. Flores-González 2017.

70. Ibid.: 117.

71. Ngai 2007.

72. Ngai 2014.

Chapter 2. United Yet Divided

1. See, e.g., Abrego 2014; Boehm 2012; Foner 1997; Foner and Dreby 2011; Glick 2010; Hondagneu-Sotelo and Avila 1997; Parrado, Flippen, and McQuiston 2005; Suárez-Orozco, Todorova, and Louie 2002.

2. Foner 2009; Kasinitz et al. 2008; Portes and Rumbaut 2001.

3. Portes and Rumbaut 2001; Zhou 1997.

4. Horton 2015.

5. Getrich 2019.

6. Migration Policy Institute 2016.

7. Gonzales 2011.

8. Abrego 2006; Abrego and Gonzales 2010; Gonzales, Suárez-Orozco, and Dedios-Sanguineti 2013; Yoshikawa and Kholoptseva 2013.

9. Vaquera, Aranda, and Sousa-Rodriguez 2017 draw on this concept first developed by Giddens 1991.

10. Vaquera, Aranda, and Sousa-Rodriguez 2017.

11. Discussed further in chapter 8.

12. Gonzales 2015.

13. Dreby 2015; Getrich 2019; Schmalzbauer 2014.

14. Horton 2015.

15. Horton 2016b.

16. Vitek, Gutierrez, and Dirrigl 2014.

Chapter 3. "Little Lies"

1. Robert Wood Johnson Foundation 2016.

2. Fleuriet and Castañeda 2017.

3. Gonzales 2015: 217.

4. Gonzales 2011.

5. De Genova 2002.

6. Horton 2016a.

7. Orne 2011. Orne's work focuses on sexual identity disclosure, but his model is particularly apt at capturing the experiences of coming out as undocumented as well. See also Muñoz 2016.

8. On social connections, see Negrón-Gonzales 2013. On interconnectedness, see Vaquera, Aranda, and Sousa-Rodriguez 2017.

9. Gleeson and Gonzales 2012.

10. Passel and Cohn 2016.

11. Center for Public Policy Priorities 2017.

12. Mangual Figueroa 2017.

13. Mangual Figueroa 2011; Valdes 1996.

14. Combs, Gonzalez, and Moll 2011; Mangual Figueroa 2011.

15. Rabin, Combs, and Gonzalez 2009.

16. Gonzales 2015: 96.

17. Ibid.: 118.

18. Dreby 2015: 159–160.

19. Other scholars have documented how regional and class stereotypes, particularly those related to indigeneity, carry over and follow migrants in the United States. See Holmes 2013 and Stephen 2007.

20. *"Fresa"* is a Mexican slang term for people who are higher class and "snobby," or "stuck up."

21. Several cities, counties, and states have proposed or enacted laws, ordinances, regulations, resolutions, policies, or other practices that shield criminals from immigration enforcement activities. This is generally accomplished by refusing to comply with requests for information, imposing conditions on detainer acceptance, denying ICE access to interview incarcerated immigrants, or otherwise impeding information exchanges between their staff and federal immigration officers.

22. Marrow 2011b.

23. Macías-Rojas 2016: 2.

24. Horton 2015.

25. De Genova 2002.

26. Danz 2000.

27. Fix and Passel 2002; Hagan et al. 2003; Huang, Yu, and Ledsky 2006; Pereira et al. 2012.

28. Luibhéid, Andrade, and Stevens 2018.

29. Pila 2016.

30. See also Cebulko 2016.

31. Reina, Lohman, and Maldonado 2013.

32. Pila 2016.

33. Cebulko and Silver 2016.

34. Muñoz 2016; Orne 2011.

35. Vargas 2011. See also Gonzales 2015: 140.

36. In *Lawrence v. Texas* (2003), the U.S. Supreme Court ruled that state laws banning homosexual sodomy are unconstitutional because they are a violation of the right to privacy.

37. See, e.g., *Borderlands/La Frontera: The New Mestiza* (1987) and *This Bridge Called My Back: Writings by Radical Women of Color* (1981).

Chapter 4. *Estamos Encerrados*

1. Lewis 1950.
2. Ibid.
3. Cresswell 2012.
4. Coutin 2010.
5. Mountz et al. 2012.
6. Coleman 2007; Rosas 2006; Stuesse and Coleman 2014.
7. Cresswell 2012.
8. Carling 2002.
9. Coutin 2010.
10. Ibid.
11. Dorsey and Díaz-Barriga 2015.
12. Coutin 2010: 200.
13. Gonzales 2015.
14. Núñez and Heyman 2007.
15. dell'Agnese and Szary 2015.
16. Carling 2002.
17. Government Accountability Office 2017.
18. American Civil Liberties Union n.d.-a.
19. American Civil Liberties Union n.d.-b.
20. Wilson 2002.
21. Ibid.
22. Dorsey and Díaz-Barriga 2015.
23. Ibid.: 217.
24. José David Saldívar (1997) discusses the symbolism of this common phrase, featured in the signature song of Los Tigres del Norte, "La Jaula de Oro" ("The Gilded Cage").
25. Vargas 2011.
26. Vargas 2014.
27. Preston and Tillman 2014.
28. Vargas 2014.
29. Heyman 2010.
30. Stuesse and Coleman 2014.
31. Sheller and Urry 2006.
32. Armenta 2017a; Stuesse and Coleman 2014; Walters 2015.
33. Stuesse and Coleman 2014.
34. Provine et al. 2016.

35. Cebulko and Silver 2016.

36. Perhaps unsurprisingly, a market for illicit driver's licenses was created at the same time. In recent years there have been cases in which DPS staff has facilitated the unlawful issuance of driver's licenses, charging undocumented persons between $1,000 and $5,000 each.

37. See e.g., del Bosque 2013; Taylor 2014.

38. Núñez and Heyman 2007.

39. Aranda and Vaquera 2015; Stuesse and Coleman 2014.

40. Gonzales 2015.

41. Gomberg-Muñoz 2016.

42. Coleman and Stuesse 2016; Stuesse and Coleman 2014.

43. Epp, Maynard-Moody, and Haider-Markel 2017.

44. Stuesse and Coleman 2014.

45. Reyna 2013.

46. Núñez and Heyman 2007.

47. Rosas 2006.

48. Stuesse and Coleman 2014.

49. Coutin 2010.

50. Dorsey and Díaz-Barriga 2015.

Chapter 5. Additional Borders

1. As mentioned in Chapter 1, this high school combines the names of two iconic presidents of Mexico and of the United States respectively, highlighting the binational identity of the region.

2. Fernandez 2011.

3. CBS 4 News Rio Grande Valley 2012.

4. Batalova and McHugh 2010; Migration Policy Institute 2016.

5. "I am Joaquín" is also the title of a famous poem from the Chicano movement in the 1960s. See Rodolfo Gonzales n.d.

6. Portes and Rumbaut 2001; Portes and Zhou 1993. See also Waldinger and Catron 2016 for a conceptual and empirical critique of modes of incorporation.

7. Gonzales 2011: 616.

8. Gonzales 2008.

9. Gonzales 2015.

10. Ibid.: 220.

11. Abrego 2006; Gleeson and Gonzales 2012.

12. Gonzales, Suárez-Orozco, and Dedios-Sanguineti 2013; Yoshikawa and Kholoptseva 2013.

13. Gonzales 2011; Gonzales and Chavez 2012.

14. Gonzales, Suárez-Orozco, and Dedios-Sanguineti 2013: 9.

15. Abrego 2006; Gonzales 2015; Vaquera, Aranda, and Sousa-Rodriguez 2017.

16. Eusebio and Mendoza 2013; Passel 2003.

17. Gonzales 2007.

18. Gonzales 2015.

19. Ibid.

20. Abrego 2006; Castro-Salazar and Bagley 2010.

21. Gonzales 2015.

22. Ibid.

23. See http://rgvfocus.org.

24. The College Assistance Migrant Program (CAMP) is an opportunity through the Department of Education that assists students who are migratory or seasonal farm-workers (or children of such workers) enrolled in their first year of undergraduate studies.

25. The Toward EXcellence, Access and Success Grant Program (TEXAS) provides need-based funding for state residents (including undocumented ones) working on their first degree in an award up to $5,000.

26. Gonzales 2015.

27. *New York Times* 2016.

28. Selby 2015.

29. Díaz-Barriga and Dorsey 2011; Dorsey and Díaz-Barriga 2011.

30. Dorsey and Díaz-Barriga 2011. They also talk about the "necro-citizenship" associated with the deaths of Mexican American service members.

31. Lavariega Monforti and McGlynn 2010.

32. Gonzales 2015.

33. González 2014.

34. U.S. Army n.d.

35. Marcos 2016.

36. Horton 2017.

37. Gonzales 2015: 122.

Chapter 6. Unequal Access

1. Enriquez 2015.

2. Castañeda and Melo 2014; Mangual Figueroa 2012; Menjívar and Abrego 2009; O'Leary and Sanchez 2011.

3. Vargas and Ybarra 2016.

4. Landale et al. 2015; Oropesa, Landale, and Hillemeier 2015; Vargas and Ybarra 2016; Yun et al. 2013.

5. Oropesa, Landale, and Hillemeier 2015.

6. Cavazos-Rehg, Zayas, and Spitznagel 2007; Dreby 2012; Williams 2003.

7. Cavazos-Rehg, Zayas, and Spitznagel 2007; Salas, Ayón, and Gurrola 2013.

8. Viruell-Fuentes, Miranda, and Abdulrahim 2012.

9. Cavazos-Rehg, Zayas, and Spitznagel 2007; Hacker et al. 2011, 2012; Sullivan and Rehm 2005.

10. Torres et al. 2018.

11. Androff et al. 2011; Cavazos-Rehg, Zayas, and Spitznagel 2007; Gonzales, Suárez-Orozco, and Dedios-Sanguineti 2013; Salas, Ayón, and Gurrola 2013; Vargas and Ybarra 2016.

12. Castañeda 2009, 2010; Castañeda et al. 2015; Waters and Pineau 2015.

13. Farmer 1999.

14. Castañeda et al. 2015.

15. Fix and Passel 2002; Hagan et al. 2003; Huang, Yu, and Ledsky 2006; Pereira et al. 2012.

16. Sommers et al. 2012.

17. Abrego and Menjívar 2011; Capps et al. 2004; Hagan et al. 2003; Xu and Brabeck 2012.

18. Vargas 2015; Vargas and Pirog 2016.

19. Castañeda and Melo 2014; Mendoza 2009; Park 2011.

20. Hagan et al. 2003: 459.

21. Hudson 2009.

22. Hagan et al. 2003; Pereira et al. 2012.

23. Fix and Passel 2002; Menjívar and Abrego 2009.

24. Abrego and Menjívar 2011.

25. Enriquez 2015.

26. Willen 2012.

27. Suárez-Orozco et al. 2011: 457.

28. O'Leary and Sanchez 2011.

29. Castañeda et al. 2010; Horton and Barker 2010; Kline 2013.

30. Horton and Barker 2010.

31. Abrego and Menjívar 2011; Menjívar and Abrego 2009.

32. See also Horton and Cole 2011.

33. Dalstrom 2012.

34. See Cunningham et al. 2018; Hellerstein 2014.

35. Mejia Lutz 2018.

36. Ibid.

37. Lee 2016.

38. See, e.g., Abrego 2011; Gonzales, Suárez-Orozco, and Dedios-Sanguineti 2013; Hacker et al. 2011; Potochnick and Perreira 2010.

39. Vargas and Ybarra 2016; Waters and Pineau 2015.

40. Valdez, Padilla, and Valentine 2013; Yoshikawa 2011.

41. Heyman et al. 2009; Maldonado et al. 2013; Rhodes et al. 2015.

42. Torres et al. 2018.

43. Lopez et al. 2017.

44. Patler and Pirtle 2017.

45. See also Abrego and Menjívar 2011; Park 2011.

46. U.S. Citizenship and Immigration Services 2011.

47. Torbati 2018.

48. Gonzales and Chavez 2012.

Chapter 7. Family Separation

1. Valdez, Padilla, and Valentine 2013.
2. Enriquez 2015.
3. Zayas 2015.
4. Hacker et al. 2011.
5. De Genova and Peutz 2010.
6. Capps et al. 2015; Chishti, Pierce, and Bolter 2017.
7. For instance, in her study on undocumented families in New Jersey and Ohio, Joanna Dreby (2015) found that around 20 percent of her respondents or their close family members or friends had experienced a deportation.
8. Nathan 2017.
9. Chaudry et al. 2010; Wessler 2011.
10. Passel, Cohn, and Gonzalez-Barrera 2012.
11. Román González and Zúñiga 2014; Zúñiga and Hamann 2015.
12. Brubeck and Xu 2010; Chaudry et al. 2010; Delva et al. 2013; Gonzales 2011.
13. Horner et al. 2014.
14. Lopez et al. 2017.
15. Allen, Cisneros, and Tellez 2015; Brabeck, Lykes, and Hunter 2014; Suárez-Orozco, Todorova, and Louie 2002.
16. Giddens 1991; Vaquera, Aranda, and Sousa-Rodriguez 2017.
17. Human Impact Partners 2013.
18. Aponte-Rivera and Dunlop 2011; Dreby 2015; Gulbas et al. 2016; Oropesa, Landale, and Hillemeier 2015; Vargas and Pirog 2016; Yoshikawa, Godfrey, and Rivera 2008.
19. Chaudry et al. 2010.
20. Capps et al. 2015.
21. Golash-Boza and Hondagneu-Sotelo 2013.
22. Montero 2017.
23. GoFundMe.com is a website that allows fund-raising for personal causes.
24. See http://notifica.us.
25. Migration Policy Institute n.d.
26. Rios 2011.
27. Slack et al. 2015; Spener 2006.
28. Vogt 2013 cites $1,500–$2,500 as the price to cross the border in 2008.
29. Ibid.

Chapter 8. Fixing Papers

1. I use this phrase throughout the chapter because it best reflects participants' conceptualization of the process.
2. Gomberg-Muñoz 2016: 134.
3. Ibid.: 231.
4. Luibhéid, Andrade, and Stevens 2017.
5. Gomberg-Muñoz 2016; Horton 2017.

6. Gomberg-Muñoz 2016; Menjívar and Kanstroom 2014.

7. Boehm 2012.

8. Gonzales 2015: 225.

9. The only quick and surefire route to lawful immigration is to be either (1) a wealthy investor or (2) the spouse, parent, or minor child of a U.S. citizen living outside the United States.

10. Travel.State.Gov. 2018.

11. Luibhéid, Andrade, and Stevens 2017.

12. Carron 2015.

13. Cacho 2012: 43.

14. Gomberg-Muñoz 2016.

15. Gonzales 2015: 188.

16. Gomberg-Muñoz 2016.

17. Ibid.: 14.

18. Gomberg-Muñoz 2016.

19. Gonzales 2015: 20.

20. Dreby 2015; Gomberg-Muñoz 2016; Schueths 2012, 2014.

21. Gomberg-Muñoz 2016: 115.

22. Ibid.: 96.

23. Suárez-Orozco et al. 2011.

24. U.S. Citizenship and Immigration Service 2013.

25. Pila 2016.

26. U.S. Citizenship and Immigration Service 2017.

27. Migration Policy Institute 2018.

28. Hidalgo County had the third highest number of DACA-eligible persons among counties in the state of Texas, at 21,000 (Migration Policy Institute 2016). However, compared to Harris (68,000) and Dallas (42,000) counties, with their huge metropolitan populations, the density of DACA-eligible persons and program recipients was much higher in the Rio Grande Valley, at approximately 2.5 percent of the total population (compared to 1.4 percent and 1.6 percent respectively).

29. McKee and Stuckler 2017; Venkataramani et al. 2017.

30. Gonzales and Bautista-Chavez 2014.

31. Gonzales and Brant 2017.

32. Pope 2016.

33. Wong et al. 2016.

34. Gonzales, Terriquez, and Ruszczyk 2014.

35. Patler and Pirtle 2017; Venkataramani et al. 2017.

36. Venkataramani et al. 2017.

37. Gonzales and Chavez 2012.

38. Menjívar and Kanstroom 2014.

39. Gomberg-Muñoz 2016: 5.

40. Menjívar 2014.

41. Gomberg-Muñoz 2016: 62.

42. Gonzales 2015: 22.

43. Gomberg-Muñoz 2016: 5.

44. This phrase also appears in numerous Spanish-language memes on the internet.

45. Cebulko 2014.

46. Gonzales 2015.

47. Ibid.: 220.

48. Nicholls 2013.

49. Gomberg-Muñoz 2016: 125.

Conclusion

1. Castañeda 2016.

2. See www.supremecourt.gov/opinions/15pdf/15-674_jhlo.pdf; Department of Homeland Security 2017.

3. Low and Merry 2010.

4. Motomura 2006.

5. Ngai 2014.

6. Abrego 2014; Dreby 2015; Gonzales 2015.

7. Chavez 2017.

8. Ibid.

9. Rosa and Bonilla 2017: 202.

10. Nicholls 2013.

11. Ibid.: 181.

12. Silbey 2005.

13. Sigona 2012: 51.

14. Greenwood 2018; Quinnipiac University 2018.

15. Sigona 2012.

16. Coutin 2010.

17. Alexander 2010.

18. Bean, Brown, and Bachmeier 2015.

19. Menjívar 2006.

20. Gonzales 2015: 219.

REFERENCES

Abrego, Leisy J. 2006. "I Can't Go to College Because I Don't Have Papers": Incorporation Patterns of Latino Undocumented Youth. *Latino Studies* 4(3): 212–231.

———. 2011. Legal Consciousness of Undocumented Latinos: Fear and Stigma as Barriers to Claims-Making for First- and 1.5-Generation Immigrants. *Law & Society Review* 45(2): 337–370.

———. 2014. *Sacrificing Families: Navigating Laws, Labor, and Love Across Borders.* Stanford, CA: Stanford University Press.

Abrego, Leisy J., and Roberto G. Gonzales. 2010. Blocked Paths, Uncertain Futures: The Postsecondary Education and Labor Market Prospects of Undocumented Youth. *Journal of Education for Students Placed at Risk* 15(1): 144–157.

Abrego, Leisy J., and Cecilia Menjívar. 2011. Immigrant Latina Mothers as Targets of Legal Violence. *International Journal of Sociology of the Family* 37(1): 9–26.

Alber, Erdmute, Cati Coe, and Tatjana Thelen. 2013. *The Anthropology of Sibling Relations: Shared Parentage, Experience, and Exchange.* London: Palgrave Macmillan.

Alexander, Michelle. 2010. *The New Jim Crow: Mass Incarceration in the Age of Colorblindness.* New York: New Press.

Allen, Brian, Erica M. Cisneros, and Alexandra Tellez. 2015. The Children Left Behind: The Impact of Parental Deportation on Mental Health. *Journal of Child and Family Studies* 24(2): 386–392.

American Civil Liberties Union (ACLU). n.d.-a. Customs and Border Protection's (CBP's) 100-Mile Radius. Factsheet prepared for the ACLU's Washington Legislative Office. www.aclu.org/other/aclu-factsheet-customs-and-border-protections-100-mile-zone?redirect=immigrants-rights/aclu-fact-sheet-customs-and-border-protections-100-mile-zone.

———. n.d.-b. Know Your Rights: The Government's 100-Mile "Border" Zone Map. https://www.aclu.org/know-your-rights-governments-100-mile-border-zone-map.

Androff, David K., Cecilia Ayón, David Becerra, Maria Gurrola, Lorraine Salas, Judy Krysik, Karen Gerdes, and Elizabeth Segal. 2011. US Immigration Policy and Immigrant Children's Well-Being: The Impact of Policy Shifts. *Journal of Sociology and Social Welfare* 38(1): 77–98.

Aponte-Rivera, Vivianne R., and Boadie W. Dunlop. 2011. Public Health Consequences of State Immigration Laws. *Southern Medical Journal* 104(11): 718–719.

Aranda, Elizabeth, and Elizabeth Vaquera. 2015. Racism, the Immigration Enforcement Regime, and the Implications for Racial Inequality in the Lives of Undocumented Young Adults. *Sociology of Race and Ethnicity* 1(1): 88–104.

Aranda, Elizabeth, Elizabeth Vaquera, and Isabel Sousa-Rodriguez. 2015. Personal and Cultural Trauma and the Ambivalent National Identities of Undocumented Young Adults in the U.S. *Journal of Intercultural Studies* 36(5): 600–619.

Arispe y Acevedo, Baltazar, Jr. 2009. The Geographic and Demographic Challenges to the Regional Institutionalization of the Lower Rio Grande Valley. *Norteamérica* 4(2): 37–69.

Armenta, Amanda. 2017a. *Protect, Serve, and Deport: The Rise of Policing as Immigration Enforcement.* Oakland: University of California Press.

———. 2017b. Racializing Crimmigration: Structural Racism, Colorblindness, and the Institutional Production of Immigrant Criminality. *Sociology of Race and Ethnicity* 3(1): 82–95.

Arreloa, Daniel D. 2002. *Tejano South Texas: A Mexican American Cultural Province.* Austin: University of Texas Press.

Bastida, Elena. 2001. Kinship Ties of Mexican Migrant Women on the United States/ Mexico Border. *Journal of Comparative Family Studies* 32(4): 549–569.

Batalova, Jeanne, and Margie McHugh. 2010. *DREAM vs. Reality: An Analysis of Potential DREAM Act Beneficiaries.* Washington, DC: Migration Policy Institute.

Bean, Frank D., Susan K. Brown, and James D. Bachmeier. 2015. *Parents Without Papers: The Progress and Pitfalls of Mexican American Integration.* New York: Russell Sage Foundation.

Blunt, Alison. 2007. Cultural Geographies of Migration: Mobility, Transnationality, and Diaspora. *Progress in Human Geography* 31(5): 684–694.

Boehm, Deborah A. 2008. "For My Children": Constructing Family and Navigating the State in the U.S.–Mexico Transnation. *Anthropological Quarterly* 81(4): 777–802.

———. 2012. *Intimate Migrations: Gender, Family, and Illegality Among Transnational Mexicans.* New York: New York University Press.

Boehm, Deborah A., and Susan J. Terrio, eds. 2018. *Illegal Encounters: Migration, Detention, and Deportation in the Lives of Young People.* New York: New York University Press.

Brabeck, Kalina, and Qingwen Xu. 2010. The Impact of Detention and Deportation on Latino Immigrant Children and Families: A Quantitative Exploration. *Hispanic Journal of Behavioral Sciences* 32(3): 341–361.

Brabeck, Kalina M., M. Brinton Lykes, and Cristina Hunter. 2014. The Psychosocial Impact of Detention and Deportation on US Migrant Children and Families. *American Journal of Orthopsychiatry* 84(5): 496–505.

Cacho, Lisa Marie. 2012. *Social Death: Racialized Rightlessness and the Criminalization of the Unprotected.* New York: New York University Press.

Capps, Randolph, Michael E. Fix, Jason Ost, Jane Reardon-Anderson, and Jeffrey S. Passel. 2004. *The Health and Well-Being of Young Children of Immigrants.* Washington, DC: Urban Institute.

Capps, Randy, Michael Fix, and Jie Zong. 2016. *A Profile of U.S. Children with Unauthorized Parents.* Washington, DC: Migration Policy Institute.

Capps, Randy, Heather Koball, Andrea Campetella, Krista Perreira, Sarah Hooker, and Juan Mendoza Pedroza. 2015. *Implications of Immigration Enforcement Activities for the Well-Being of Children of Immigrant Families.* Research report prepared for the Migration Policy Institute, September. https://www.urban.org/sites/default/files/alfresco/publication-exhibits/2000405/2000405-Implications-of-Immigration-Enforcement-Activities-for-the-Well-Being-of-Children-in-Immigrant-Families.pdf.

Carling, Jørgen. 2002. Migration in the Age of Involuntary Immobility: Theoretical Reflections and Cape Verdean Experiences. *Journal of Ethnic and Migration Studies* 28(1): 5–42.

Carron, Anna. 2015. Marriage-Based Immigration for Same-Sex Couples After DOMA: Lingering Problems of Proof and Prejudice. *Northwestern University Law Review* 109(4): 1021–1052.

Castañeda, Heide. 2009. Illegality as Risk Factor: A Survey of Unauthorized Migrant Patients in a Berlin Clinic. *Social Science & Medicine* 68(8): 1552–1560.

———. 2010. Im/migration and Health: Conceptual, Methodological, and Theoretical Propositions for Applied Anthropology. *Annals of Anthropological Practice* (formerly *NAPA Bulletin*) 34(1): 6–27.

———. 2016. What Does the Supreme Court's Deadlocked Decision on Deferring Deportations Mean for Immigrant Families? Policy brief prepared for the Scholars Strategy Network, July 1. www.scholarsstrategynetwork.org/brief/what-does-supreme-courts-deadlocked-decision-deferring-deportations-mean-immigrant-families.

Castañeda, Heide, Iraida Carrion, Nolan Kline, and Dinorah Martinez Tyson. 2010. False Hope: Effects of Social Class and Health Policy on Oral Health Inequalities for Migrant Farmworker Families. *Social Science & Medicine* 71(11): 2028–2037.

Castañeda, Heide, Seth M. Holmes, Daniel S. Madrigal, Maria-Elena DeTrinidad Young, Naomi Beyerle, and James Quesada. 2015. Immigration as a Social Determinant of Health. *Annual Review of Public Health* 36: 375–392.

Castañeda, Heide, and Milena A. Melo. 2014. Health Care Access for Latino Mixed-Status Families: Barriers, Strategies, and Implications for Reform. *American Behavioral Scientist* 58(14): 1891–1909.

Castles, Stephen, and Alastair Davidson. 2000. *Citizenship and Migration.* New York: Routledge.

Castro-Salazar, Ricardo, and Carl Bagley. 2010. "Ni de aquí ni from there": Navigating Between Contexts; Counter-Narratives of Undocumented Mexican Students in the United States. *Race Ethnicity and Education* 13(1): 23–40.

Cavazos-Rehg, Patricia A., Luis H. Zayas, and Edward L. Spitznagel. 2007. Legal Status, Emotional Well-Being and Subjective Health Status of Latino Immigrants. *Journal of the National Medical Association* 99(10): 1126–1131.

CBS 4 News Rio Grande Valley. 2012. Joaquin Luna's Mother "Hopeful" About New Immigration Policy for Youth. YouTube video, 08:56, posted June 18. https://www.youtube.com/watch?v=h6QJAG6Ppis.

Cebulko, Kara. 2014. Documented, Undocumented, and Liminally Legal: Legal Status During the Transition to Adulthood for 1.5-Generation Brazilian Immigrants. *The Sociological Quarterly* 55(1): 143–167.

———. 2016. Marrying for Papers? From Economically Strategic to Normative and Relational Dimensions of the Transition to Adulthood for Unauthorized 1.5-Generation Brazilians. *Sociological Perspectives* 59(4): 760–775.

Cebulko, Kara, and Alexis Silver. 2016. Navigating DACA in Hospitable and Hostile States: State Responses and Access to Membership in the Wake of Deferred Action for Childhood Arrivals. *American Behavioral Scientist* 60(13): 1553–1574.

Center for Public Policy Priorities. 2017. State of Texas Children 2017. https://forabettertexas.org/images/2017_SOTC_RioGrande.pdf.

Chaudry, Ajay, Randolf Capps, Juan Pedroza, Rosa Maria Castañeda, Robert Santos, and Molly M. Scott. 2010. *Facing Our Future: Children in the Aftermath of Immigration Enforcement*. Washington, DC: Urban Institute.

Chavez, Leo R. 1988. *Shadowed Lives: Undocumented Immigrants in American Society*. New York: Harcourt Brace College Publishers.

———. 2007. The Condition of Illegality. *International Migration* 45(3): 192–196.

———. 2014. Illegality Across Generations: Public Discourse and the Children of Undocumented Immigrants. In *Constructing Immigrant "Illegality": Critiques, Experiences, and Responses*, edited by Cecilia Menjívar and Daniel Kanstroom, 84–110. Cambridge: Cambridge University Press.

———. 2017. *Anchor Babies and the Challenge of Birthright Citizenship*. Stanford, CA: Stanford University Press.

Chishti, M., S. Pierce, and J. Bolter. 2017. The Obama Record on Deportations: Deporter in Chief or Not? Migration Policy Institute, January 26. http://www.migrationpolicy.org/article/obama-record-deportations-deporter-chief-or-not.

Coe, Cati. 2011. What Is Love? The Materiality of Care in Ghanaian Transnational Families. *International Migration* 49(6): 7–24.

Coleman, Mathew. 2007. A Geopolitics of Engagement: Neoliberalism, the War on Terrorism, and the Reconfiguration of US Immigration Enforcement. *Geopolitics* 12(4): 607–634.

Coleman, Mathew, and Angela Stuesse. 2014. Policing Borders, Policing Bodies: The Territorial and Biopolitical Roots of U.S. Immigration Control. In *Making the*

Border in Everyday Life, edited by Reece Jones and Corey Johnson, 33–63. Farnham, UK: Ashgate.

———. 2016. The Disappearing State and the Quasi-Event of Immigration Control. *Antipode* 48(3): 524–543.

Combs, Mary Carol, Norma Gonzalez, and Luis C. Moll. 2011. US Latinos and the Learning of English: The Metonymy of Language Policy. In *Ethnography and Language Policy*, edited by Teresa L. McCarty, 185–204. New York: Routledge.

Correa, Jennifer G. 2013. "After 9/11 Everything Changed": Re-formations of State Violence in Everyday Life on the US–Mexico Border. *Cultural Dynamics* 25(1): 99–119.

Correa, Jennifer G., and James M. Thomas. 2015. The Rebirth of the U.S.–Mexico Border: Latina/o Enforcement Agents and the Changing Politics of Racial Power. *Sociology of Race and Ethnicity* 1(2): 239–254.

Coutin, Susan Bibler. 2003. *Legalizing Moves: Salvadoran Immigrants' Struggle for U.S. Residency*. Ann Arbor: University of Michigan Press.

———. 2007. *Nations of Emigrants: Shifting Boundaries of Citizenship in El Salvador and the United States*. Ithaca, NY: Cornell University Press.

———. 2010. Confined Within: National Territories as Zones of Confinement. *Political Geography* 29: 200–208.

Cresswell, Tim. 2006. The Right to Mobility: The Production of Mobility in the Courtroom. *Antipode* 38(4): 735–754.

———. 2012. Mobilities II: Still. *Progress in Human Geography* 36: 645–653.

Cunningham, Scott, Jason M. Lindo, Caitlyn Myers, and Andrea Schlosser. 2018. How Far Is Too Far? New Evidence on Abortion Clinic Closures, Access, and Abortions. National Bureau of Economic Research Working Paper No. 23366. http://www.nber.org/papers/w23366.

Dalstrom, Matthew. 2012. The Mexican Health Care Solution? American Anthropological Association blog on *Huffington Post*, August 22. www.huffingtonpost.com/american-anthropological-association/mexico-health-care-tourism_b_1729100.html.

Danz, Shari M. 2000. A Nonpublic Forum or a Brutal Bureaucracy? Advocates' Claims of Access to Welfare Center Waiting Rooms. *New York University Law Review* 75(4): 1004–1044.

Dauvergne, Catherine. 2008. *Making People Illegal: What Globalization Means for Migration and Law*. Cambridge: Cambridge University Press.

De Genova, Nicholas, and Nathalie Puetz. 2010. *The Deportation Regime: Sovereignty, Space, and the Freedom of Movement*. Durham, NC: Duke University Press.

De Genova, Nicholas P. 2002. Migrant "Illegality" and Deportability in Everyday Life. *Annual Review of Anthropology* 31: 419–447.

del Bosque, Melissa. 2013. DPS Checkpoints Create Fear, Havoc in the Rio Grande Valley. *Texas Observer*, October 4. www.texasobserver.org/dps-checkpoints-create-fear-havoc-rio-grande-valley.

De León, Jason. 2015. *The Land of Open Graves: Living and Dying on the Migrant Trail*. Berkeley: University of California Press.

Dell'Agnese, Elena, and Anne-Laure Amilhat Szary. 2015. Borderscapes: From Border Landscapes to Border Aesthetics. *Geopolitics* 20(1): 4–13.

Delva, Jorge, Pilar Horner, Ramiro Martinez, Laura Sanders, William D. Lopez, and John Doering-White. 2013. Mental Health Problems of Children of Undocumented Parents in the United States: A Hidden Crisis. *Journal of Community Positive Practices* 13(3): 25–35.

Department of Homeland Security. 2017. Rescission of Memorandum Providing for Deferred Action for Parents of Americans and Lawful Permanent Residents ("DAPA"). Fact sheet released June 15. www.dhs.gov/news/2017/06/15/rescission -memorandum-providing-deferred-action-parents-americans-and-lawful.

Díaz-Barriga, Miguel, and Margaret Dorsey. 2011. Border Walls and Necro-Citizenship: The Normalization of Exclusion and Death on the U.S.–Mexico Border. In *The American Wall,* edited by Maurice Sherif, 17–23. Austin: University of Texas Press.

Dorsey, Margaret E., and Miguel Díaz-Barriga. 2010. Beyond Surveillance and Moonscapes: An Alternative Imaginary of the U.S.–Mexico Border Wall. *Visual Anthropology Review* 26(2): 128–135.

———. 2011. Patriotic Citizenship, the Border Wall, and the "El Veterano" Conjunto Festival. In *Transnational Encounters: Music and Performance at the U.S.– Mexico Border,* edited by Alejandro L. Madrid, 207–227. Oxford: Oxford University Press.

———. 2015. The Constitution Free Zone in the United States: Law and Life in a State of Carcelment. *Political and Legal Anthropology Review* 38(2): 204–225.

Dreby, Joanna. 2012. The Burden of Deportation on Children in Mexican Immigrant Families. *Journal of Marriage and Family* 74(4): 829–845.

———. 2015. *Everyday Illegal: When Policies Undermine Immigrant Families.* Berkeley: University of California Press.

Enriquez, Laura E. 2015. Multigenerational Punishment: Shared Experiences of Undocumented Immigration Status Within Mixed-Status Families. *Journal of Marriage and Family* 77(4): 939–953.

Epp, Charles R., Steven Maynard-Moody, and Donald Haider-Markel. 2017. Beyond Profiling: The Institutional Sources of Racial Disparities in Policing. *Public Administration Review* 77(2): 168–178.

Eusebio, Catherine, and Fermín Mendoza. 2013. *The Case for Undocumented Students in Higher Education.* Oakland, CA: Educators for Fair Consideration.

Farmer, Paul. 1999. *Infections and Inequalities: The Modern Plagues.* Berkeley: University of California Press.

Fernandez, Manny. 2011. Disillusioned Young Immigrant Kills Himself, Starting an Emotional Debate. *New York Times,* December 10, A25. http://www.nytimes .com/2011/12/11/us/joaquin-luna-jrs-suicide-touches-off-immigration-debate .html.

Fix, Michael E., and Jeffrey S. Passel. 2002. *Lessons of Welfare Reform for Immigrant Integration.* Washington, DC: Urban Institute. http://www.urban.org/url.cfm?ID =900497.

Fleuriet, K. Jill, and Heide Castañeda. 2017. A Risky Place? Media and the Health Landscape in the (In)secure U.S.–Mexico Borderlands. *North American Dialogue* 20(2): 32–46.

Flores-González, Nilda. 2017. *Citizens But Not Americans: Race and Belonging Among Latino Millennials.* New York: New York University Press.

Foner, Nancy. 1997. The Immigrant Family: Cultural Legacy and Cultural Changes. *International Migration Review* 31(4): 961–974.

———, ed. 2009. *Across Generations: Immigrant Families in America.* New York: New York University Press.

Foner, Nancy, and Joanna Dreby. 2011. Relations Between the Generations in Immigrant Families. *Annual Review of Sociology* 37: 545–564.

Garcia, Maribel. 2006. Life Along the NAFTA Highway: Transnational Living Strategies on the US/Mexico Border. *Cultural Dynamics* 18(2): 139–161.

Garip, Filiz. 2017. *On the Move: Changing Mechanisms of Mexico-U.S. Migration.* Princeton, NJ: Princeton University Press.

Gee, Lisa Christensen, Matthew Gardner, Misha E. Hill, and Meg Wiehe. 2017. *Undocumented Immigrants' State and Local Tax Contributions.* Report for the Institute on Taxation and Economic Policy, March. https://itep.org/wp-content/uploads/ITEP-2017-Undocumented-Immigrants-State-and-Local-Contributions.pdf.

Getrich, Christina. 2019. *Border Brokers: Children of Mexican Immigrants Navigating U.S. Society, Laws, and Politics.* Tucson: University of Arizona Press.

Giddens, Anthony. 1991. *Modernity and Self-Identity: Self and Society in the Late Modern Age.* Redwood City, CA: Stanford University Press.

Gleeson, Shannon, and Roberto Gonzales. 2012. When Do Papers Matter? An Institutional Analysis of Undocumented Life in the United States. *International Migration* 50(4): 1–19.

Glick, Jennifer E. 2010. Connecting Complex Processes: A Decade of Research on Immigrant Families. *Journal of Marriage and Family* 72(3): 498–515.

Golash-Boza, Tanya Maria. 2015. *Deported: Immigrant Policing, Disposable Labor, and Global Capitalism.* New York: New York University Press.

Golash-Boza, Tanya Maria, and Pierette Hondagneu-Sotelo. 2013. Latino Immigrant Men and the Deportation Crisis: A Gendered Racial Removal Program. *Latino Studies* 11(3): 271–292.

Gomberg-Muñoz, Ruth G. 2016. *Becoming Legal: Immigration Law and Mixed-Status Families.* Oxford: Oxford University Press.

Gonzales, Roberto G. 2007. *Wasted Talent and Broken Dreams: The Lost Potential of Undocumented Students.* Washington, D.C.: Immigration Policy Center.

———. 2008. Left Out But Not Shut Down: Political Activism and the Undocumented Student Movement. *Northwestern Journal of Law and Policy* 3(2): 219–239.

———. 2011. Learning to Be Illegal: Undocumented Youth and Shifting Legal Contexts in the Transition to Adulthood. *American Sociological Review* 76(4): 602–619.

———. 2015. *Lives in Limbo: Undocumented and Coming of Age in America.* Berkeley: University of California Press.

Gonzales, Roberto G., and Angie M. Bautista-Chavez. 2014. *Two Years and Counting: Assessing the Growing Power of DACA*. Special report prepared for the American Immigration Council. https://www.americanimmigrationcouncil.org/research/two-years-and-counting-assessing-growing-power-daca.

Gonzales, Roberto G., and Kristina Brant. 2017. Analysis: DACA Boosts Young Immigrants' Well-Being, Mental Health. NBC News, June 15. https://www.nbcnews.com/news/latino/amp/analysis-daca-boosts-young-immigrants-well-being-mental-health-n772431.

Gonzales, Roberto G., and Leo R. Chavez. 2012. "Awakening to a Nightmare": Abjectivity and Illegality in the Lives of Undocumented 1.5-Generation Latino Immigrants in the United States. *Current Anthropology* 53(3): 255–281.

Gonzales, Roberto G., and Ariel G. Ruiz. 2014. Dreaming Beyond the Fields: Undocumented Youth, Rural Realities and a Constellation of Disadvantage. *Latino Studies* 12(2): 194–216.

Gonzales, Roberto G., Carola Suárez-Orozco, and Maria Cecilia Dedios-Sanguineti. 2013. No Place to Belong: Contextualizing Concepts of Mental Health Among Undocumented Immigrant Youth in the United States. *American Behavioral Scientist* 57(8): 1174–1199.

Gonzales, Roberto G., Veronica Terriquez, and Stephen P. Ruszczyk. 2014. Becoming DACAmented: Assessing the Short-Term Benefits of Deferred Action for Childhood Arrivals (DACA). *American Behavioral Scientist* 58(14): 1852–1872.

Gonzales, Rodolfo C. n.d. I Am Joaquin. Latinamericanstudies.org, http://www.latinamericanstudies.org/latinos/joaquin.htm.

González, Daniel. 2014. Undocumented Immigrants May Be Allowed into Military. AZcentral.com, September 26. www.azcentral.com/story/news/2014/09/26/undocumented-immigrants-may-allowed-military/16304969.

Government Accountability Office. 2017. *Border Patrol: Issues Related to Agent Deployment Strategy and Immigration Checkpoints*. Report to Congressional Requesters. GAO-18-50.

Greenwood, Max. 2018. Poll: Nearly 9 in 10 Want DACA Recipients to Stay in US. *The Hill*, January 18. http://thehill.com/blogs/blog-briefing-room/news/369487-poll-nearly-nine-in-10-favor-allowing-daca-recipients-to-stay.

Grimes, Andrea. 2016. Texas Relents on Birth Certificates for Children of Undocumented Immigrants. *Texas Observer*, July 25. https://www.texasobserver.org/texas-birth-certificate-settlement.

Gulbas, Lauren E., Luis H. Zayas, Hyonwoo Yoon, Hannah Szlyk, Sergio Aguilar-Gaxiola, and Guillermina Natera. 2016. Deportation Experiences and Depression Among U.S. Citizen-Children in Undocumented Mexican Families. *Child: Care, Health, and Development* 42(2): 220–230.

Hacker, Karen, Jocelyn Chu, Lisa Arsenault L., and Robert P. Marlin. 2012. Provider's Perspectives on the Impact of Immigration and Customs Enforcement (ICE) Activity on Immigrant Health. *Journal of Health Care for the Poor and Underserved* 23(2): 651–665.

Hacker, Karen, Jocelyn Chu, Carolyn Leung, Robert Marra, Alex Pirie, Mohamed Bra-himi, Margaret English, Joshua Beckmann, Dolores Acevedo-Garcia, and Robert P. Marlin. 2011. The Impact of Immigration and Customs Enforcement on Immigrant Health: Perceptions of Immigrants in Everett, Massachusetts, USA. *Social Science & Medicine* 73(4): 586–94.

Hagan, Jacqueline, Nestor Rodriguez, Randy Capps, and Nika Kabiri. 2003. The Ef-fects of Recent Welfare and Immigration Reforms on Immigrants' Access to Health Care. *International Migration Review* 37(2): 444–463.

Hannam, Kevin, Mimi Sheller, and John Urry. 2006. Mobilities, Immobilities and Moorings. *Mobilities* 1(1): 1–22.

Harvey, Mark. 2010. Welfare Reform and Household Survival in a Transnational Com-munity: Findings from the Rio Grande Valley, Texas. *The Applied Anthropologist* 30(1–2): 19–26.

Heidbrink, Lauren. 2014. *Migrant Youth, Transnational Families, and the State: Care and Contested Interests*. Philadelphia: University of Pennsylvania Press.

Hellerstein, E. 2014. The Rise of the DIY Abortion in Texas. *The Atlantic Monthly*, June 2014. http://www.theatlantic.com/health/archive/2014/06/ the-rise-of-the-diy -abortion-in-texas/373240/.

Hendricks, Tyche. 2010. *The Wind Doesn't Need a Passport: Stories from the U.S.–Mexico Borderlands*. Berkeley: University of California Press.

Heyman, Josiah McC. 1991. *Life and Labor on the Border: Working People of Northeast-ern Sonora, Mexico, 1886–1986*. Tucson: University of Arizona Press.

———. 1999. United States Surveillance over Mexican Lives at the Border: Snapshots of an Emerging Regime. *Human Organization* 58(4): 429–437.

———. 2002. U.S. Immigration Officers of Mexican Ancestry as Mexican Americans, Citizens, and Immigration Police. *Current Anthropology* 43(3): 479–507.

———. 2008. Constructing a Virtual Wall: Race and Citizenship in U.S.–Mexico Border Policing. *Journal of the Southwest* 50(3): 305–333.

———. 2010. The State and Mobile People at the U.S.–Mexico Border. In *In Class, Con-tention, and a World in Motion*, edited by Winnie Lem and Pauline Gardiner Barber, 58–78. Oxford: Berghahn Books.

Heyman, Josiah McC., Guillermina Gina Núñez, and Victor Talavera. 2009. Health-care Access and Barriers for Unauthorized Immigrants in El Paso County, Texas. *Family and Community Health* 32(1): 4–21.

Heyman, Josiah McC., and John Symons. 2012. Borders. In *A Companion to Moral Anthropology*, edited by Didier Fassin, 540–557. Malden, MA: Wiley-Blackwell.

Hollifield, James F. 2004. The Emerging Migration State. *International Migration Review* 38(3): 885–912.

Holmes, Seth. 2013. *Fresh Fruit, Broken Bodies: Migrant Farmworkers in the United States*. Berkeley: University of California Press.

Hondagneu-Sotelo, Pierrette, and Ernestine Avila. 1997. "I'm Here, But I'm There": The Meanings of Latina Transnational Motherhood. *Gender and Society* 11(5): 548–571.

Hordge-Freeman, Elizabeth. 2015. *The Color of Love: Racial Features, Stigma, and Socialization in Black Brazilian Families.* Austin: University of Texas Press.

Horner, Pilar, Laura Sanders, Ramiro Martinez, John Doering-White, William Lopez, and Jorge Delva. 2014. "I Put a Mask On": The Human Side of Deportation Effects on Latino Youth. *Journal of Social Welfare and Human Rights* 2(2): 33–47.

Horton, Alex. 2017. U.S. Army Kills Contracts for Hundreds of Immigrant Recruits: Some Face Deportation. *Washington Post*, September 15. https://www.washington post.com/news/checkpoint/wp/2017/09/15/army-kills-contracts-for-hundreds -of-immigrant-recruits-sources-say-some-face-deportation/?utm_term= .95e92b8cfad5.

Horton, Sarah B. 2015. Identity Loan: The Moral Economy of Migrant Document Exchange in California's Central Valley. *American Ethnologist* 42(1): 55–67.

———. 2016a. From "Deportability" to "Denounce-ability": New Forms of Labor Subordination in an Era of Governing Immigration Through Crime. *Political and Legal Anthropology Review* 39(2): 312–326.

———. 2016b. *They Leave Their Kidneys in the Fields: Illness, Injury, and Illegality Among U.S. Farmworkers.* Berkeley: University of California Press.

Horton, Sarah B., and Judith Barker. 2010. Stigmatized Biologies: Examining the Cumulative Effects of Oral Health Disparities for Mexican American Farmworker Children. *Medical Anthropology Quarterly* 24(2): 199–219.

Horton, Sarah B., and Stephanie Cole. 2011. Medical Returns: Seeking Health Care in Mexico. *Social Science & Medicine* 72(11): 1846–1852.

Huang, Zhihuan Jennifer, Stella M. Yu, and Rebecca Ledsky. 2006. Health Status and Health Service Access and Use Among Children in U.S. Immigrant Families. *American Journal of Public Health* 96(4): 634–640.

Hudson, Julie L. 2009. Families with Mixed Eligibility for Public Coverage: Navigating Medicaid, CHIP, and Uninsurance. *Health Affairs* 28(4): w697–w709.

Human Impact Partners. 2013. Family Unity, Family Health: How Family-Focused Immigration Reform Will Mean Better Health for Children and Families. https:// www.familyunityfamilyhealth.org/#findings.

Inda, Jonathan Xavier, and Julie A. Dowling. 2013. Governing Migrant Illegality. In *Governing Immigration Through Crime: A Reader,* edited by Julie A. Dowling and Jonathan Xavier Inda, 1–36. Stanford, CA: Stanford University Press.

Joseph, Tiffany D., and Helen B. Marrow. 2017. Health Care, Immigrants, and Minorities: Lessons from the Affordable Care Act in the U.S. *Journal of Ethnic and Migration Studies* 43: 1965–1984.

Kasinitz, Philip, John H. Mollenkopf, Mary C. Waters, and Jennifer Holdaway. 2008. *Inheriting the City: The Children of Immigrants Come of Age.* New York: Russell Sage Foundation.

Kline, Nolan. 2013. "There's Nowhere I Can Go to Get Help, and I Have Tooth Pain Right Now": The Oral Health Syndemic Among Migrant Farmworkers in Florida. *Annals of Anthropological Practice* 36(2): 387–401.

Landale, Nancy S., Jessica Halliday Hardie, R. S. Oropesa, and Marianne M. Hillemeier. 2015. Behavioral Functioning Among Mexican-Origin Children: Does Parental Legal Status Matter? *Journal of Health and Social Behavior* 56(1): 2–18.

Lavariega Monforti, Jessica, and Adam McGlynn. 2010. The Poverty Draft? Exploring the Role of Socioeconomic Status in the U.S. Military Recruitment of Hispanic Students. Presentation prepared for the American Political Science Association Annual Meeting, Washington, DC, September 2–5. https://www.researchgate.net /publication/228212120_The_Poverty_Draft_Exploring_the_Role_of_Socio economic_Status_in_US_Military_Recruitment_of_Hispanic_Students.

Lee, Esther Yu Hsi. 2016. Meet Eveyln, An Immigrant Who's Trapped Between Border Checkpoints in Texas. Thinkprogress.com, May 5. https://thinkprogress.org/meet -evelyn-an-immigrant-whos-trapped-between-border-checkpoints-in-texas -c8a96a9c5d6a.

Lewis, C. S. 1950. *The Lion, the Witch and the Wardrobe.* New York: Scholastic.

López, Leslie. 2005. De Facto Disentitlement in an Information Economy: Enrollment Issues in Medicaid Managed Care. *Medical Anthropology Quarterly* 19(1): 26–46.

Lopez, William D., Daniel J. Kruger, Jorge Delva, Mikel Llanes, Charo Ledón, Adreanne Waller, Melanie Harner, Ramiro Martinez, Laura Sanders, Margaret Harner, and Barbara Israel. 2017. Health Implications of an Immigration Raid: Findings from a Latino Community in the Midwestern United States. *Journal of Immigrant and Minority Health* 19(3): 702–708.

Low, Setha M., and Sally Engle Merry. 2010. Engaged Anthropology: Diversity and Dilemmas: An Introduction to Supplement 2. *Current Anthropology* 51(52): S203–S226.

Luibhéid, Eithne, Rosi Andrade, and Sally Stevens. 2017. Intimate Attachments and Migrant Deportability: Lessons from Undocumented Mothers Seeking Benefits for Citizen Children. *Ethnic and Racial Studies* 41(1): 17–35.

Luna, Sarah. 2018. Affective Atmospheres of Terror on the Mexico–U.S. Border: Rumors of Violence in Reynosa's Prostitution Zone. *Cultural Anthropology* 33(1): 58–84.

Macías-Rojas, Patrisia. 2016. *From Deportation to Prison: The Politics of Immigration Enforcement in Post–Civil Rights America.* New York: New York University Press.

Maldonado, Cynthia Z., Robert M. Rodriguez, Jesus R. Torres, Yvette S. Flores, and Luis M. Lovato. 2013. Fear of Discovery Among Latino Immigrants Presenting to the Emergency Department. *Academic Emergency Medicine* 20(2): 155–161.

Mangual Figueroa, Ariana. 2011. Citizenship and Education in the Homework Completion Routine. *Anthropology & Education Quarterly* 4(3): 263–280.

———. 2012. "I Have Papers So I Can Go Anywhere!" Everyday Talk About Citizenship in a Mixed-Status Mexican Family. *Journal of Language, Identity & Education* 11(5): 291–311.

———. 2017. Speech or Silence: Undocumented Students' Decisions to Disclose or Disguise Their Citizenship Status in School. *American Educational Research Journal* 54(3): 485–523.

Marcos, Cristina. 2016. House Rejects Efforts to Ban Illegal Immigrants from Military Service. *The Hill*, June 16. http://thehill.com/policy/finance/283762-house-rejects -effort-to-ban-illegal-immigrants-from-enlisting-in-military.

Marrow, Helen. 2011a. *New Destination Dreaming: Immigration, Race, and Legal Status in the Rural American South*. Stanford, CA: Stanford University Press.

———. 2011b. When We All Become the Immigration Police. Latino Decisions, December 19. www.latinodecisions.com/blog/2011/12/19/when-we-all-become-the -immigration-police.

———. 2012. Deserving to a Point: Unauthorized Immigrants in San Francisco's Universal Access Healthcare Model. *Social Science & Medicine* 74(6): 846–854.

Massey, Douglas S., Jorge Durand, and Nolan J. Malone. 2003. *Beyond Smoke and Mirrors: Mexican Immigration in an Era of Economic Integration*. New York: Russell Sage Foundation.

Mathema, Silva. 2016. *Keeping Families Together: Why All Americans Should Care About What Happens to Unauthorized Immigrants*. Report by the Center for American Progress and USC Dornsife Center for the Study of Immigrant Integration. https:// cdn.americanprogress.org/content/uploads/2017/03/15112450/KeepFamilies Together-brief.pdf.

McKee, Martin, and David Stuckler. 2017. The Deferred Action for Childhood Arrivals Programme: A Quasi-Experiment in Giving Hope to Migrants. *The Lancet* 2(4): e160–e161.

Mejia Lutz, Elena. 2018. At Border Patrol Checkpoints, an Impossible Choice Between Health Care and Deportation. *Texas Observer*, February 13. https://www.texas observer.org/border-patrol-checkpoints-impossible-choice-health-care -deportation.

Melo, Milena A. 2017a. Enacting Life: Dialysis Among Undocumented Mexican Immigrants in the U.S.–Mexico Borderlands. PhD diss., University of San Antonio.

———. 2017b. Stratified Access: Seeking Dialysis Care in the Borderlands. In *Unequal Coverage: The Experience of Health Care Reform in the United States*, edited by Jessica M. Mulligan and Heide Castañeda, 59–78. New York: New York University Press.

Mendoza, Fernando S. 2009. Health Disparities and Children in Immigrant Families: A Research Agenda. *Pediatrics* 124(S3): S187–S195.

Menjívar, Cecilia. 2006. Liminal Legality: Salvadoran and Guatemalan Immigrants' Lives in the United States. *American Journal of Sociology* 111(4): 999–1037.

———. 2014. Immigration Law Beyond Borders: Externalizing and Internalizing Border Controls in an Era of Securitization. *Annual Review of Law and Social Science* 10: 353–369.

Menjívar, Cecilia, and Leisy Abrego. 2009. Parents and Children Across Borders: Legal Instability and Intergenerational Relations in Guatemalan and Salvadoran Families. In *Across Generations: Immigrant Families in America*, edited by Nancy Foner, 160–189. New York: New York University Press.

Menjívar, Cecilia, and Daniel Kanstroom, eds. 2014. *Constructing Immigrant "Illegality": Critiques, Experiences, and Responses*. Cambridge: Cambridge University Press.

Migration Policy Institute. 2016. Unauthorized Immigrant Population Profiles. www
.migrationpolicy.org/programs/us-immigration-policy-program-data-hub
/unauthorized-immigrant-population-profiles.

———. 2018. DACA Recipients & Program Participation Rate, by State, MPI Data Hub.
https://www.migrationpolicy.org/programs/data-hub/deferred-action-childhood
-arrivals-daca-profiles.

———. n.d. Profile of the Unauthorized Population: Hidalgo County, TX. Unauthorized Immigrant Population Profiles, MPI Data Hub. www.migrationpolicy.org/data
/unauthorized-immigrant-population/county/48215.

Montero, David. 2017. Fearful Parents Sign Papers for Friends to Care for Kids in Case
They're Deported. *Los Angeles Times*, March 13. www.latimes.com/nation/la-na
-immigration-power-attorney-2017-story.html.

Motomura, Hiroshi. 2007. *Americans in Waiting: The Lost Story of Immigration and
Citizenship in the United States.* Oxford: Oxford University Press.

Mountz, Alison, Kate Coddington, R. Tina Catania, and Jenna M. Loyd. 2012. Con-
ceptualizing Detention: Mobility, Containment, Bordering, and Exclusion. *Progress
in Human Geography* 37(4): 522–541.

Muñoz, Susana M. 2016. Undocumented and Unafraid: Understanding the Disclosure
Management Process for Undocumented College Students and Graduates. *Journal
of College Student Development* 57(6): 715–729.

Najarro, Ileana, and Jenny Deam. 2017. Fearing Deportation, Undocumented Immigrants in Houston Are Avoiding Hospitals and Clinics. *Houston Chronicle*, December 27. https://www.houstonchronicle.com/news/houston-texas/houston/article
/Fearing-deportation-undocumented-immigrants-are-12450772.php.

Nájera, Jennifer R. 2015. *The Borderlands of Race: Mexican Segregation in a South Texas
Town.* Austin: University of Texas Press.

Nathan, Debbie. 2017. ACLU Texas: Immigrants Versus Alt-Facts in South Texas. *Rio
Grande Guardian*, March 10. http://riograndeguardian.com/aclu-texas-immigrants
-versus-alt-facts-in-south-texas.

Negrón-Gonzales, Genevieve. 2013. Navigating "Illegality": Undocumented Youth &
Oppositional Consciousness. *Children and Youth Services Review* 35(8): 1284–1290.

Nevins, Joseph. 2008. *Dying to Live: A Story of U.S. Immigration in an Age of Global
Apartheid.* San Francisco: City Lights.

New York Times. 2016. Transcript: Donald Trump's Comments About Women. October 8. www.nytimes.com/2016/10/08/us/donald-trump-tape-transcript.html?mcubz
=1&_r=0.

Ngai, Mae M. 1999. The Architecture of Race in American Immigration Law: A Reex-
amination of the Immigration Act of 1924. *Journal of American History* 86(1):
67–92.

———. 2007. Birthright Citizenship and the Alien Citizen. *Fordham Law Review* 75(1):
2521–2530.

———. 2014. *Impossible Subjects: Illegal Aliens and the Making of Modern America—
Updated Edition.* Princeton, NJ: Princeton University Press.

Nicholls, Walter J. 2013. *The DREAMers: How the Undocumented Youth Movement Transformed the Rights Debate*. Stanford, CA: Stanford University Press.

Núñez, Guillermina G., and Josiah Heyman McC. 2007. Entrapment Processes and Immigrant Communities in a Time of Heightened Border Violence. *Human Organization* 66(4): 354–365.

O'Leary, Anna Ochoa, and Azucena Sanchez. 2011. Anti-Immigrant Arizona: Ripple Effects and Mixed Immigration Status Households Under "Policies of Attrition" Considered. *Journal of Borderlands Studies* 26(1): 115–133.

Orne, Jason. 2011. "You Will Always Have to 'Out' Yourself": Reconsidering Coming Out Through Strategic Outness. *Sexualities* 14(6): 681–703.

Oropesa, R. S., Nancy S. Landale, and Marianne M. Hillemeier. 2015. Family Legal Status and Health: Measurement Dilemmas in Studies of Mexican-Origin Children. *Social Science & Medicine* 138: 57–67.

Park, Lisa Sun-Hee. 2011. Criminalizing Immigrant Mothers: Public Charge, Health Care, and Welfare Reform. *International Journal of Sociology of the Family* 37(1): 27–47.

Parrado, Emilio A., Chenoa A. Flippen, and Chris McQuiston. 2005. Migration and Relationship Power Among Mexican Women. *Demography* 42(2): 347–372.

Parreñas, Rhacel Salazar. 2005. *Children of Global Migration: Transnational Families and Gendered Woes*. Stanford, CA: Stanford University Press.

Passel, Jeffrey S. 2003. *Further Demographic Information Relating to the DREAM Act*. Washington, DC: Urban Institute.

———. 2011. Demography of Immigrant Youth: Past, Present, and Future. *The Future of Children* 21(1): 19–41.

Passel, Jeffrey S., and D'Vera Cohn. 2016. *Children of Unauthorized Immigrants Represent Rising Share of K–12 Students*. Washington, DC: Pew Hispanic Center. http://www.pewresearch.org/fact-tank/2016/11/17/children-of-unauthorized-immigrants-represent-rising-share-of-k-12-students/.

———. 2017. As Mexican Share Declined, U.S. Unauthorized Immigrant Population Fell in 2015 Below Recession Level. Pewresearch.org, April 25. www.pewresearch.org/fact-tank/2017/04/25/as-mexican-share-declined-u-s-unauthorized-immigrant-population-fell-in-2015-below-recession-level.

Passel, Jeffrey S., D'Vera Cohn, and Ana Gonzalez-Barrera. 2012. *Net Migration from Mexico Falls to Zero—and Perhaps Less*. Washington, DC: Pew Hispanic Center.

Patler, Caitlin, and Whitney Laster Pirtle. 2017. From Undocumented to Lawfully Present: Do Changes to Legal Status Impact Psychological Wellbeing Among Latino Immigrant Young Adults? *Social Science & Medicine* 199: 39–48.

Pereira, Krista M., Robert Crosnoe, Karina Fortuny, Juan Pedroza, Kjersti Ulvestad, Christina Weiland, Hirokazu Yoshikawa, and Ajay Chaudry. 2012. *Barriers to Immigrants' Access to Health and Human Services Programs*. Washington, DC: Urban Institute. http://aspe.hhs.gov/hsp/11/ImmigrantAccess/Barriers/rb.pdf.

Pew Research Center. 2010. *Household Structure; Mixed Families*. www.pewhispanic.org/2010/08/11/iii-household-structure-mixed-families.

———. 2016. U.S. Unauthorized Immigration Population Estimates. http://www.pewhispanic.org/interactives/unauthorized-immigrants/

Pila, Daniela. 2016. "I'm Not Good Enough for Anyone": Legal Status and the Dating Lives of Undocumented Young Adults. *Sociological Forum* 31(1): 138–158.

Pope, Nolan G. 2016. The Effects of DACAmentation: The Impact of Deferred Action for Childhood Arrivals on Unauthorized Immigrants. *Journal of Public Economics* 143: 98–114.

Portes, Alejandro, and Rubén G. Rumbaut. 2001. *Legacies: The Story of the Immigrant Second Generation*. Berkeley: University of California Press.

Portes, Alejandro, and Min Zhou. 1993. The New Second Generation: Segmented Assimilation and Its Variants. *Annals of the American Academy of Political and Social Science* 530(1): 74–96.

Potochnick, Stephanie R., and Krista M. Perreira. 2010. Depression and Anxiety Among First-Generation Immigrant Latino Youth: Key Correlates and Implications for Future Research. *Journal of Nervous and Mental Disease* 198(7): 470–477.

Preston, Julia. 2016. Lawsuit Forces Texas to Make It Easier for Immigrants to Get Birth Certificates for Children. *New York Times*, July 24, A17. https://www.nytimes.com/2016/07/25/us/lawsuit-texas-immigrants-birth-certificates.html?_r=o.

Preston, Julia, and Laura Tillman. 2014. Immigration Advocate, Detained on Texas Border, Is Released in Visa Case. *New York Times*, July 15, A13. https://www.nytimes.com/2014/07/16/us/Jose-Antonio-Vargas-immigrant-advocate-arrested.html.

Provine, Doris Marie, Monica W. Varsanyi, Paul G. Lewis, and Scott H. Decker. 2016. *Policing Immigrants: Local Law Enforcement on the Front Lines*. Chicago: University of Chicago Press.

Quinnipiac University. 2018. Helping Dreamers Can't Get U.S. Voters over the Wall, Quinnipiac University Poll Finds; Support for Infrastructure Almost 10–1. News release, Quinnipiac University, January 18. https://poll.qu.edu/national/release-detail?ReleaseID=2514.

Rabin, Nina, Mary Carol Combs, and Norma Gonzalez. 2009. Understanding Plyler's Legacy: Voices from Border Schools. *Journal of Law and Education* 37(1): 15–82.

Reina, Angelica S., Brenda J. Lohman, and Marta María Maldonado. 2013. "He Said They'd Deport Me": Factors Influencing Domestic Violence Help-Seeking Practices Among Latina Immigrants. *Journal of Interpersonal Violence* 29(4): 593–615.

Reyna, Hugo. 2013. "Alerta de Retenes 956" Causa Furor en Redes Sociales. *La Prensa*, October 2. http://laprensa.mx/notas.asp?id=231511.

Rhodes, Scott D., Lilli Mann, Florence M. Simán, et al. 2015. The Impact of Local Immigration Enforcement Policies on the Health of Immigrant Hispanics/Latinos in the United States. *American Journal of Public Health* 105(2): 329–337.

Richardson, Chad. 1999. *Batos, Bolillos, Pochos and Pelados: Class and Culture on the South Texas Border*. Austin: University of Texas Press.

Richardson, Chad, and Michael J. Pisani. 2012. *The Informal and Underground Economy of the South Texas Border*. Austin: University of Texas Press.

Richardson, Chad, and Rosalva Resendiz. 2006. *On the Edge of the Law: Culture, Labor and Deviance on the South Texas Border*. Austin: University of Texas Press.

Rios, Victor. 2011. *Punished: Policing the Lives of Black and Latino Boys*. New York: New York University Press.

Robert Wood Johnson Foundation. 2016. *County Health Rankings and Roadmaps*. http://www.countyhealthrankings.org.

Román González, Betsabé, and Víctor Zúñiga. 2014. Children Returning from the U.S. to Mexico: School Sweet School? *Migraciones Internacionales* 7(27): 277–286.

Romero, Mary. 2008. The Inclusion of Citizenship Status in Intersectionality: What Immigration Raids Tells Us About Mixed-Status Families, the State and Assimilation. *International Journal of Sociology of the Family* 34(2): 131–152.

Rosa, Jonathan, and Yarimar Bonilla. 2017. Deprovincializing Trump, Decolonizing Diversity, and Unsettling Anthropology. *American Ethnologist* 44(2): 201–218.

Rosas, G. 2006. The Managed Violences of the Borderlands: Treacherous Geographies, Policeability, and the Politics of Race. *Latino Studies* 4(4): 401–418.

Salas, Lorraine Moya, Cecilia Ayón, and Maria Gurrola. 2013. Estamos Traumados: The Effect of Anti-Immigrant Sentiment and Policies on the Mental Health of Mexican Immigrant Families. *Journal of Community Psychology* 41(8): 1005–1020.

Sassen, Saskia. 2000. Regulating Immigration in a Global Age: A New Policy Landscape. *Annals of the American Academy of Political and Social Science* 570(1): 65–77.

Schmalzbauer, Leah. 2014. *The Last Best Place? Gender, Family, and Migration in the New West*. Stanford, CA: Stanford University Press.

Schueths, April M. 2012. "Where Are My Rights?" Compromised Citizenship in Mixed-Status Marriage—A Research Note. *Journal of Sociology and Social Welfare* 39(4): 97–109.

———. 2014. "It's Almost Like White Supremacy": Interracial Mixed-Status Couples Facing Racist Nativism. *Ethnic and Racial Studies* 37(13): 2438–2456.

Selby, W. Gardner. 2015. In Context: Barack Obama's Call for a Veterans Hospital in the Rio Grande Valley. Politifact: Texas, February 4. http://www.politifact.com/texas/article/2015/feb/04/context-barack-obama-promise-veterans-hospital.

Sheller, Mimi, and John Urry. 2006. The New Mobilities Paradigm. *Environment and Planning* 38(2): 207–226.

Sigona, Nando. 2012. "I've Too Much Baggage": The Impact of Legal Status on the Social Worlds of Irregular Migrants. *Social Anthropology/Anthropologie Sociale* 20(1): 50–65.

Silbey, Susan S. 2005. After Legal Consciousness. *Annual Review of Law and Society* 1: 323–68.

Slack, Jeremy, Daniel E. Martinez, Scott Whiteford, and Emily Peiffer. 2015. In Harm's Way: Family Separation, Immigration Enforcement Programs and Security on the US–Mexico Border. *Journal on Migration & Human Security* 3(2): 109–128.

Sommers, Benjamin D., Meredith Roberts Tomasi, Katherine Swartz, and Arnold M. Epstein. 2012. Reasons for the Wide Variation in Medicaid Participation Rates

Among States Hold Lessons for Coverage Expansion in 2014. *Health Affairs* 31(5): 909–919.

Spener, David. 2006. *Clandestine Crossings: Migrants and Coyotes on the Texas-Mexico Border*. Ithaca, NY: Cornell University Press.

Stephen, Lynn. 2007. *Transborder Lives: Indigenous Oaxacans in Mexico, California, and Oregon*. Durham, NC: Duke University Press.

Stuesse, Angela, and Mathew Coleman. 2014. Automobility, Immobility, Altermobility: Surviving and Resisting the Intensification of Immigrant Policing. *City & Society* 26(1): 51–72.

Suárez-Orozco, Carola, Irina L. G. Todorova, and Josephine Louie. 2002. Making Up for Lost Time: The Experience of Separation and Reunification Among Immigrant Families. *Family Process* 41(4): 625–643.

Suárez-Orozco, Carola, Hirokazu Yoshikawa, Robert Teranishi, and Marcelo M. Suárez-Orozco. 2011. Growing Up in the Shadows: The Developmental Implications of Unauthorized Status. *Harvard Educational Review* 81(3): 438–473.

Sullivan, Margaret M., and Roberta Rehm. 2005. Mental Health of Undocumented Mexican Immigrants: A Review of the Literature. *Advances in Nursing Science* 28(3): 240–251.

Taylor, Steve. 2014. Valley Residents: DPS Not Being Honest over Random Checkpoint Operations. *Rio Grande Guardian*, September 25. http://riograndeguardian.com/valley-residents-dps-not-being-honest-over-random-checkpoint-operations.

Torbati, Yeganeh. 2018. Exclusive: Trump Administration May Target Immigrants Who Use Food Aid, Other Benefits. Reuters.com, February 8. www.reuters.com/article/us-usa-immigration-services-exclusive/exclusive-trump-administration-may-target-immigrants-who-use-food-aid-other-benefits-idUSKBN1FS2ZK.

Torres, Jacqueline M., Julianna Deardorff, Robert B. Gunier, Kim G. Harley, Abbey Alkon, Katherine Kogut, and Brenda Eskenazi. 2018 Worry About Deportation and Cardiovascular Disease Risk Factors Among Adult Women: The Center for the Health Assessment of Mothers and Children of Salinas Study. *Annals of Behavioral Medicine* 52(5): 186–193. https://doi.org/10.1093/abm/kax007.

Travel.State.Gov. 2018. Visa Bulletin for June 2018. https://travel.state.gov/content/travel/en/legal/visa-lawo/visa-bulletin/2018/visa-bulletin-for-june-2018.html.

Tsing, Anna Lowenhaupt. 2015. *The Mushroom at the End of the World: On the Possibility of Life in Capitalist Ruins*. Princeton, NJ: Princeton University Press.

Ura, Alexa. 2016. Latest Census Data Shows Poverty Rate Highest at Border, Lowest in Suburbs. *Texas Tribune*, January 19. www.texastribune.org/2016/01/19/poverty-prevalent-on-texas-border-low-in-suburbs.

U.S. Army. Additional Incentives: MAVNI. www.goarmy.com/benefits/additional-incentives/mavni.html.

U.S. Citizenship and Immigration Services (USCIS). 2011. Public Charge Fact Sheet. https://www.uscis.gov/news/fact-sheets/public-charge-fact-sheet.

———. 2013. Parole in Place Memorandum. Policy memorandum PM-602-0091, November 15. https://www.uscis.gov/sites/default/files/USCIS/Laws/Memoranda/2013/2013-1115_Parole_in_Place_Memo_.pdf.

———. 2017. *DACA Performance Data, FY 2017, Qtr 2.* https://www.uscis.gov/sites/default/files/USCIS/Resources/Reports%20and%20Studies/Immigration%20Forms%20Data/All%20Form%20Types/DACA/daca_performancedata_fy2017_qtr2.pdf.

U.S. Department of State. 2018. Country Information: Mexico. https://travel.state.gov/content/travel/en/international-travel/International-Travel-Country-Information-Pages/Mexico.html.

Valdes, Guadalupe. 1996. *Con Respeto: Bridging the Distances Between Culturally Diverse Families and Schools.* New York: Teachers College Press.

Valdez, Carmen R., Brian Padilla, and Jessa Lewis Valentine. 2013. Consequences of Arizona's Immigration Policy on Social Capital Among Mexican Mothers with Unauthorized Immigration Status. *Hispanic Journal of Behavioral Sciences* 35(3): 303–322.

Valerio-Jiménez, Omar. 2013. *River of Hope: Forging Identity and Nation in the Rio Grande Borderlands.* Durham, NC: Duke University Press.

Vaquera, Elizabeth, Elizabeth Aranda, and Isabel Sousa-Rodriguez. 2017. Emotional Challenges of Undocumented Young Adults: Ontological Security, Emotional Capital, and Well-Being. *Social Problems* 64(2): 298–314.

Vargas, Edward D. 2015. Immigration Enforcement and Mixed-Status Families: The Effects of Risk of Deportation on Medicaid Use. *Children and Youth Services Review* 57: 83–89.

Vargas, Edward D., and Maureen A. Pirog. 2016. Mixed-Status Families and WIC Uptake: The Effects of Risk of Deportation on Program Use. *Social Sciences Quarterly* 97(3): 555–572.

Vargas, Edward D., and Vickie D. Ybarra. 2016. U.S. Citizen Children of Undocumented Parents: The Link Between State Immigration Policy and the Health of Latino Children. *Journal of Immigrant and Minority Health* 19(4): 913–920.

Vargas, Jose Antonio. 2011. My Life as an Undocumented Immigrant. *New York Times Magazine,* June 22, MM22. https://www.nytimes.com/2011/06/26/magazine/my-life-as-an-undocumented-immigrant.html?pagewanted=all.

———. 2014. Trapped on the Border. *Politico Magazine,* July 11. http://www.politico.com/magazine/story/2014/07/texas-border-trapped-108826.html#.VB8kMRaG3J4.

Vélez-Ibáñez, Carlos G. 1996. *Border Visions: Mexican Cultures of the Southwest United States.* Tucson: University of Arizona Press.

Venkataramani, Atheendar S., Sachin J. Shah, Rourke O'Brien, Ichiro Kawachi, and Alexander C. Tsai. 2017. Health Consequences of the US Deferred Action for Childhood Arrivals (DACA) Immigration Programme: A Quasi-Experimental Study. *Lancet Public Health* 2(4): e175–e181.

Vilanova, Nuria. 2002. Another Textual Frontier: Contemporary Fiction on the Northern Mexican Border. *Bulletin of Latin American Research* 21(1): 73–98.

Viruell-Fuentes, Edna A., Patricia Y. Miranda, and Sawsan Abdulrahim. 2012. More Than Culture: Structural Racism, Intersectionality Theory, and Immigrant Health. *Social Science & Medicine* 75(12): 2099–2106.

Vitek, Christopher J., Joann A. Gutierrez, and Frank J. Dirrigl Jr. 2014. Dengue Vectors, Human Activity, and Dengue Virus Transmission Potential in the Lower Rio Grande Valley, Texas, United States. *Journal of Medical Entomology* 51(5): 1019–1028.

Vogt, Wendy A. 2013. Crossing Mexico: Structural Violence and the Commodification of Undocumented Central American Migrants. *American Ethnologist* 40(4): 764–780.

Waldinger, Roger, and Peter Catron. 2016. Modes of Incorporation: A Conceptual and Empirical Critique. *Journal of Ethnic and Migration Studies* 42(1): 23–53.

Walters, William. 2015. Migration, Vehicles, and Politics: Three Theses on Viapolitics. *European Journal of Social Theory* 18(4): 469–488.

Warren, Robert, and Donald Kerwin. 2017. The 2,000 Mile Wall in Search of a Purpose: Since 2007 Visa Overstays Have Outnumbered Undocumented Border Crossers by a Half Million. *Journal on Migration and Human Security* 5(1): 124–136.

Wasem, Ruth Ellen. 2012. *Unauthorized Aliens' Access to Federal Benefits: Policy and Issues.* Congressional Research Service. https://fas.org/sgp/crs/homesec/RL34500.pdf.

Waters, Mary C., and Marisa Gerstein Pineau, eds. 2015. *The Integration of Immigrants into American Society.* Washington, DC: National Academies Press.

Wessler, Seth Freed. 2011. *Shattered Families: The Perilous Intersection of Immigration Enforcement and the Child Welfare System.* New York: Applied Research Center.

Willen, Sarah S. 2007. Toward a Critical Phenomenology of "Illegality": State Power, Criminalization, and Abjectivity Among Undocumented Migrant Workers in Tel Aviv, Israel. *International Migration* 45(3): 8–38.

———. 2012. Migration, "Illegality," and Health: Mapping Embodied Vulnerability and Debating Health-Related Deservingness. *Social Science & Medicine* 74(6): 805–811.

Williams, Gareth H. 2003. The Determinants of Health: Structure, Context and Agency. *Sociology of Health and Illness* 25(3): 131–154.

Wilson, Steven Harmon. 2002. *The Rise of Judicial Management in the U.S. District Court, Southern District Texas, 1955–2000.* Athens: University of Georgia Press.

Winton, Ailsa. 2015. Violence, Borders, and Boundaries: Reframing Young People's Mobility. In *Movement, Mobilities and Journeys: Geographies of Children and Young People,* edited by Caitriona Ni Laoire, Allen White, and Tracey Skelton, 131–149. Singapore: Springer.

Wong, Tom K. 2016. United We Dream, National Immigration Law Center, and Center for American Progress National Survey. 2016 Survey Results. https://cdn.american progressaction.org/content/uploads/2016/10/21111136/2016-daca_survey_draft _updated-FINAL2.pdf.

Wong, Tom K., Greisa Martinez Rosas, Adrian Reyna, Ignacia Rodriguez, Patrick O'Shea, Tom Jawetz, and Philip E. Wolgin. 2016. New Study of DACA Beneficiaries

Shows Positive Economic and Educational Outcomes. Americanprogress.org, October 18. https://www.americanprogress.org/issues/immigration/news/2016/10/18/146290/new-study-of-daca-beneficiaries-shows-positive-economic-and-educational-outcomes.

Xu, Qingwen, and Kalina Brabeck. 2012. Service Utilization for Latino Children in Mixed-Status Families. *Social Work Research* 36(3): 209–221.

Yarris, Kristin E. 2017. *Care Across Generations: Solidarity and Sacrifice in Transnational Families*. Stanford, CA: Stanford University Press.

Yoshikawa, Hirokazu. 2011. *Immigrants Raising Citizens: Undocumented Parents and Their Young Children*. New York: Russell Sage Foundation.

Yoshikawa, Hirokazu, Erin B. Godfrey, and Ann C. Rivera. 2008. Access to Institutional Resources as a Measure of Social Exclusion: Relations with Family Process and Cognitive Development in the Context of Immigration. *New Directions for Child and Adolescent Development* 121: 63–86.

Yoshikawa, Hirokazu, and Jenya Kholoptseva. 2013. *Undocumented Immigrant Parents and Their Children's Development: A Summary of the Evidence*. Washington, DC: Migration Policy Institute. http://www.migrationpolicy.org/pubs/COI-Yoshikawa.pdf.

Yun, Katherine, Elena Fuentes-Afflick, Leslie A. Curry, Harlan M. Krumholz, and Mayur M. Desai. 2013. Parental Immigration Status Is Associated with Children's Health Care Utilization: Findings from the 2003 New Immigrant Survey of US Legal Permanent Residents. *Maternal and Child Health Journal* 17(10): 1913–1921.

Zayas, Luis H. 2015. *Forgotten Citizens: Deportation, Children, and the Making of American Exiles and Orphans*. New York: Oxford University Press.

Zhou, Min. 1997. Growing Up American: The Challenge of Confronting Immigrant Children and Children of Immigrants. *Annual Review of Sociology* 23: 63–95.

Zúñiga, Víctor, and Edward T. Hamann. 2015. Going to a Home You Have Never Been To: The Return Migration of Mexican and American-Mexican Children. *Children's Geographies* 13(6): 643–655.

INDEX

WITHDRAWN

CPSIA information can be obtained
at www.ICGtesting.com
Printed in the USA
LVHW030922010721
691577LV00008B/1237

9 781503 607910